CARDINAL O'CONNELL OF BOSTON

Cardinal O'Connell of Boston

A BIOGRAPHY OF
WILLIAM HENRY O'CONNELL
1859–1944

BY

Dorothy G. Wayman

FARRAR, STRAUS AND YOUNG
NEW YORK

Nihil Obstat

> Rt. Rev. Edward G. Murray, D.D.
> Diocesan Censor

Imprimatur

> ✠ Richard J. Cushing
> Archbishop of Boston
> November 8, 1954

Library of Congress catalog card number: 55-5834

First printing, 1955

Manufactured in the United States of America
by American Book–Stratford Press, Inc., New York

IN MEMORIAM

William Cardinal O'Connell, Archbishop of Boston, built a mortuary chapel beneath the windows of his residence in the grounds of the Archdiocesan Seminary. He built it as a *memento mori,* a reminder that death comes to all—and then, Eternity!

"Someday someone who knows only a little of the facts will attempt to write my life and . . . then not the truth, but fiction, will be given to the public," wrote the Cardinal.[1]

It is, admittedly, impossible for any human to know all the truth about another human being. However, fiction has been excluded from this book as rigidly as research could ensure. Instead, a mosaic has been built up, composed of dates, documents, reminiscences, photographs, correspondence.

A mosaic, viewed through centuries by millions who have visited the basilica of St. Peter in Rome, is that called the Navicella, above the entrance. It is not a lifelike portrait of the Fisherman of Galilee, but those who look on it, carry away an indelible impression of the role of Peter, the Rock chosen by Christ on which to found His Church.

Let this book, then, be regarded as a mosaic portraying the role of a Cardinal of the Holy Roman Catholic Church, whose life spanned the last half of the Nineteenth, the first half of the Twentieth Century.

For the keynote of this work, certain other words, spoken by the Cardinal himself about another priest, have been kept in mind:

"This is not a gathering for a process of canonization. (He) would be the last to pretend that he was without failing, fault or defect. The highest saints had these, because they were all human. In the daily life of any man, be he priest or layman, there are diffi-

v

culties which try his soul to its last faculty, and no one escapes them all. To be always right is the privilege of one only, God.

"But the will to be right and to do the right, that is God acting in man. The instrument is defective but the will is true. . . . However far from perfection he himself may be, the priest holds within his soul a message, a power which comes from God. . . . The voice is God's—the lips are clay." [2]

D. G. W.

CONTENTS

FOREWORD

IN TWO weeks time I shall have completed a decade as Archbishop of Boston. They have been busy years and in them with God's help the growth of Catholic life has found many new manifestations within the Archdiocese. Yet as I review the works that have been brought to accomplishment, I cannot regard them as altogether new activities. Time and time again it has been brought home to me that we have for the greatest part built upon foundations prudently laid by my predecessor, the late William Cardinal O'Connell.

It is this sense of our obligation to the memory of the late Cardinal that has prompted my encouragement of the biography of his late Eminence. He was, himself, conscious in the extreme of the similar debt he owed to the work of his predecessor, Archbishop Williams, and in his brochure "A Tribute of Affectionate Memory," he set forth the terms of his obligation in his own warm phrases and distinctive style.

It could be stated that ten years are too short a time in which to assess the measure of such a man's influence upon his own day and the future growth of the Church. In many ways this is true. The further removed from it we are, the more clearly we can measure the special impact of a personality without reference to the charm it may have exercised over its contemporaries. Yet with these thoughts in mind, I feel that now rather than later is the time for the life of Cardinal O'Connell. There are still living so many of those who can bring their personal witness to his deeds and their intentions, and who would not survive to tell their story to the biographer of a later day. Among these I dare count myself not the least since I was among those closely associated with him almost from the time of my ordination until his death. It should be brought in mind, too, that Miss Wayman has not attempted what might be called a conventional biography of the late Cardinal. Absent from these pages are most of the accomplishments which belong to history, and absent by consequence, any value-judgments in their regard. The monumental *History of the Archdiocese of Boston,* commissioned by Cardinal O'Connell, and the fruit of a dozen years of research, was published within a few weeks of his

death and contains most of the historical facts of his long episcopate. At that time it was not possible to explore, as it now is, the
personality of the Cardinal, to see what manner of human being
it was who, aided richly by divine grace, governed the Church of
Boston for thirty-seven years. That inquiry is the specific task to
which Miss Wayman has set herself and the result is what you will
read in her fascinating story.

It is unusual to attempt such a character study of an eminent
ecclesiastic along the lines of modern biographical scholarship.
Before giving the enterprise my encouragement, I consulted with
the family of the late Cardinal and those who had been closer to
him than myself in their personal and official capacities. They all
expressed their entire willingness to cooperate, and this they did
and many of them have read the manuscript prior to publication.
It is a measure of the help which was so willingly given in every
quarter to see the long list of acknowledgments which Miss Wayman includes in her preface. There were literally no doors closed
to her in her investigation and I know from many conferences with
her that she accepted nothing in evidence unless her independent
research commended it to her.

Together the pontificates of Archbishop Williams and Cardinal
O'Connell embraced the period between 1866 and 1944. We are
told that when Archbishop Williams was a boy he knew by name
all the Catholic families living in the city of Boston. By the death
of his successor the growth of the Church had been such that it
seemed almost unreal that a short century before the number of
the faithful had been so few.

It was due to the unhappy circumstances of their native lands
beyond the seas that so many Catholics came to these parts during
the last century. It was due to their poverty in great measure that
so many settled by these northeastern shores lacking the funds to
share the great push to the West which was occupying so much
of the energies of the nation. Once settled here, they followed a
pattern of sending for the members of their families to join them
here. Such would be the historical reasons behind the great number
of Catholics who began life anew in the storied towns and cities
of New England.

Yet more than this is needed to account for their integration into their social and political communities, and the maintenance among so many diverse strains of the unity of the Church. Fortunate indeed was the See of Boston to have had two such leaders during the critical years of its formation. They were prepared to do everything to make the newcomer feel at home. They prudently saw to the provision of churches and priests for the various language groups. However, they always preached a devotion to America and her ideas which would make the need of national churches a temporary one, while safeguarding always the contribution each group had to make to the riches of our American cultural diversity. It was no accident that bequeathed to me ten years ago such a united priesthood and laity.

When Cardinal O'Connell came to Boston as the Coadjutor of Archbishop Williams in 1906, he came as one whose chief task was to lighten the declining years of that great prelate. So he expressed himself to the priests of the Archdiocese in a memorable sermon on that occasion. He lived himself to the venerable age of his predecessor and to the last he remained the directing force of the Archdiocese, unfatigued in will by the decline of his bodily powers.

One aspect of Cardinal O'Connell which it was mine to know in personal fashion was his ability to delegate responsibility without abrogating it. To those who worked with him, as I did, in the various curial offices of the Archdiocese, he gave a very great area of initiative, which derived from the trust he placed in them. Yet there was no one who looked upon himself as doing other than furthering the Cardinal's ideas. He accepted ultimate responsibility for whatever was done in his name.

Given the personality with which God endowed him, it was perhaps inevitable that Cardinal O'Connell might seem to many a remote being, while to the lesser number who had occasion to know him well, he was a thoughtful, provident, prayerful shepherd, and a truly gifted and beloved friend. The sense of his office was never absent from him at any time and he was instinct with what he used to call *Romanita,* the Roman sense of things, in which he had lived so long, and which had become part of him. If in a sense he reminded us of a prelate of the Old World, it was because he had this sense of tradition and it was because of this that he was able to accomplish so much in accommodating the best traditions of the Old World to the special circumstances of the New, as for example his reorganization of the Curia, almost fifty years ago, which, little changed, endures to this day.

In many things that he did and said he was a figure of controversy. It was not in his nature to await a change in the climate of opinion before doing that which he felt must be done here and now. This book does not enter in any considerable degree into these controversies, but it may make more plain the utterly fearless person around whom they centered. Since none of us is gifted with a total recall of past events there are even now divergent opinions as to the facts in controversy. Now is not the time to attempt a final resolution of these, yet I have learned in good part from Cardinal O'Connell, in good part through my years as Archbishop, how often decisions must be made in the light of all the facts, when only the decisions and not the facts themselves can be made public.

Each of the Bishops and Archbishops of Boston has brought some special gift to his office. This is a theme upon which it was mine to enlarge only a few weeks ago at the time of the consecration of my newest Auxiliary, Bishop Minihan, former secretary to Cardinal O'Connell. To all of these great men we of today owe our debts of gratitude. Since to most of us Cardinal O'Connell was the one whose long span of years reaching within a few weeks of his diamond jubilee in the priesthood made him best known, and whose works are closest to us, we pay in this volume our tribute of respect and of gratitude. The Church moves on in each generation, but her progress is best when she remembers the path that has brought her to her present station. Separated now by years, but brought together by the same burden of responsibility, I am happy to salute the memory of my great predecessor, and father in the Lord, Cardinal O'Connell, and to pray that everlasting rest be his portion.

✠ RICHARD J. CUSHING
Archbishop of Boston
October 18, 1954

CARDINAL O'CONNELL OF BOSTON

CHAPTER ONE

IRISH ANCESTRY

. . . lo cammin corto
di quella vita che al termine vola.
Dante: Purgatorio, Canto xx, 38-39

> *(The short pilgrimage of life still speed-
> ing to its close on restless wing.)*
>
> Cary, tr.

To THE new industrial city of Lowell, Massachusetts, about
1850, came a family from County Cavan, Ireland. It included
John O'Connell, aged forty years; his wife Brigid, eight years
younger; and seven children. Four more children would be born
to them in Lowell, the youngest being the subject of this biography.

Already many Irish people and priests from County Cavan had
emigrated to the then Diocese of Boston in which the city of Lowell
is included.[1]

County Cavan, which had a fine classical school, was a great
mother of vocations in the early Nineteenth Century. The tradition
and example of St. Patrick, sent to evangelize Ireland by Pope Ce-
lestine, in 430 A.D., urged many to volunteer for the mission field
of the young United States of America.

Father Thomas Lynch, ordained by Bishop Fenwick in Boston
in 1833 and first pastor of old St. Patrick's Church on Northampton Street, Boston, was a native of Lurgan, County Cavan, close

3

to the ancestral home of the O'Connells. A nephew of Brigid O'Connell was Rev. Patrick Farrelly, long a laborer in the Lord's vineyard in California until his death in 1910. From the same clan came the late Bishop John P. Farrelly of Cleveland, Ohio, born of Irish parents at Memphis, Tennessee, in 1856. Another scion of the same stock is now Bishop of Lismore, New South Wales, Australia, the Most Reverend Patrick J. Farrelly, D.D. Ancestors of the late John Cardinal Farley of New York lie buried in Temple Ceallaigh in the parish of Mullagh.

In many Irish families, the hardships of the nation cause gaps in official records. However, it is recorded that one ancestor of the future first Cardinal of Boston, a Brian O'Connell, had his estate in Raffeny, in the parish of Mullagh. It was confiscated in the reign of James I of England, in 1605. They must have been sturdy, hard-working stock for after the Cromwellian campaign of 1649-50, a Philip O'Connell by 1664 was owner again of a farm in Mullagh parish. The family tradition always held a kinship, too, with Patrick O'Connell, Canon of Kilmore Cathedral in 1542. Kilmore is the diocese which includes County Cavan and one of Cardinal O'Connell's last acts before his death would be to send a substantial contribution towards the new Kilmore Cathedral.

Family names were repeated lovingly from generation to generation. The Lurgan parish register, dating from 1754 to 1790, records the baptism of William O'Connell's grandfather, John O'Connell, son of Patrick and Eileen (Smith) O'Connell, on December sixth, 1766.

The bitter years of the Protestant Ascendancy and first years of the Union with Britain interrupted the keeping of records by hunted parish priests from 1790 to 1821. The census of 1821 brings John O'Connell to view again, now listed as a farmer of Fartagh, aged fifty-five years, with his wife Judith, three sons and three daughters. Mrs. Judith, her daughter Margaret, nineteen and daughter Brigid, seventeen, are described as "flax-spinners." Farmer John had ten acres of land for the growing of the flax.

The son John, father of the future Cardinal, was born February 23, 1809 and, on January 15, 1838, was married in the Lurgan parish church to Brigid Farrelly of Cargagh Simon, the adjoining townland. John was given a portion of the family farm at his marriage and built a home for his bride. To them in the next eleven years were born six children.[2] An elder brother of John, James O'Connell was to inherit the farm and live there until, in the 1880's, his family was evicted and the old house fell into ruins.[3]

Young John O'Connell, educated at a "hedge school" in County Cavan, was educated in the classics, English and Gaelic. He was said to be an accomplished musician and sang in the choir of the old chapel at Maghera where the family went to Mass on Sundays and holy-days. This talent for music and love of reading were traits evidently inherited by his youngest son, the future Cardinal.

In 1846-47 came the terrible blight of the potato crop which, coupled with the unrelenting pressure for high rents from the landlord class, destroyed over a million of Ireland's population and drove hundreds of thousands overseas.

A vivid picture of those dark days is given in the diary of Brigid Farrelly O'Connell's cousin, Father Peter Edward O'Farrelly (1794-1873), who after education and ordination in Paris, was a priest of the Archdiocese of Dublin till his death.[4]

No one who knows the long, long Via Crucis of Ireland, between landlord troubles, religious persecution and the potato blight, would wonder why John and Brigid O'Connell made a bitter North-Atlantic voyage in an emigrant ship around 1850. The only wonder is how the gallant mother survived those weeks of seasickness, of crowded quarters, of home-fetched provisions of porridge, bacon and hardtack, with six children, ranging from twelve-year-old Julia to the babe-in-arms, Matthew, and brought all safely to land at Montreal.

They settled first at Malone, New York, a centrally situated city on the railroad linking Lake Champlain with Ogdensburg on the St. Lawrence below Lake Ontario. In the foothills of the Adirondack mountains, only ten miles from the Canadian border, the Salmon River gives it abundant power for paper, pulp and other manufacturing interests.

The father of the family, John O'Connell, was a brick mason by profession and the factories of that era were chiefly of brick construction. He had no difficulty in finding employment. Malone later became famous as the gathering point of two Fenian raids over the Canadian border, so doubtless they had many friends there, of Irish birth. Their seventh child, Simon, was born at Malone, April 1, 1851.

The northern climate, with its deep snows, probably did not agree with the family, after the mild climate of Ireland, and the decision to move to Lowell was doubtless motivated by two factors, the mill-building there which promised employment to the brick mason and the presence of Brigid Farrelly O'Connell's sister, Mrs. Sarah Fay.

John O'Connell must have been a good earner, and his wife a thrifty manager. When they settled in Lowell, they bought a neat cottage on the outskirts of the new city and, in a short time, had built for rental three more houses, forming a little court on their property on Gorham Street.

In Lowell were born Sarah, May 21, 1853; Richard, September 8, 1855; Edward, September 4, 1857; and William Henry, December 8, 1859.

The future Cardinal was thus the eleventh child of his parents. His mother was forty-one years old at the time of his birth. Family tradition states that the anxious father carried the infant for baptism at St. Peter's Church only a few hours after his birth. The eighteen-year-old brother John ingeniously rigged a home-made incubator, by arranging the cradle near the open oven door of the kitchen stove, to supply artificial warmth for the frail baby.

At the very beginning of William O'Connell's life, the historian is faced with a contradiction. The municipal records of the City of Lowell give his birth date as December twenty-second, 1859; "William O'Connell, male, white, born at Gorham Street, Lowell, parents John and Bridget O'Connell, both born in Ireland, father's occupation, laborer." This discrepancy in dates was brought to the Cardinal's attention late in his life when public recognition of his birthday in Boston became a custom. It did not seem important enough to him to take steps to have the Lowell record corrected.

He had always known his birthday was December eighth, and it was so listed in all official documents, such as those concerned with his ordination as a priest. Moreover, he knew that the correct date was written in the original baptismal record of St. Peter's Church in Lowell,[5] in the middle of the page for December, routinely entered in ink with the rest of the babies baptized that month by the pastor, Rev. Peter Crudden. The date is given as December eighth, "William O'Connell, son of John O'Connell and Bridget Farley; sponsors, John O'Connell and Sarah Fay." Sarah Fay was sister to Mrs. Brigid O'Connell, aunt to the new baby; the godfather presumably the child's brother.

It is likely that the record down at City Hall reflects the mistake of a clerk in transcribing the date when the physician's return was made, rather than the actual birth date.

William Henry O'Connell, however, should furnish consolation to readers of his life who, themselves, have difficulty in remembering dates or anniversaries. This man, who as a youth took highest honors in college; who spoke Latin, Italian, French, German and Spanish; who recalled literally thousands of names and who administered superbly affairs running into millions of dollars, frequently got his dates wrong in other matters.

If he spoke of history, he often got the year wrong. As most of his adult life was passed in positions of honor or authority, people tended not to correct or challenge his dates and so he, himself, was unconscious of this rather common human defect. A family man generally gets picked up on dates by wife, children or friends. A Cardinal is accorded such deference that his mistakes go uncorrected.

For instance, O'Connell said his First Holy Mass on the eighth of June at the shrine of Our Lady of Perpetual Help in Rome, and mixed that date up with June seventh, when he had been ordained. He gave June eighth as the day of his ordination in his sketch for "Who's Who in America." Probably the eighth stuck in his mind because of his birthday being on the eighth of December. In short, the Cardinal had a poor memory for dates—a common human failing.

CHAPTER TWO

THE FAMILY IN LOWELL

La maggior valle in che l'acqua si spanda,
. . . Di quelle valle fu' io littorano.
Dante: Paradiso, Canto ix, 82, 88

(The great valley in which water stretcheth
. . . of this valley was I shoresman.)
Wicksteed, tr.

THE VALLEY of the Merrimack River, in Eastern Massachusetts, after precipitous descent from its beginnings in the foothills of the White Mountains, spreads out in a fertile plain and doubles back upon itself, finding the sea eventually at Newburyport on the East, instead of to the South. Perhaps, long ages ago, some yet unthawed dam of glacial ice so diverted it.

There, in primeval forests, the red men, Indians of the Pennacook tribe, had their villages at Pawtucket Falls on the Merrimack and Wamesit Falls on its tributary, the Concord River. Thence they went forth hunting deer, bear, wild turkey or beaver; or speared alewives and salmon swarming up the river in Spring, or tickled for trout in the forest brooks, for unrecorded years. Their chieftain Passaconway, in 1644, made treaty with newcomers, the white settlers of Massachusetts Bay. In 1647, Rev. John Eliot began his journeys thither from Roxbury, to bring them the gospel, the good tidings of Christ.

By 1652 white men were exploring the valley of the Merrimack River by boat, ascending from the sea as far as Lake Winnepesaukee; and, in 1655, the area including the future city of Lowell was incorporated by the General Court of Massachusetts as the town of Chelmsford. A century of peaceful cultivation of farms ensued.

Sheep were an important factor in the economy of rural New England. A mill for carding wool was built in what is today Lowell, in 1801, using water-power from the Merrimack. Disruption of trade, due first to the Napoleonic wars in Europe and the embargo leading to the War of 1812 with Britain, resulted in establishment of Lowell's first cotton-spinning mill in 1813.

Meantime, the man whose name is remembered in that of the city, Francis Cabot Lowell, had been sojourning in England and Scotland to learn the carefully-guarded industrial secrets of the power loom. British law forbade export of machines or plans for their building, but Francis Lowell had a retentive memory. "It was these secrets of manufacture intangibly hidden in his brain that were to create the huge factories of Lowell and Lawrence." [1]

The first mills, in Waltham, started by Lowell and his relatives, were soon paying twenty percent in dividends. The promoters, in 1821, organized the Merrimack Company; by 1830 they had promoted the Boston and Lowell Railroad to carry to market the products of their new mills on the Merrimack. It opened for traffic in 1835.

William Henry O'Connell was born in the little village of East Chelmsford, which had been incorporated into the City of Lowell. A hundred thousand spindles were whirling at five great mills of the Merrimack Company, with twenty-five hundred looms clacking. Some seventeen hundred 'teen-age girls from all over Northern New England worked in the mills and lived in the company boarding houses that Dickens described in his *American Notes*. Seven hundred men found employment, and lived in cottages on the hills above the river, like John O'Connell. Other mills, dye-works, machine shops and bleacheries congregated around the river banks.

Lowell, in the first years of its phenomenal growth and prosperity, was a Yankee community, but the digging of the canal and grading of the railroad attracted Irish laborers, Catholic in religion. In 1830, Kirk Boott, manager of the Merrimack Company, gave to Bishop Benedict J. Fenwick, S.J., land on which to build St. Patrick's Chapel. By 1854, Irish Catholics had so increased in numbers as to need and to build a $75,000 church on the site.

The South Common was laid out as a public park in 1840, by Gorham Street where, in 1842, a second Catholic church, St. Peter's, was established. In 1856 were built in that neighborhood the great stone walls of Lowell Jail for which Cardinal O'Connell, years later, would find a better purpose.

Old residents, Protestant by faith, viewed with distrust the rapid growth of the Catholic community. Shortly before William O'Connell's birth, the first lodge in Massachusetts of the notorious American Protestant Association, named for Plymouth Rock, was chartered in Lowell [2] on March second, 1859. Catholic celebrities entertained in Lowell, while William O'Connell was still in his cradle, were Prince Jerome Napoleon, with his wife Princess Clothilde.[3] No one could imagine, on that day of September twenty-fourth, 1861, that his sister-in-law, Queen Margherita of Italy, would come to kneel in Rome in the church of which William O'Connell would be rector.

Charles Dickens, visiting Lowell in 1842, gave a disheartening picture in his *American Notes* of railroad cars "like shabby omnibuses," on the single track from Boston through mile after mile of stunted trees, stagnant pools, stations in the woods; "mud almost knee-deep" in Lowell streets; new unpainted wooden buildings, the mills, "fresh buildings of bright-red brick." He praised the boarding houses where the mill girls lived; and pointed out that children could only work nine months a year and must have three months of schooling. Recalling the wording of the Anglican catechism "to do my duty in that station to which it has pleased God to call me," Dickens wrote of the girls:

"It is their station to work. And they do work . . . in these mills twelve hours a day, and pretty tight work, too."

Dickens spent about six hours in Lowell. Rev. Henry A. Miles,

who lived in Lowell, could tell how the three-story company board-
ing-houses, with a common dining room and kitchen on the first
floor, the rest given over to sleeping-rooms, up to six girls crowded
into a single room, did not have proper ventilation. Breakfast was
scheduled "so early as to begin work as soon as it is light"; supper
came after work around seven-thirty in the evening. Thirty minutes
were allowed at noon to run home, eat, and be back to work. Girls
paid $1.25, men $1.75 for board for a week and beginners' wages
were fifty cents above the charge for board. A skilled operative
could make up to $4 a week—but a boarding-house keeper, going
in debt for furnishing the house, in eleven years could pay all debts
and have $1,400 in the savings bank.[4]

Several of the O'Connell boys and girls worked in the Lowell
mills as their first employment, to aid their mother during John
O'Connell's lingering illness from cancer of the throat. One of William O'Connell's earliest memories was of being roused from sleep
to kneel, reciting the rosary at his father's deathbed, on the night
of September twenty-second, 1865. His only other memory of his
father was at family gatherings on Saturday evenings, reading aloud
to the children the then newly published poems of Whittier and
Longfellow. The custom was continued by their mother.

"My mother was always the major-general and director of our
home," said the son. "And the family never failed, before going to
bed, to kneel together and say their beads. I can see her now, a
stately figure with silver-gray hair, very beautiful, sacrificing herself
for us as only a mother can." [5]

Brigid O'Connell reared all of her children in a strong Catholic
faith, in habits of industry and thrift, and in virtue of character. A
precious family memory was of her welcome home of her oldest
son, at the close of his service in the Union Navy during the Civil
War. Her happiness was not in the six hundred dollars he had
saved to give her, but in himself that he had come back with his
ideals of purity untarnished, as she had taught them to him.

After the father's death, Julia became the mother's right hand
in care of the home and of the younger children. With the aid of
the older boys and girls and by prudent management of the prop-

erty left by her husband, Mrs. O'Connell purchased land on Fay Street, building a comfortable home and setting off portions, as her children married, so that they might build homes close to her.

There was never poverty in the household on Gorham Street, but neither were there riches. William's boyhood included learning to ride the family horse, a cob,[6] which his Irish heritage soon taught to jump fences or hedges around the countryside. There was swimming in the Concord River nearby and diving, from the old six-arch bridge; boating on the river, up the Merrimack to Tyngsboro Island; apple orchards to raid in the autumn; baseball on the Common in the Spring and football scrimmages when the frost came.

He attended the Edson Grammar School, unhappy because he felt the Protestant teachers despised the Irish Catholic minority. The memory of one Good Friday, when with other boys, he absented himself to serve on the altar at the Mass of the Pre-Sanctified, rankled deep for sixty years.

"Immediately on the opening of class (the next) morning, the teacher, a rabid anti-Catholic, called our names and bade us rise in our places. . . . With a sneer, she told the whole class that that was no reason whatever. 'Good Friday!' she said. 'I want you to know that all Fridays are good, and the boys who absented themselves may now come forward for punishment.' " [7]

CHAPTER THREE

SCHOOL DAYS

Io veggio ben' che giammai non si sazia
nostro intelletto.
> Dante: Paradiso, Canto iv, 124-5

> *(Now I see that never can our intellect
> be sated.)*
> Wicksteed, tr.

HOWEVER HAPPY may be childhood's hours of play and of maternal affection in the home, few would deny that the process of education is painful in some degree.

There is the effort to grasp unfamiliar techniques and to satisfy new authorities. There is the uncertainty as to vocation and future. Even a child knows vaguely that schooling leads to the day when he must stand alone, and knows worry as to where his lines shall lie, how he is to make his living.

Brigid O'Connell soon realized that her youngest son had the best mind in the family. He had a gift for music, fostered by piano lessons at home, progressing to ambitious efforts at the church organ. From the first, she was resolved that he should not become a mill-hand.

As a youngster, William O'Connell had a strong-willed independent nature. He had been petted by older brothers and sisters, thwarted by the anti-Catholic environment in school and commu-

13

nity. His mother learned to rule him by love and by indirection. So, probably, did Sister Mary Gabrielle who came Sundays from the Notre Dame convent to teach Sunday School. "We boys thought her the most beautiful woman in the world." [1] Public school hours were not so happy.

The year of his graduation from grammar school, young O'Connell had the idea that going to work in the mill would be pleasanter than more years of school. His wise mother acquiesced, woke him the next morning in time to answer the six o'clock bell at the mill gate, handed him a sandwich wrapped in paper as he started.

"For the first hour or two, I had the greatest delight in scattering the fluffy cotton . . . on the carding machine and watching it with fascinated eyes pass through the machinery. . . . The poetry of mechanical motion began to turn into a very serious prose. I began to feel faint from the disgusting smell of the oil . . . the roar of the noise . . . deafened my ears and numbed my brain. . . . I staggered feebly on . . . until the noon bell rang . . . I left the mill then and I never returned. . . . I took the uneaten sandwich from my pocket and sat down to a refreshing meal with my brothers and sisters. During all my life, that sandwich was a perpetual joke in my family." [2]

The practice of early First Holy Communion was not, at that period, encouraged to the degree that it would be, later. William O'Connell was nearly twelve years old before the day came for him, in the octave of the feast of the Assumption, August 21, 1870. He carefully preserved all his life the certificate signed by Father Thomas Norris. [3]

In June of 1876, William O'Connell was graduated from the Lowell High School. He had found its teachers more congenial, the studies more interesting than those of grammar school. Latin, physics, chemistry and geology he enjoyed. Spelling gave him trouble. He was furious at himself after an examination in which he had spelled a word "elickser," only, on walking home to see it in a drugstore sign as "elixir."

Furious, because already he had dreams of a vocation to the priesthood and knew he must do well in his studies to achieve it.

He mentions, in the summer of 1876, a long conversation with his confessor, who was probably Father Peter Crudden, pastor of old St. Peter's. O'Connell later described him as "a refined, cultivated man of amiable disposition."

The Catholic atmosphere of his home had its influence on him, too. Family tradition held that a priest-uncle,[4] before William was a week old, had predicted "This boy will be a priest." Brigid O'Connell, as Irish mothers do, must have prayed often that one, at least, of her children might serve God in His Church.

Nightly, as she led her brood in recitation of the rosary, her silent invocation must have ascended. Regularly she put aside savings towards the sum that might be needed to educate a priest. O'Connell himself recorded that from his fifteenth year he felt an attraction to the priesthood although, on graduating from high school, he still had no distinct sense of a vocation.[5] A long conversation with his confessor finally decided him to enter St. Charles' College in Maryland. He was not yet seventeen years old and, on his way South "spent a week of intense interest" visiting at Philadelphia the colorful Centennial Exposition, celebrating one hundred years of American Independence.

Then he went on to Baltimore and thence to Ellicott City where the tall-towered granite seminary stood on the former estate of Charles Carroll, Catholic signer of the Declaration of Independence.

The plunge into seminary life, straight from a co-educational public school was hard for William O'Connell. At first view, he could write home cheerfully of the Catholic atmosphere, of the crucifix in each classroom, religious pictures, statues and shrines honoring Christ, the Blessed Virgin, the saints. Daily Mass in the lovely Gothic chapel with white marble altar and stained glass windows was truly devotional. As at old St. Peter's, O'Connell was soon in the choir and presently was made its director.[6]

However, to the unsophisticated youth, accustomed to the blunt, genial ways of Irish priests who wore, in house or street, the ordinary garb of civilians around them, there was something chilling in his first contact with the French Sulpicians with their clerical garb, ascetic life, strict discipline and supervision. It was not easy for a boy, used to the freedom of his home and of the fields and river in Lowell, the unfettered conversation and companionship of brothers and sisters to learn to sleep in a proctored dormitory, to keep silence in corridor and refectory, to observe the rules in study-hall or classroom.

After the few hours daily of secular teachers in high school in Lowell, the steady discipline of the Sulpicians galled O'Connell. He hinted at his own trials in writing home of how Archbishop James Gibbons, when a student at St. Charles', had been punished for a false accent in Latin by having to kick a wooden post forty times, while repeating the word correctly. Boy-like, too, he poked fun at the devoted priests for their French accent in English. He was too young, too inexperienced to understand how they knew his difficulties and tried, gently, to give his impetuous nature an outlet by special privileges. One day, as an educator himself, he would realize what wise surveillance lay behind the sudden appearance of Père Denis, the President, three months after O'Connell's induction at the college:

"Wandering in the basement under the Chapel," wrote Willy O'Connell,[7] "I came across a wheezy little melodeon . . . I pumped for dear life on the pedals . . . to make the old thing echo the *Parigi, o cara* from Traviata . . . I turned to look over my shoulder and there in the gloom, wrapped in his long black mantle was— Père Denis, the President."

The upshot was that the gentle Sulpician said only: "You love music? Well, that, too, is a gift of the good God." Shortly thereafter, young O'Connell was working with Père Menu, the music master who, to the student's surprise, called on him to direct the students' choir.

Père Denis was perhaps disturbed about his young pupil when the new Archbishop James Gibbons made a visitation to his Alma Mater in November of 1878. Recollection, as taught by the Sulpicians, was getting Willy O'Connell down. His impetuous nature required the stimulus of notice, of admiring glances, of kindly conversation.

He lurked—no other word expresses his intention and action—
in the corridor. "After a while he (Archbishop Gibbons) came out
of Professor Griffin's room and I went over, rather sheepishly, and
asked if he would kindly bless my rosary." [8]

What else could the Archbishop do? But what did Père Denis
think about his student's self-seeking? It was not as though the
Sulpicians had not made every endeavor to ameliorate for William
O'Connell the transition from secular to seminary life. He had had
the advantage of many hours of the informal society of John Tabb,
convert clergyman from the Episcopal Church, who was teaching
English at St. Charles', before entering the Catholic priesthood.

Poet, scholar and musician, Tabb was encouraged by the Sulpicians to lighten young O'Connell's recreation hours with Bach,
Chopin, Schubert and Schumann.

"Once he sang to me the 'Erl King,' " remembered O'Connell,
fifty years later. "Here was magic of vivid description both in words
and music. I have heard the Erl King sung by singers renowned
for their artistic fame but never have I heard it interpreted as . . .
in that little room by one unknown and unhonored in the out-of-
the-way college of St. Charles'." [9]

None of the efforts of the Sulpicians succeeded in moulding the
fiery spirit of William O'Connell, as they had moulded James Gibbons or John J. Williams, Archbishop of Boston, to a pattern of
gentleness, patience, meekness.

The summer of 1878 brought it out strongly. O'Connell was
home in Lowell. The tendrils of home twined around his heart, as
he watched his mother's sorrow and resignation in the lingering
death from tuberculosis of thirty-year-old daughter Mary, veteran
of the lint-laden air of the textile mills in Lowell.

"She suffers very much, not only from weak spells but most of
all from the dreadful bed-sores, owing to her months of prostra-
tion," he wrote, ". . . I think I am going to have a bad time trying
to get my mind on studies. . . . I am at the beginning of a year's
hard work." [10]

He had found the work hard already. In his first year at St.
Charles', he had taken honors in Latin and French. In the second

year, no honors. Now he went back, reluctant, and did even more unsatisfactorily. By December he was sure that St. Charles' was not the place for him, but he remained cheerful.

"I spend at least two hours every day in the saddle. I have the dearest little cob you ever saw . . . I canter out in the country all alone and the fresh air and the riding are very exhilarating . . . mother says I begin to look like myself. . . . I am going in for my examination at Boston College in a few weeks." [11]

"This riding and freedom and home food are just what I need," [12] O'Connell wrote a chum at St. Charles' in January, 1879. He meant, although he would not have recognized or admitted it then, that they were just what his independent and loath-to-be-ruled disposition craved.

In March, 1879, because his pride would not let him leave school without a degree, he matriculated at Boston College, for the second semester. It speaks well for the teaching he had had at St. Charles' that the Jesuits found him qualified to enter at mid-term. He had come far enough to admit—just to himself—that he *was* running away in leaving St. Charles'; but he was still a bit immature about it all. He expected God to give him a sign.

"Somehow I felt that if God really wanted me to be a priest, He was going to give me a sign, and that sign would be my success in the coming exam." There was no realization in his mind that, contributing to success would be the natural endowments God had implanted in him at birth, the efforts of teachers in the Lowell schools and at St. Charles'. It never even entered his thought that the Rector, Father Robert Fulton, S.J., long experienced in educating boys, might have purposely left him waiting an hour for the interview; an hour in which to think, to hope, to pray, before the oral examination began.

"I got on swimmingly. I never felt so clear. I began to wonder at myself."

Finally good Father Fulton rose, picked up his biretta, led William O'Connell to a classroom.

"I have come to bring you a new student," said Father Fulton. "If you boys don't work hard, he will take all the honors."

In the end, with that spur, that challenge, that is just what William O'Connell did. For a year and a half, every morning he rose in time to take the seven o'clock train to the old depot in Boston, walk a mile and a half in all weathers across the Common to old Boston College on Harrison Avenue in the South End; recite, and perform the journey home to Lowell again. The train journey took an hour each way, time for studying his lessons. He got in an hour's ride before supper on the little cob.

He even found time for his music, when a vacancy occurred in the parish church of Wakefield, a few miles from Lowell, and he took on the job of directing the choir and playing the organ. The Wakefield pastor made it easy, by inviting him to supper and overnight on Saturdays—incidentally giving William O'Connell his first experience of the life of a parish priest.

In June, 1881, William O'Connell was graduated with the class he had joined in mid-course less than two years before. The Governor of Massachusetts, John D. Long, presented the prizes. William O'Connell was called three times to the platform: for first gold medal in Philosophy; first silver medal in Physics; second medal in Chemistry.

"God bless you, child," said his mother, when they were home in Lowell that night. "You must be very happy."

But he was not happy. He had not yet resolved the question of his life's career. Attendance at the Jesuit day college in the city had afforded opportunities on Saturday afternoons, or week-day evenings to enjoy the theatres. The Boston College debating society had fired many a student with a desire to study law or to go into politics.[13] His prowess in physics and chemistry offered a vista of a career in science, a professorship, perhaps, at some great university. There were all kinds of possibilities, but down underneath, the still small voice kept whispering. His mother saw his restlessness. Finally, he broached his indecision to her.

"Pray, son, pray," was all the advice she offered.

"So I began a novena to our Blessed Mother," he recalled.

It was in his mind that he might, temporarily, find a position as lay-instructor at Boston College. There is no other reason why a young man from Lowell should be walking up Washington Street in Boston's South End on a blazing hot morning of the sixth of July.

The way to Boston College from the former Lowell railroad depot in Boston passes the Cathedral of the Holy Cross. William O'Connell saw many carriages with their horses tethered around the cathedral, a great crowd of people going into the granite Gothic structure. He followed them, idly, curiously, little knowing that in the next hour the Finger of God would give him the sign he had wanted.

Archbishop John J. Williams, born, 1822, in Boston, educated by the Sulpicians in Montreal and Paris, ordained in Notre Dame Cathederal there in 1845; Metropolitan of New England since 1875, was noted for his reluctance to preach. Taciturn in the highest degree even in conversation, he avoided public utterances as much as possible.

On that July morning, however, he ascended the pulpit (half-way down the tremendous nave, before the invention of microphones and loud-speakers) to deliver a eulogy on the young rector of the cathedral whose bier stood in the aisle.

Simply, yet eloquently, the Archbishop told of this young priest, born in Lowell (William O'Connell, standing at the rear of the crowded cathedral, started at the name of the city). He described how John B. Smith had come to him for permission to study for the priesthood; how he, the Archbishop, had sent him as one of the first young men from Boston diocese, in 1869, to the new North American College in Rome.

"He came back to us from Rome" said the Archbishop, "where he already had given promise of all he has now fulfilled of the power and holiness of a priestly life. He loved Rome as a child loves a dear, tender mother, and he taught us by that love to cherish Rome more. May God send this Church and this Diocese many priests like him."

The words winged through the great cathedral straight to the heart of William O'Connell.

"I got down on my knees . . . those around me must have

thought I was some dear friend of the dead rector, overcome with grief. An usher came to offer me a place in a pew. How little they knew. Not grief, but joy was bursting my heart, overflowing in tears of thanksgiving. I left the Church and fairly ran to the station for the train home."

William O'Connell would never know a more sincere moment in all his long life—but the sincerity would never fade.

He had no thought of ambition or self-seeking at that moment. He could not look into the future and know that thirty years later, in the scarlet and ermine of a Cardinal he, Willy O'Connell of Lowell, would pontificate in that very cathedral on whose floor he humbly knelt that August morning. He knew only, at last, that he wanted to serve God.

There it was. Out of the early death of a beloved young priest, out of the reluctant preaching of a taciturn archbishop, out of the aimless footsteps of a twenty-two-year old college graduate, God's Providence forged the shining steel of a purpose to serve Him in His Church on three continents for the next half-century.

William O'Connell was back in Boston next morning, at the cathedral rectory on Union Park Street where Archbishop Williams lived with his clergy. The Archbishop recognized the honor scholar he had seen at Boston College Commencement a few days earlier. He listened to him sympathetically.

"Would you like to study in Rome?" asked the Archbishop, thinking of the boy he had sent to Rome ten years ago and had buried yesterday.

CHAPTER FOUR

SEMINARIAN IN ROME

Qual sole o quai candele, ti stenebraron si,
che tu drizzasti poscia di retro al
pescator le vele?
>   Dante: Purgatorio, Canto xxii, 1 61-63

>   *(What sun or candle dispelled the darkness so
>   that thou henceforth set thy sails to
>   follow the Fisherman?)*
>   Okey, tr.

WILLIAM O'CONNELL had not realized how long, how confidently his mother had prayed for his vocation until, as she presented her bankbook at the cashier's cage, he heard her say cheerfully:

"All, please."

It shamed him, hurt him to think of using her last hoarded penny to buy his passage to Rome. He protested.

"Not as bad as all that," she answered, smiling but with the glint of a tear.

"I put this away, bit by bit through the years, with a prayer for this one purpose. And I want you to go by way of Ireland for a greeting to my old home there for me."

How many times in the thirty years since she left County Cavan, must Brigid O'Connell have felt the tight grip of homesickness take her heart. How often she must have longed to see once again the dear land, the familiar faces, hear the home-speech. But she would not spend the money on herself. She had dedicated it to give God a priest—a true widow's mite such as earned Our Lord's blessing long ago.

Two months after Archbishop Williams had accepted him, young O'Connell sailed from East Boston on the old Cunarder *Marathon* for Queenstown. A fellow-passenger was another Boston candidate for the North American College, John F. Ford.

It was a bit of a marathon that the pair made, on landing at Queenstown. First to Dublin to see the Book of Kells, that priceless illuminated manuscript from the Eighth Century; then to the town of Kells to see the old stone church still called "St. Colmcille's House" and the beautiful stone Celtic crosses, only five miles from County Cavan and the little town of Virginia on the wooded shores of Loch Ramor. It was from Virginia that John and Brigid O'Connell had emigrated thirty years earlier. Nearby was the parish church of Lurgan where they had been married. The old O'Connell homestead at Fartagh was no longer in the family's possession; but at Enagh, he found his mother's brother, Uncle John Farrelly.

With cordial Irish hospitality, the two youths were entertained and William must talk late into the night, telling all the kinsfolk the news of the family in Lowell. By day, walking about the green countryside, he recognized each view, each place from his mother's tales of them—especially the Hill of Bruise, towering six hundred feet above the plain, dear to the heart in memory of County Cavan natives.

Rome was calling and the travelers' time all too short. O'Connell and Ford, stopping briefly (and most economically) in London and Paris for a bit of sight-seeing, arrived by train in Rome early on the morning of October twenty-seventh, 1881. They loaded their bags into one of the open carriages, with the *vetturino* sitting high in front, his feet on a bundle of green fodder. The horse clumped off over the cobblestones, up the Esquiline hill and down and around to the narrow Via dell' Umiltá, and the recessed doorway in the high, blank wall of Number Thirty.

The hour was so early that the students' Mass was not yet ended. The porter left them to wait in the palm-shaded garden court inside the rectangle formed by the ancient structure.

So historic and beautiful are this ancient cloister and church that, in 1951, the Italian Government officially declared them a National Monument: [1] and they are justly cherished in the memories of every American priest who has lived and studied there.[2]

They were rich traditions that young O'Connell and Ford and Deasy from Boston [3] inherited when they entered the North American College in 1881. Five Boston men had been ordained there between 1869 and 1874. For several years, there had been no Boston representatives. Now the newcomers found three comrades from Boston to welcome them; James F. Talbot and Nicholas B. Walsh, sent by Archbishop Williams in 1878; and Charles F. Glennon who had come in 1880.

The first student whom the newcomers met, however, was the prefect, August J. Schulte of Philadelphia, who took them to a huge and gloomy cell, brick-floored, with stone walls; lighted by brass handlamps burning olive oil. There was no heat, no plumbing. Two iron cots with cornhusk mattresses, two deal chests, two wooden desks and two chairs comprised the furnishings. At first the two young Americans looked around in dismay. They read the marble tablet, stating that Francesca Baglioni lived twenty-six years in this room before she died in 1626.

"Well," said Ford, making the best of it. "If she could stand it, I guess we can."

There was novelty in laying away their civilian clothes in camphor in the chests, and donning the knee breeches and long black stockings as foundation for their new cassocks. The garment seemed medieval to youths fresh from America where even their Archbishop wore sober black secular suits with shirtstuds and neckties.

They were to learn that students of most of the eight national colleges for seminarians in Rome were distinguished by the colors of their soutanes. They made a bright touch in the streets, going on their walks, two by two, or to classes. At the Pontifical Seminary, the cassock was purple; at the Propaganda, black with red piping and sash; the German College was all scarlet; the Scots, purple with a red sash; the Greek, blue with a red sash. Originally, for distinctiveness, it had been planned to have green cassocks for the Americans. The first students protested so passionately at parading the streets like parrakeets, that plain black was substituted, with a dark red cincture, three red buttons at the neck,[4] a white clerical collar, and blue facings. This satisfied the seminarians as representing the "Red-White-and-Blue," and it was this costume which O'Connell and Ford now donned for the first time. The "leading strings" of their sleeveless *soprano* were a novelty, but they soon learned that all students had the two broad strips of cloth hanging down the back from the shoulders, to represent that they were not yet ordained.

The Americans were not long in falling into the pattern of seminary life. Up at five-thirty every morning, for prayers and meditation; Mass at six; breakfast; tidy their rooms. At ten minutes of eight, fall in two by two with the *camerata* for the ten-minute march down the street to the old Urban College for classes. March home again at ten for two hours of study; examen of conscience; dinner at noon. Forty-five minutes for siesta or recreation; the march again for two hours of afternoon class; then a five-mile walk, still two by two, through the city to one of the famous churches where Forty Hours was being held, and to the Pincian Gardens or some other park. Home again for study; rosary and supper at eight o'clock; recreation and, at nine-thirty, night prayers and bed. This was the regimen for nine months of the year. August, September, October, when, in the old days, malaria was prevalent in Rome, were spent in the Alban hills, in a villa at Grottoferrata.

Students, schoolboys, soldiers in barracks and prisoners in jails notoriously complain of institutional fare. William O'Connell was no exception. He said that in the refectory, at each table seating six students, "a watery concoction that had not even the merit of being hot" was ladled from soup-tureens. "Then came a platter of meat, cut in the merest slivers, excellent Italian greens . . . dessert in the form of the tiniest little russet apple—supplemented on feast days by a piece of cheese. At the side of each plate was a hard crust of excellent bread, and before each student a small bottle of wine, a little over half a pint."

The meal was eaten in silence, with spiritual reading as accompaniment by a reader in a pulpit over the door. Supper consisted of "an almost invisible portion of cold meat or a few sardines on fast days." However, he admitted, after their afternoon walk, they had "a half-glass of wine and a biscuit." Breakfast was "coffee and a biscuit."

The wine as beverage, of course, was "the custom of the country," in a day when no prophylaxis was known against typhoid or cholera and the lack of sanitation made drinking of water too hazardous. It was "an excellent red wine—rather a bitter taste," [5] non-intoxicating in the quantities allotted to the students.

Even so, the young Americans at the college were getting heartier fare than the native Italians had. The Pope, like the humblest peasant, ate only one meal, in the middle of the day, before the siesta, with perhaps a cup of soup and some fruit before bed. It suited the climate, said the Italians, and suited them; but hearty, husky young Americans expected more.

The classes at the Urban College were an eye-opener to O'Connell. Boston College had already introduced him to lectures in Latin, but that had been beginners' Latin. Here in Rome, were experts who could talk in Latin, vividly, naturally, learnedly, for two hours without a pause, on abstruse topics of philosophy or theology. Textbooks were not employed in the classroom; instead the students took voluminous notes, to study and compare in their own rooms. Physics, Hebrew and Greek and mathematics completed the first-year curriculum. In the ensuing years came dogmatic theology, moral theology, Church history, Sacred Scripture, liturgy. Gregorian chant was taught and practised in classes at the American College.

Young O'Connell never liked the Rector of his day, Rt. Rev. Louis E. Hostlot, "a face and manner quite Napoleonic" was his

description, "courteous enough—perhaps a trifle peremptory."
Other students recalled that Monsignor Hostlot was very fond of
music. "We could judge of his happy or melancholy moods by
hearing him accompanying himself and singing in the Sala." [6]

The students, of course, had no idea of Monsignor Hostlot's
problems that contributed to his occasional "melancholy"; but
only six months before O'Connell and Ford reached Rome, the
Italian Government had launched a program of confiscating and
auctioning off church property. As the property was held in the
name of the Sacred Congregation of Propaganda, the Rector and
the American Archbishops were worried for fear of losing the in-
vestment of about a quarter of a million dollars of American money
over the past twenty years in improvement, furnishings and endowment for scholarships in the property in Rome. The seizure
was fought from court to court, on appeal until, early in 1884,
the Court of Cassation, highest in Italy, ruled against the Church.
The blow, undoubtedly, contributed to Monsignor's sudden death
by a heart attack in March of 1884, and the long-drawn out
suspense had given him anxiety all through O'Connell's student
years.

In the crisis caused by Hostlot's sudden death and the impending government confiscation, the college in Rome was saved by
the prompt initiative of its alumnus Bishop Michael A. Corrigan
of New York. President Chester A. Arthur chanced to be staying
in New York that week, and Corrigan put the case before the
President. The result was that Secretary of State Frederick T.
Frelinghuysen cabled American Ambassador William Waldorf
Astor to interview the Italian Foreign Minister Mancini. On hearing from the American authorities, the Italian government recognized the North American College as American property and
exempted it from the seizure.

Young O'Connell, his mind stuffed with as yet undigested Latin,
Greek and Hebrew paradigms, philosophical propositions and theological dogmas, had little grasp of Italian politics and no idea
of how near he was to having the roof sold over his head. He just
put Monsignor Hostlot down as a moody Napoleonic character.

He admired the professor of theology, Doctor Checchi, who had "a manner so simple and utterly self-effacing" as he made "sublime doctrine clear as crystal." He found the Greek professor of liturgy, Archbishop Stephanopoli, picturesque in loose-flowing, wide-sleeved habit, jet-black beard and long hair, with his way of taking snuff from a silver snuffbox and flicking the grains from his beard with a silk handkerchief. He enjoyed the students' joke on gullible Doctor Pennachi, who asked the variegated class to give specimens of addresses, each in their native language. The Spaniards, the French, the Egyptians, Chinese performed punctiliously. The English orated in clipped syllables. The North American representative rose and, poker-faced, delivered a string of gibberish concocted the night before hilariously at the college. The tongue, he solemnly informed the group, was "native American Choctaw." The professor was not quite as simple as they thought. Thereafter, in calling on Americans, he was apt to say "No more Choctaw, please!"

Of all his professors, in the three years that William O'Connell was at North American College, the one whose influence was to count for most in his life was Francesco Satolli, whose subject was Scholastic Theology. There were no schoolboy pranks played in Satolli's class at Propaganda; the students were spellbound by his personality.

"Middlesized, very swarthy, lean and angular; but he has a brain, and an eye and a tongue . . . which simply sets the classroom on fire with enthusiasm," wrote William O'Connell to his friend in 1883.[7]

One thing a study of Catholic biography shows is that God can use all kind of characters and dispositions in His service, granted the will and intention to serve Him. At the very time that William O'Connell was a student in Rome, another student was pursuing his studies more quietly with better recollection than the impetuous young American from Lowell. This was Achille Ratti, who had been ordained in 1879 but was still pursuing his doctorate at the Gregorian. The first time that William O'Connell met Achille

Ratti, however, was on the sixth of February, 1922, when he knelt before him as the newly elected Pope Pius XI.

In 1882, however, both Ratti and O'Connell were working away at their studies, unaware of what the future held. Bit by bit, precept upon precept, line upon line, the influence of the devoted teachers, the atmosphere of the solemn ceremonies in the beautiful old shrines, the impact of a tradition stemming from the days when Peter and Paul trod the same streets, had its effect in forming the character of William O'Connell.

He gave an unconscious picture writing to his mother in May, 1882: "On the feast of St. Philip we all went to assist at Vespers in the great Basilica of Sant' Apostoli. . . . The Cardinal Vicar, Monaco La Valetta, officiated and the students assisted . . . we sat upright for hours. It was wonderfully grand, but my! so fatiguing. How the poor Cardinal is able to go through such interminable functions again and again is surely a mystery. . . . As we went back into the sacristy in procession with the Cardinal it was already nearly dark. I wish you could have seen . . . the great gloomy church lit dimly by the great torches, the Cardinal in that wonderful red Cappa, the train yards behind carried by the train-bearer; his chaplain and gentleman-in-waiting in costume—it was certainly very, very beautiful.

"They are all so very gracious and amiable, these great Roman prelates. After being disrobed, His Eminence sat in a great gold chair and received us. Such a charming manner—a little word for each, sometimes a tap on the cheek or a pat on the head—but all so charmingly amiable . . . he was escorted to the carriage by the *parroco* and all the monks bearing lighted torches—a little wave of the hand, a bow and His Eminence entered, the door closes with a click and off the black horses trot . . . and we, too, trot around the corner back to Umiltá and our books." [8]

The boy from Lowell was beginning to absorb the lesson that an ambassador of Christ disciplines himself to reverence during ceremonies, hardens himself to bear the weight of heavy robes and the toll of long hours; and still is "charming" and "amiable" to those about him, strangers though they may be. Example is often a better teacher than text, and Holy Mother Church has known this for many a century.

Even as the Sulpicians, so Monsignor Hostlot recognized that for William O'Connell, music was a release of tension. O'Connell was soon given responsibility as director of the seminary choir and he had tremendous happiness in the praise accorded a musical composition of his—the motet *Juravit Dominus,* first sung by the seminary choir and ever since the official American College anthem at ordinations. Even after Cardinal O'Connell's death, it would continue to be sung in the Boston archdiocese, too, and was heard on the first televised ordination, in the chapel of St. John's Seminary in Boston on February 1, 1953.

The North American College, being supported by the American bishops, was also their usual stopping place on visits to Rome. In the late fall of 1883, most of the Archbishops of America were there, for consultations over the Plenary Council to be held at Baltimore in the Spring. O'Connell thus saw at close quarters the "giants" who had borne the heat and burden of the early days of the Church in the Nineteenth Century;—Archbishop James Gibbons; Monsignor Chatard representing the Indianapolis diocese (he had been the second Rector of the College 1868-78); Archbishop Patrick J. Ryan of Philadelphia, a noted orator; Archbishop Peter Richard Kenrick of St. Louis.

"To my mind, the prince of them all is our own Archbishop," wrote O'Connell of John J. Williams. "In appearance and manner and carriage he is certainly an imposing prelate. He says very little, curtly refusing to address the students. They say he does not excel in that sort of work, although I shall never forget the sermon he preached in our Cathedral at the death of Father Smith. I serve his Mass and he looks like a saint at the altar . . . his face is a combination of severe dignity and genuine goodness." [9]

On the agenda discussed for the coming Plenary Council was the regulation of clerical garb for priests and bishops in America, now that anti-Catholic hostility and prejudice were waning. The students were amused by Father William J. Daly, pastor of St.

Joseph's Church in Boston's West End, who had accompanied Archbishop Williams on the voyage to Rome.

"He was a jolly, rotund man . . . who wore a wide open vest displaying a great white shirtfront, decorated with three enormous emerald studs. One of the prelates, speaking about requiring the Roman collar and long black coat, pointed laughingly at Father Daly and said: 'This sort of array will end pretty soon.' Most of us agreed it was time," [10] wrote young O'Connell, thoroughly habituated to his own black soutane and the ecclesiastical dress of the Roman clergy by now.

CHAPTER FIVE

ORDAINED A PRIEST

L'esercito di Cristo, che si caro coste a
riarmo, retro all' insegno si movea.
Dante: Paradiso, Canto xii, 37-38

*(Christ's army, which it cost so dear to re-equip,
was following His standard.)*

Wicksteed, tr.

THE VITAL years in the whole life of any priest, are those spent in the seminary, preparing for ordination.

Whatever the future holds for a man—be he destined for a pastorate, for the missions, for the purple or, even, for the tiara of the Papacy—in the seminary is forged the dedication to Christ's service, the self-abnegation necessary to perseverance, after his consecration "according to the order of Melchisedech."

In the seminary, too, are acquired the fundamental training in theology and liturgy, the habits of study by which a priest, the rest of his years, will continue to form himself as a teacher, a spiritual guide and a sacramental minister to his people.

These things are taught in every Catholic seminary in the world. In Rome, the surroundings and atmosphere impart special lessons.

Rome of 1881, as young O'Connell first saw it, was only ten years divorced from centuries of Papal administration despite occasional stormy interregna. The Nineteenth Century's bent to-

wards Nationalism, to culminate in two World Wars in the Twentieth Century, however, had brought Victor Emmanuel II's cannon
crashing through the ancient wall at Porta Pia, in 1870 naming a
street newly Via Venti Settembre. The King of unified Italy by
1881 lived in the old palace of the Popes on Quirinal hill. The
pope, Pius IX, had died a self-immured prisoner in the Vatican.
Only three months before O'Connell's arrival, a sacrilegious mob
had battled with the papal funeral cortege on the bridge over the
Tiber, hoping to fling the body in the river before it could be
buried at St. Laurence's-without-the-Walls.

The excesses of a revolutionary, anti-clerical mob necessitated
strict observance of ancient Vatican rules that no cardinal go on
the streets alone. They must drive in carriages, accompanied by a
secretary and coachman. The seminarians were by old custom forbidden to walk abroad alone. Always they went in *Camerata,* fifteen or twenty strong, walking two by two.

Skulking through the crowds, too, were anarchist-conspirators,
ever hoping for a chance to kill the King, though it would be
twenty years yet before King Umberto I was assassinated at Monza.

"Is Your Majesty not afraid to drive so informally through the
streets?" Umberto was asked, after the attempt on his life at
Naples, 1878. "You might be assassinated."

"Comment donc! C'est un des ennuis de notre metier!" said the
king.[1] (Oh well, that is one of the annoyances of my job!)

The superiors and professors of O'Connell's day still remembered when Pius IX lived in the Quirinal palace and could walk, in
his white robes, down the hill to hear Vespers at San Clemente and
on to St. John Lateran, with the people kneeling for his blessing as
he passed. Now, in 1881, the new Pope, Leo XIII, sat in Peter's
Chair and took his solitary exercise only behind the high walls of
the Vatican gardens.

Yet, for all the temporal political changes, Rome remained—
and still remains—the Eternal City, the heart's home of every
ardent Catholic. Young O'Connell soon felt it, like every pilgrim.

It strikes home with the first step inside the bronze doors of St.
Peter's basilica, when, in the distance, six hundred feet away, be-

yond the flicker of ninety-five lamps perpetually burning above the tomb of the Apostle, the golden light streams in a glory of radiance through the window of the Holy Ghost above Peter's Chair.

In lingering visits, the pilgrim will come to know the individual monuments; the colossal statues, the marble cherubs upholding the holywater fonts, the glorious mosaics, the beauty of the sixteen side chapels, each a church by itself; the detail of the papal altar beneath the bronze canopy with twisted mighty columns. But never will be forgotten that first symbolic vista of a forest of pillars and statues, illuminated by the light of Heaven shining through to a troubled world.

The North American seminarians, in their daily afternoon walks, visited all the historic shrines that evoke so powerfully the abiding sense of the continuity of the Catholic faith, the procession of generations of the Church which is the Mystical Body of Christ, its members each a branch of the True Vine, nourished by the same Sacrament, linked in the same profession of Faith.

There were plenty of ancient churches for the seminarians to visit. St. John Lateran, with its attached palace where the Popes had dwelt in the first ten centuries, now embellished with rare marbles and paintings, and the silver reliquaries containing the heads of St. Peter and St. Paul; or Santa Maria Maggiore, with its gorgeous ceiling embossed with the first gold brought from the American continent after Columbus' discovery; and the beautiful Borghese chapel where a boy of O'Connell's day would say his First Holy Mass, all unconscious that O'Connell one day would vote for him as Pope.[2]

The Rome of O'Connell's seminary days existed in a world that has vanished. It knew no telephones, no radio nor television. Its traffic was composed of carriages drawn by horses, carts hitched to donkeys or oxen; burdens balanced gracefully on the heads of men and women. Every *piazza* or square had its colorful outdoor stalls for merchandise. The immense flight of the Spanish Stairs, curving up to the twin-towered church of Trinita dei Monti, was banked with masses of fresh-cut flowers for sale, and thronged

with dark-eyed, curly-headed Roman women and children waiting
to be hired as models by the art students and artists of all nations
studying in the artistic capital of the world.

Day by day, over the seminary years, the walks for the *camerata*
were planned to show the students one or another of Rome's four
hundred and more ancient, storied churches, her catacombs, her
ruins. Day by day their spirits absorbed the lessons of history, the
traditions of the Faith, the enlargement of the mind's horizon that
is the gift of Rome above all of other cities, unique in its inter-
weaving of temporal and spiritual heritage.

If the *camerata,* in O'Connell's day, took their afternoon walk
westward, they passed the church of St. Ignatius with the time
ball on its roof, of which the dropping at noon was signal for the
cannon to be fired from the Janiculum by which all Rome set its
clocks and watches. Victor Emmanuel had seized the ancient
Collegio Romano, where the Jesuits had taught from the Sixteenth
century, to make a museum of it. The Gregorian University, since
1873, had to hold its classes in the Palazzo Borromeo.

There was no tunnel in the old days, under the Quirinal hill.
The *camerata* might climb to the Piazza del Quirinale, with its
obelisk and the four mighty marble horses, and down the steps,
perhaps, to the church of Santa Croce dei Lucchesi to hear the
nuns singing vespers.

Or, in early January, perhaps they would visit Santa Maria in
Ara Coeli, the lofty brown church on the site of the Roman temple
that Augustus erected when the Sibyl prophesied "A Hebrew
child, in God Himself and stronger than all the gods, bids me leave
Heaven to give Him place. Invoke me then no more." It was a
solemn thing for young seminarians, looking back over twenty
centuries of history to realize that their lesson in Gregorian chant
that morning, perhaps, had referred to this, in the marvelous Sequence of the Mass for the Dead:

> Dies irae, dies illa
> Solvet saeclum in favilla
> Teste David *cum Sibylla.*

After Epiphany, in old Rome, soon would come the week-long Carnival before Lent, when people drove up and down the Corso tossing flowers, bonbons and confetti to the crowds in the street, and, in the late afternoon, a herd of wild horses would be loosed in the Piazza del Populo to race, goaded by the yells of close-packed spectators down the narrow mile of the Corso to Piazza Venezia. Carnival ended on Shrove Tuesday night with everyone carrying a lighted candle through the streets, all trying gaily to guard their own and extinguish their neighbor's taper.

Snow lay rarely in the streets of Rome. By March everywhere in park or field the bright cyclamens, anemones, purple violets would spangle the young green grass, and shrubs and ferns and masses of white or yellow roses masked the as yet unexcavated ruins of the Forum or the Baths of Caracalla.

O'Connell and the other seminarians would see, in March of 1883, the great display of fireworks from Castel Sant' Angelo, honoring the state visit of the Crown Prince of Germany to King Humbert.

All around them, too, were pointed out ancient buildings associated with great names. The English poet John Milton had been a guest of Cardinal Barberini, brother of Urban VIII, in 1638 and had studied Greek manuscripts in the Vatican library. In their Dante, they might read

> Quivi era storiata l'alta gloria
> Del roman principato, il cui valore
> Mosse Gregorio alla sua gran vittoria
> Io diso di Traiano imperadore.[3]

and, that same afternoon, take their walk through the Forum of Trajan in the steps of Gregory the Great who prayed there that the soul of so noble a pagan might be saved. Daily they might pass the Church of San Andrea delle Fratte where Alphonse Ratisbonne on January 20, 1842, had the vision of Our Lady; and so by Via di Mercede past the house where Sir Walter Scott once lived; or the house where Keats died. They might visit San Pietro in Montorio across the Tiber and muse by the gravestones of Hugh

O'Neil of Tyrone and that dated 1608 of O'Donnell of Tyrconnell, who fled to Rome from the persecution of James I and died here. If they went to the Church of St. Agatha on via Panisperna, built by the Goths in the fifth century, then attached to the Irish College, William O'Connell could gaze, with a surge of Irish emotion, at the monument to Daniel O'Connell, great champion of Irish freedom, who willed his heart to be buried there in Rome, in 1847.

Day by day these stones once pressed by the feet of Apostles, the dust once reddened with the blood of martyrs, the ancient churches built by the faithful, ruined by barbarians, rebuilt by the Church which suffers all, endures through all, made their mark on the young American seminarian. More and more he felt gratitude to God for his vocation and the resolution to serve God, wherever it might please his Master to call him.

The test was nearer than he could guess. He looked forward to graduate study for his doctorate, for which his high scholastic standing qualified him, after his ordination in June of his third year. Instead, in February, 1884, influenza struck him down for a month, in his brickfloored, unheated cell, and, during his illness, he received a great shock.

"Pacifico, as he opened the door with my breakfast, gasped, 'Il Rettore e morto!' Weak as I was, I dressed and crawled down stairs, with Pacifico's aid, to the Rector's apartment. The house was ghostly still; the students were all in chapel for Mass. The door of the bedroom was open and there, true enough, lay the poor dead form of our Rector, so white and still. He had died suddenly in the night. I entered softly, knelt at the bedside and prayed. I was chattering with a chill and Pacifico forced me back to my room . . . Thus began another wicked stage in my illness—the worst yet." [4]

O'Connell had done so well in his studies, that the acting-Rector, Rev. August Schulte, arranged for his ordination, with several men longer at the college than he, on June seventh, at St. John Lateran. The Prefect of the Congregation of Propaganda Fidei, John Cardinal Simeoni, officiated since the United States were still a mission territory under the direction of Propaganda.

O'Connell had received First Tonsure on December fifteenth and Minor Orders on the seventeenth and twenty-third of the same month in 1882, a year after his arrival in Rome. On May first, 1883, he lay prostrate before the altar for ordination to the Sub-diaconate, and on May nineteenth he was made a Deacon. Cardinal Simeoni officiated at all the ceremonies.

The Retreats of May, 1882, and June, 1883, prior to Ordination were held under the direction of the Redemptorists in their large house on Via Merulana, adjoining the Church of St. Alphonsus. This beautiful church was not ancient, having been built only in 1859, the year of O'Connell's birth. Unlike most churches of Rome, its architecture was Gothic, representing a thank-offering to God of the Scottish convert, Father Edward Douglas.

Kneeling in this church, William O'Connell had impressed upon his heart the title under which for the rest of his life, he would particularly honor his patroness, the Blessed Mother of God, Our Lady of Perpetual Help. Above the main altar he saw enshrined the ancient picture of Mary, in dark blue robe, with undergarment of red, and spreading crown of gold. The Infant, also crowned and dressed in green, with golden cloak, is seated on her left arm, clasping the thumb of her right hand in His two tiny hands. Angels, in pink with green wings, hover on either side, holding the instruments of Our Lord's Passion.

He conceived a deep affection for this representation of the Virgin and Child. He bought for himself a small triptych, in a portable gold case and for sixty years, until his death, it stood always by his bed, last thing he saw at night, and first in the morning.[5]

The church of St. John Lateran to which the Popes used to go in procession, riding on their white mules, to take possession by right of their original title of Bishop of Rome, did not look in 1884 as we of today see it. For nearly ten years, since 1876, the apse with the high altar, and both transepts had been closed off to the public, while workmen labored at the restoration undertaken by Leo XIII, the first Pope who had not been able to visit his titular church because of the Italian occupation. The ordination, in 1884, was held

in the imposing nave, bordered by gigantic statues of the Apostles.
"The ordination was a severe test for me, I felt so weak," O'Connell wrote to his brother. "But oh! the happiness, the indescribable
joy gave me strength to spare.

"There was a large number for ordination . . . we were there
from early morning until one in the afternoon . . . the Cardinal
was so calm, so comfortable-looking that you would never think
it was so huge a task as it must have been for a man of seventy-five.
But these Roman ecclesiastics are gentility itself . . . they are always
there, bringing order out of chaos." [6]

None of William O'Connell's family could afford to go from
Lowell for the ordination in the basilica of St. John Lateran. Much
as he missed having them there, it is readily imagined what a
sacrifice it was on Brigid O'Connell's mother heart to have given
all her savings to educate her son for the priesthood, and have
none left to see him made a priest and receive his first blessing.

Perhaps it was to spare his mother's heart a pang of holy envy,
that young Father O'Connell did not write her of the imparting
of his first blessing. Perhaps it was not until many years later that
he knew that it was to the Dana family of Cambridge that he owed
the scholarship at North American College bestowed on him. Undoubtedly, however, Archbishop Williams had reported on the
scholarship holder and his excellent progress.

"When the day of my ordination in Rome came, my first thought
and prayer were for her, still in the little cottage thousands of miles
away across the sea . . . and, as I turned from the altar, a gentle
old lady . . . timidly approached me.

" 'You are thinking of your mother far away. Will you give me
your blessing for her?' and she knelt before me on the bare pavement of St. John Lateran's and, with my hands trembling with
emotion, I imparted to her, for my mother, my first priestly Benediction. She then arose and said, with the sweetest of smiles, 'I am
Miss Charlotte Dana of Cambridge. . . . I am leaving for home
tomorrow and will carry your first blessing to your dear mother.' " [7]

And so, on the rolls of the Recording Angel, were written the
names of two women who, unknown to each other, had sacrificed

and spent to give God one more young priest. Charlotte Dana, a convert, was a cousin of Henry Wadsworth Longfellow and a sister of Richard Henry Dana who wrote *Two Years Before the Mast.*

Vice-Rector Schulte and the physician to the American College were worried about the persistent cough and weakness of the new young priest. Directly after his ordination, he was sent for a stay at the seashore village of Anzio to recuperate. He had said his first Mass on June eighth in the Redemptorists' church of St. Alphonsus on Via Merulana at the shrine of Our Lady of Perpetual Help to ask her to restore his health.

For two months he lived in the village, drinking goat's milk, from the flock in the piazza, putting to sea with the fishermen in the salt sunshine and warm breezes; walking over the hills to Nettuno. He enjoyed the beauty of the countryside, the relaxation from studies, the chance to perfect his Italian talking with the friendly people.

By the end of August he felt well and rejoined the seminarians at their summer villa at Grottaferrata, taking his place as first prefect. With the others he climbed the mountain beyond Frascati to the peaceful community of the Camaldolese monks, white-robed with black scapular and hood. He saw the tiny individual cottages in which they lived, the church where they gathered for singing of the office. He felt the attraction of such a life, devoted in peace and silence to contemplation and prayer; but he knew it could never be for him.

"America will not produce Camaldolesi for several centuries more of rush and riot and energy," he predicted,[8] little dreaming of the surge of vocations for other contemplative orders—Trappists —Carmelites—Carthusians—that would follow release of young American men and women from the armed services after World War II.

In October, they were all back in Via dell' Umilta, and Fr. William O'Connell promptly fell sick again, with congestion of the lungs. The history of tuberculosis in his family forbade Vice-Rector Schulte and the physicians to keep him another winter in the chilly cell and halls of the old building. In December, he was counselled to return home.

He was too disheartened, at this blow to his ambition and hope of the doctorate degree that would normally crown his years of study, to do any sight-seeing on the journey home. He took the train to Switzerland, Paris, crossed to England and sailed from Liverpool for New York in time to be with his mother for Christmas.

This time there was no uncertainty, no craving for freedom and gallops over the countryside on the little cob. In his years in Rome, William O'Connell had learned two great lessons of a life dedicated to religion—resignation to the Will of God; and obedience to superiors.

His first call, back in America, was at the Union Park rectory, to report to Archbishop Williams. Two days after Christmas, came a letter to the Gorham Street cottage in Lowell notifying Father William O'Connell of his assignment as a curate at St. Joseph's Church, Medford.

CHAPTER SIX

FIRST PARISH WORK

Che studio di ben far grazia rinverda—
Dante: Purgatorio, Canto xviii, L 104-5

> *(Hearty zeal to serve re-animates*
> *celestial grace.)*
>
> Cary, tr.

LOOKING BACK over half a century in the priesthood, William O'Connell recalled the trepidation, the inexperience, the humility with which a young priest enters on his first parish work.

"The priest trembles at the thought of his own weakness. As the days pass and one year succeeds another, he receives reminders that he is made of flesh and blood. Like everyone else, the priest is sensitive and he can be stung by injustice. . . .

"No one really knows the life of a priest but the priest himself. No one but he can appreciate his difficulties and the endless problems he must solve. No one but he can realize the enormous patience required to conduct even the smallest parish. . . . Living very close to a parish priest, it would be a miracle if you did not find some things that you think are defects and shortcomings, because, when Almighty God sends his ministers among His people, he does not send angels or archangels. Who of us are worthy to have archangels minister to us?" [1]

Archbishop Williams had postponed assignment to give young Father William O'Connell Christmas at home.

"My dear mother is so happy since my return that she grows younger every day," he realized. "She came to my every Mass and knelt like one transfixed, just thanking God all the time, she says, that He has spared her to see this day."

The first of January the pastor of St. Peter's in Lowell got out his sleigh and personally drove his one-time altar boy to his first parish work at St. Joseph's, Medford. It seemed novel, after Rome, to be back in New England with crisp white snow drifted over the landscape, bare leafless trees, jingle of sleigh bells in the air, skating on the Mystic River just behind the Church. The brisk air outdoors, the furnace-warmed comfort of the rectory indoors were a tonic that soon had O'Connell putting on weight, regaining strength and vigor.

The parish was almost as new as O'Connell's priesthood. Separated from the mother-parish of the Immaculate Conception in Malden two years earlier, its building had been remodelled from an old Congregational meeting house on High Street. The congregation was about eight hundred souls, a little island of Catholicity in the Yankee city.

Fresh from crowded hours of lecture, study and spiritual exercises, and the constant companionship of his fellow-seminarians, O'Connell found himself a stranger, living in a rambling rectory with a sick man. The pastor, Rev. Richard Donnelly, was rapidly becoming a bed-patient with tuberculosis. There were not yet sanitaria, nor realization of the danger of infection from tubercular patients. It was not only Christian charity but normal procedure of the day for the young priest to become sick-nurse to the dying man. The duties were not unfamiliar; eight years before he had served at the bedside of his own sister Mary, suffering from the same "white plague."

Meanwhile, the neophyte also had to carry on the work of the parish; Masses, Sunday school, preparations for First Holy Communion or Confirmation; marriages, baptisms, sick calls, funerals. He had to count the cash from collections; keep the parish books and register; hear confessions; consult with the organist and choir; look after the sacred vessels, and drill the altar-boys.

His first sermon threw him into terror. Throat parched, heart beating like trip-hammer, he gabbled through his prepared address too fast and had to extemporize weakly, to fill out the time.[2]

The young curate never forgot the day the Archbishop came for Confirmation at St. Joseph's, driving out from Boston in the buggy with the fast little horse he loved. He climbed the stairs for a visit with Father Donnelly in his sickroom, and then was escorted by the curate to the sacristy to vest. O'Connell took a quick check in the church. Vespers was to begin at three o'clock, followed by Confirmation. The pews were crowded, with little boys in neat dark suits, little girls like flowers in their white dresses and veils; beaming mothers and fathers, uncles and aunts and onlookers. But, from the choir, came a signal of distress. The organist had not shown up!

As this dawned on Father O'Connell, Father Sullivan [3] from Malden walked into the sacristy. The day was saved; he took Vespers and O'Connell hastily climbed the gallery steps to play the organ for the choir. The belated organist arrived after the Magnificat and took over. Archbishop Williams had not overlooked the unorthodox scurrying of the curates. Taking off his vestments in the sacristy, he said drily:

"It is a good thing to be able to shoe a horse or play a jews-harp. You can never tell when you may be called on."

Father Donnelly died on October seventh, 1886. Father O'Connell carried on for a month until Father Michael Gilligan was appointed pastor, with O'Connell moving to Gilligan's place as assistant at another St. Joseph's in Boston's West End on Allen Street.

One of the responsibilities of a bishop is to try to give his clergy well-rounded experience. Archbishop Williams had placed O'Connell in the country parish originally because of the report from Rome that his lungs seemed delicate. Now that his health was robust again and it was obvious that one priest could carry the parish in Medford, O'Connell was to see the seamy side of life in a city parish numbering some twelve thousand souls. Instead of the home-like rectory in Medford, with tall elm trees and green lawn running down to the river, the young curate's room would be up three flights in a brick rookery at 6 Allen Street, with the parlor bell ringing all day and all through the night.

A young Boston settlement worker, a pioneer at that same period in America's "new gospel" of sociology, made a detailed study of the West End during O'Connell's ten years there. Robert A. Woods recorded [4] that after the razing of old Fort Hill, which had harbored hundreds of Irish immigrant families, the former Yankee homes of the West End were made over into tenements, renting for eighty cents per room per week. A hundred years earlier, the West End had been Boston's fashionable section. Remnants of its magnificence are seen today in the stately brick mansion of old Governor Harrison Gray Otis (preserved as a museum by the Society for the Preservation of N.E. Antiquities) and the classic beauty of the West (Congregational) Church (now the West End Branch of the Boston Public Library). The first minister of the West Church was Charles Lowell (whose brother's descendant, Abbott Lawrence Lowell, would be President of Harvard and whose family gave its name to O'Connell's native city of Lowell).

There were virtually no Catholics in the West End in 1804 when young Charles Lowell went on the usual "Grand Tour" of Europe made by the wealthy, to form his impressions in Rome as a sightseer: "You see Dapper Priests in stockings of bright purple with hats girt with the same color," he wrote home,[5] "tripping it lightly from the shop of the Friseur. The Rich and Proud Cardinal, too, wrapped in his double folds of purple, arrayed with proud magnificence and accompanied with his princely train of liveried domestics, rolls along, unheeding the objects of horror (beggars) which meet him on every side."

The United States had a new Cardinal in 1886, the year that O'Connell went to the West End, for, on June seventh, Leo XIII had elevated James Gibbons of Baltimore to the Roman purple, although Gibbons had no princely train of liveried domestics and was neither rich nor proud!

South of St. Joseph's Church, bought in 1862 from a Unitarian congregation, rose historic Beacon Hill, with its brick mansions, its view of the elms of Boston Common through purple panes and its population of Boston Brahmins, of whom Henry Cabot Lodge wrote, in 1891: "race-pride or race-prejudice . . . has never been wholly lost and probably never will be. More interesting than pride of race has been the development of early Puritan qualities . . . the conflict which all unconsciously the Puritans planted in Boston, when they established a narrow theocracy as the government of a united Church and State, and then placed on the one side of it political liberty and on the other the free school." [6]

The priests of St. Joseph's knew well that they were but ministers of God's grace and of the merits of Christ and the saints, won in sacrifice, for sinful souls. Priests like William O'Connell lived in the cramped, shabby rectory in the crowded West End of Boston; endured the stifling summer heat, gave themselves day or night to the service of God in a church that well-to-do Unitarians were glad to abandon because of its unsavory neighborhood.

No longer of Him be it said
"He hath no place to lay His head."

In every land a constant lamp
Flames by His small and mighty camp.

Cloistered beside the shouting street.
Silent, He calls me to His feet.*

* *Poems, Essays and Letters,* by Joyce Kilmer. Copyright 1914, 1917, 1918 by Doubleday & Co., Inc. By permission.

CHAPTER SEVEN

OLD BOSTON DAYS

Se tu segui tua stella
Non puoi fallire al glorioso porto.
                    Dante: Inferno,
                    Canto xv, 11 55-56

(If you follow your star
You cannot fail of a glorious port.)
                    Cary, tr.

THERE WERE eighty-eight saloons in old Ward Eight, around
St. Joseph's Church. Boston's houses of ill fame were concentrated there in the decade that William O'Connell was an
assistant to the pastor, Vicar-General William F. Byrne. When
O'Connell first went there, in 1886, the good Irish cops of the Joy
Street Police station used to belabor with their billy-clubs evil men
who solicited trade for these houses. However, the landlords of
houses, who did not live in the West End, brought pressure from
above and the police eventually were forbidden to use their night-
sticks.

Corruption and "protection" were rife in the politics of the day.
The slang expression "bay window" for a portly belly originated
because landlords, greedy for extra rental, paid twenty-five dollars
to a certain Republican alderman for each bay window illegally

built out over the narrow streets. The Alderman was of corpulent
build and soon was nicknamed "Bay Window." [1]

Five thousand families lived in tenements, above alleys littered
with garbage and filth; in bedrooms without window or airshaft;
fire-traps of rickety wooden stairs; one toilet common to all, on
landing or in the back yard. One survey showed sixty-seven toilets
in a total of one hundred and eighteen houses inhabited by five
hundred and forty poor people, seventeen of them "out-of-order"
when inspected. Yet, in such quarters, until the Legislature of 1891
took action, piecework for the sweated garment and millinery in-
dustries was carried on by women and children for long hours at
incredibly small wages.

The majority of Irish men in the West End worked as unskilled
laborers for two dollars a day, when the sun shone and they could
find a job. Of a Sunday, the throngs that flocked to Mass at St.
Joseph's filled the large church and spread out over the steps,
kneeling on the sidewalk or street like a swarm of bees.

Jewish immigrants from Russia's persecutions were just beginning to arrive in O'Connell's day. By 1895, when he left, the
census noted "Americans," 4,800; Irish, 7,200; Italians, 1,100; and
Jews, 6,300. Little Catholic boys built up a trade on Saturdays and
Jewish holidays, calling "Fire! Fire!" while looking up for beckon-
ing hands inviting them to tend the stoves and gas lights that ritual
forbade a Jew to light on the Sabbath.

The rectory bell was ringing all around the clock and life in the
rectory knew little recreation. "But in the evening about nine we
(curates) all meet in someone's room and a genial hearty company
we are," wrote William O'Connell. "There is not as much general
conversation at table as there might be—the pastor at times is very
didactic and prone to make long and fatiguing soliloquies upon the
learned articles he is reading."

The confinement was hard for young O'Connell, too, after long
daily walks in *camerata* through the years in Rome, or rambles
with his dog around Medford's countryside. Night after night, he
slipped out to take a hard fast walk of a mile around the Charles
River Basin between the two bridges at Cambridge and Causeway

Street. As a curate, Fr. O'Connell had more than the usual share
of experiences of human misery, since the West End parish ministered to local jail, prison and hospital, as well as a congested,
under-privileged population.

Hearing confessions was a task to wear down the spirit. There
was no form of wickedness, no perversion or sin, no vile temptation, no human weakness that was not poured into the ears of the
priests behind the green curtains at St. Joseph's. Here came the
habitual drunkard, ready to "take the pledge" in a spasm of re-
morse; and maybe in the gutter again before the week was out.
Here came pitiful young servant girls, betrayed into pregnancy
and frightened at the consequence. Here were underpaid clerks,
living in cheap lodginghouses, who could not keep their hands
from picking and stealing. Again, it might be a man with murder
on his soul.

Revolting, disgusting, discouraging, the torrent of whispers of
sins was enough to make a man lose his faith; until he won through
to the realization that the very fact of confession testified to God's
grace, His mercy, His unending love for human beings. For these
unlovely or repulsive people, Jesus Christ had given Himself to
be crucified. The priest, despite his repugnances and his own temptations and weaknesses, was Christ's ambassador.

O'Connell was wise enough to realize that he must have some intellectual occupation interspersed with physical preoccupations. He
had to teach thirteen hundred Sunday School children to sing
hymns and repeat their catechism, with expeditions to the sacristy
to administer a bit of the birch to unruly boys whom a later generation, sparing the rod, would term "juvenile delinquents."

"We have an occasional tough customer," wrote O'Connell,
"who always sneaks in late for Mass, never knows his lesson and
behaves generally unexorcised. We have a system for him—behind
closed doors in the sacristy . . . a few taps on a certain tender spot
with a nice polished piece of birch . . . just enough to make him
realize physically that it is pleasanter all around to keep in order.
. . . Naturally, such children are the ones whose parents are care-

less and neglectful of their duty at home. Some of them after this little disciplining have become my best boys." [2]

O'Connell, in evenings, and moments between calls on "parlor duty," took up the study of Spanish. Parlor calls were unpredictable. One day came "a nice-looking chap who wanted some advice. I asked him his occupation. He pinched his cheek between thumb and forefinger and drew out the skin to an alarming distance, saying: 'I am the elastic-skin man at Stone's Museum.'"

Hospital and sick calls were harrowing, but they broadened his circle by friendships with the great physicians of his day, devoted to service of their neighbor. Father O'Connell made a lifelong friendship with Dr. William Dunn, in the winter of 1895 when he climbed four flights of stairs to find a dying woman in an attic from which every stick of furniture had been pawned.

"Two little children, half dressed, sat on the floor by the mother who lay on a pallet of straw . . . the walls covered in black patches with roaches, the stove broken, the windows stuffed with paper and bits of clothing . . . and yet all through faith had kept the flame alive of hope until now the only hope was for Heaven . . . I sat almost stunned at the perfect patience and heroic resignation her quivering lips unfolded.

"Confession, communion, anointing all finished . . . I hurried to Doctor Dunn's. Together we went back with a nurse and provisions. She was brought down to a clean, comfortable room. The children were washed and dressed. She kissed them tenderly and let us take them to the Home. I saw Doctor Dunn go to the window to hide the tears streaming down his cheeks." [3]

Dr. Dunn, at this time, was as new to human misery as had been Father O'Connell eight years earlier. He had just been graduated from Harvard Medical School and opened his office on Chambers Street in 1895. He, like O'Connell, was an honor graduate of Boston College and had aided Father Fulton, S.J., to found the Young Men's Catholic Association.

Many first-generation immigrants in the West End had had little or no schooling at home. Cynical politicians, rounding them up at election time with promises of city jobs in the future if they voted right, bade them "go over the ballot with a fine-tooth comb." The comb, fitting snugly in a pocket, accompanied them into the voting booth. Its teeth had been cut in a pattern which, when laid over the ballot, covered all but the name of the "right" candidate.

Young Father O'Connell could speak Italian, but he had not the Gaelic. That was the asset of the most widely-known resident of the old West End—Martin Lomasney. Martin spoke Gaelic fluently and his brother Joseph had learned the deaf-and-dumb alphabet of the fingers. Political opponents said: "What chance have you against the pair of them!"

Martin Lomasney and William O'Connell were of an age; Lomasney born December 3 and O'Connell December 8, 1859; the one in Boston, the other in Lowell.

When O'Connell first knew Lomasney, both were twenty-seven years old. O'Connell had had the best education his day afforded. Lomasney, orphaned, left school at thirteen. O'Connell was a priest at St. Joseph's in old Ward Eight. Lomasney had just opened his famous Hendricks Club, at the corner of Lowell and Causeway streets; had a job as a health inspector of the City of Boston at $1,800 a year; and went to Mass and confession at the Jesuit Church of St. Mary's in another ward, although he lived at 27 Mc-Lean Street, in St. Joseph's parish.

Lomasney, when he died, August 12, 1933, and was buried from St. Joseph's Church, West End, had been for fifty years a chief political factor in Boston. Their lifelong relations, Cardinal and Catholic political "boss," perhaps are summed up in the fact that Lomasney left his $200,000 estate, not to "the Archbishop of Boston, a corporation sole," which, in 1933, would have been O'Connell; but to provide "a memorial for Archbishop John J. Williams," predecessor of O'Connell in the See. Archbishop Cushing, on October 7, 1945, eighteen months after O'Connell's death, would dedicate the Catholic Boys Guidance Center, made possible by the Lomasney money, as a memorial to Archbishop Williams.[4]

The Hendricks Club, named for Thomas A. Hendricks, vice-president of the United States under Grover Cleveland, opened on December 20, 1885, just a few months before Father O'Connell moved from St. Joseph's on the Mystic River to St. Joseph's near the Charles River. In 1892, while O'Connell was still a curate, Lomasney split the Democratic vote to get himself elected as an Alderman in Boston's then bi-cameral city government. Political feelings and maneuvers ran so high in those days that a disgruntled West End property-owner, on whom Lomasney, when health inspector, had put some pressure, shot and wounded Lomasney in the City Hall on School Street.

For ten years politician and priest lived as neighbors in the West End without becoming friends. Lomasney with his gray-blue eyes, handlebar mustache, jutting jaw, and O'Connell cleanshaven, with prominent brown eyes, were of the same age, same racial and religious background; even had the same fundamental ideals. Both believed in temperance and decency in family life, justice for the poor, loyalty to land and to Church, but their education had been different and their careers diverged.

It was a pity, since both became leaders in the community, that temperamental difference kept them from becoming friends. Perhaps each had too much of the leader in his make-up to run placidly in double harness. The history of politics in Boston might have been different had the churchman been able to have the cooperation of the politician.

Lomasney was always passionate for having the United States and the Democratic Party embroil themselves in the Irish fight for freedom. O'Connell, sympathetic to Ireland's cause, nevertheless felt that the Church should leave foreign affairs to the United States Department of State. Lomasney, a staunch Catholic, a total abstainer from alcoholic drinks or tobacco, a generous patron of the Catholic Home for Destitute Children, as a politician was an opportunist. For the sake of wielding power, he would make temporary alliance with any faction that could give him victory and influence. William O'Connell eschewed partisan politics and intervened only on questions of morality.

So, of an evening, young Father O'Connell would not be found sitting around the Hendricks Club; nor would Martin Lomasney be dropping in at 6 Allen Street for a chat with the curates.

Friendships formed with the curates in the next decade at St. Joseph's would endure through the years to come. O'Connell, when Cardinal, would advance them. In 1912, he obtained papal honors for Monsignor Edward J. Moriarty and appointed him to the pastorate of historic St. Thomas Aquinas Church in Jamaica Plain. The same year on June 2, he went to Medford to dedicate for Father Thomas L. Flanagan the beautiful new St. Joseph's Church, in the Medford parish where O'Connell had served his first curacy in the converted old meetinghouse. Father Denis J. Wholey had his promotion in 1890, when Archbishop Williams gave him the responsibility of forming a new parish. Wholey earned the honor and credit of building Sacred Heart Church in Newton where, years later, a future Pope, Cardinal Eugenio Pacelli, would be entertained by a future Cardinal, Francis Spellman; and where, too, O'Connell's successor as Archbishop of Boston, Richard J. Cushing, would live as Auxiliary Bishop.

The curate for whom Cardinal O'Connell was to do most, however, was the youngest, Joseph G. Anderson, graduate of Boston College in 1887, seminarian at St. John's in Brighton, ordained in 1892. His native parish of St. Joseph's in the West End was his first assignment. When O'Connell came back to Boston and became Archbishop in 1907, one of his first appointments was of Father Anderson as Director of the new Catholic Charitable Bureau; in 1911, while in Rome to receive his red hat, O'Connell procured nomination of Anderson as Auxiliary Bishop, and appointed for his residence the fine parish of St. Peter's in Dorchester.

Young Father O'Connell knew quite well that a man was likely to serve thirty years as an assistant in various parishes before the great day came when he might be appointed pastor of a parish. Routine work went on day after day, and a man did not fret, nor repine, because that was what he had signed up for, when he offered his life in Christ's service.

Nevertheless, being neither an angel nor an archangel, once in a while the young curates craved a bit of mild recreation. O'Connell's way of "breaking out" was to make a rendezvous with one of his former companions at the North American College and "pretend" with him that they were back in Rome. A carriage and coachman would be hired from Kenny and Clark's livery and the pair, riding around the milldam and the Back Bay in the sunshine would discourse in Italian like a couple of cardinals taking their airing back in Rome; and end up having dinner at the old Hotel Victoria, with a bottle of Chianti and a couple of good cigars. The play-acting was needed relief from the never-ending toll of human misery in their daily lives.

CHAPTER EIGHT

FORMATIVE INFLUENCES

Fui conosciuto da un che mi prese
per lo lembo e grido: "Qual maraviglia!"
Dante: Inferno, Canto xv, 23-24

*(I was known by one who, plucking my garment,
cried "What a wonder!")*

Carlyle, tr.

THE LIFE of any man or woman knows unplanned encounters which determine the future. If Maud Howe, daughter of Julia Ward Howe of Boston, for instance, had not been a passenger in a stagecoach, sightseeing in Italy, she would never have met and married the English artist, John Elliott. Had Isabel Perkins of Boston not visited the Elliotts in Rome, she might never have met and married Larz Anderson of Cleveland, Ohio.[1]

William O'Connell, as a priest, had no intentions of matrimony; but had he not studied his philosophy lessons well under Francesco Satolli, he would never have found himself in Rome, dining with the Elliotts and Andersons.

It was Satolli who brought about the extraordinary change soon to happen in the career of the young curate at St. Joseph's in Boston's West End.

It was detectible in O'Connell's youth, and very marked in his later years of public life that his nature was independent, proud

55

and extremely resistant to ideas or suggestions from his associates. In eighty-odd years of his life, only three men broke through his shell of self-reliance and effected an influence on his character and actions. They were of very different types; the only common trait was that all three were signally devoted priests.

Robert Fulton, S.J., Rector of Boston College when O'Connell was a student, is the only educator of whom O'Connell never uttered a criticism. Since O'Connell was critical by nature, that in itself was remarkable; but Fulton's life was remarkable in many ways.

Born in 1826, son a wealthy Virginian, he was left fatherless at an early age. When at sixteen, he told his mother of his desire to enter the Jesuit Order, she outdid him in generous desire to serve God. The slaves of their establishment were given their freedom, twenty years before the Emancipation Proclamation; and the mother became a Visitation nun, living forty years in religion until her death. Father Fulton, ordained in 1857, was sent to Boston in 1861, was prefect of studies when Boston College was opened in 1864, and its president from 1870 through 1879. His second tenure of office, starting in 1888 saw the enlargement of the buildings on James Street that doubled the classroom capacity. More important than his executive ability, was his radiant personality. In an age when first the Know-Nothings and later the A.P.A. hated the Jesuits even more than they did other Catholics, Father Fulton was loved and admired throughout Boston. Oliver Wendell Holmes, Louis Agassiz were among the non-Catholics who sought his company. There was universal regret when sickness caused his retirement in October, 1890. His death did not come until five years later, but his memory was still cherished. It is not the custom of the Jesuits to pronounce eulogies on members of their own Order; but the hosts of alumni and friends wished one, and Father William O'Connell was the one they wanted to make it. But men look in vain through the eleven volumes of printed Sermons and Addresses of Cardinal O'Connell to find the text of this eulogy.

Robert Fulton, priest, educator, man with charity and charm for all, left a deep impress on William O'Connell. Through the years, he would remember Father Fulton, try to imitate him; in moments of humility, recognize how far short he fell of the example. He had too little pride in his eulogy to print it.

The second man to influence William O'Connell was Archbishop John J. Williams, whose words, heard by chance, in the Boston cathedral, had crystallized O'Connell's vocation in 1881. Pope Leo XIII was reported to have said: "Archbishop Williams must be a great man. He writes me not to make him a Cardinal. I never got a letter like that from anyone else!" [2]

The Archbishop, taciturn, reticent as a rule, was fond of saying that he was born in Boston when it was only a small town. It was true, the city's charter became effective three days after his birth in 1822. His parents were early immigrants from Ireland. His father died when he was eight and his mother re-married. The family lived in the original Cathedral parish, when the Cathedral stood on Franklin Street, near the present Diocesan office building, and Bishop Benedict Joseph Fenwick, S.J., interested himself in the boy, sending him, at the age of eleven, in Montreal to the college of Sulpician Fathers; and, in 1841 to the Grand Seminaire de Theologie in Paris, where he was ordained May 17, 1845.

Despite the kindly interest of both Jesuit and Sulpician, John Williams' vocation was for the work of a parish priest. He returned to the Cathedral parish in Boston and served the mission chapel in a re-modeled blacksmith's shop in the West End that would develop into St. Joseph's on Allen Street where Father William O'Connell was curate. His benefactor, Bishop Fenwick, died August 11, 1846 and was succeeded by another Boston boy he had sent to the Sulpicians, the 34-year-old Coadjutor Bishop John Bernard Fitzpatrick. Williams, in his turn, was named coadjutor January 8, 1866, a month before Bishop Fitzpatrick's death.

To Bishop Williams, then it fell, to represent Boston at the historic Vatican Council of 1869-70, in the last year that a Pope was temporal ruler of Rome, dwelling summers in the Quirinal Palace. He also took part in the Second Plenary Council of Baltimore in October, 1866 under Baltimore Archbishop Martin J. Spalding and again, in the Third Baltimore Council of 1884. He had been Archbishop since 1875, when Boston was made a metropolitan see, along with Philadelphia, Sante Fe and Milwaukee. His, thus, had been a long and responsible share in the councils of the American hierarchy. He had to build the immense Gothic cathedral of the Holy Cross in Boston; to cope with the provision of new parishes and churches, necessitated by the great influx of Irish, German, Italian, Portuguese and Polish Catholic immigrants in the forty-odd years of his episcopate.

O'Connell, who served Archbishop Williams' Mass during one of the latter's visits at the North American College in Rome, said at the time, "He looks like a saint at the altar. Such a majestic walk —so regal in all his manner. I cannot take my eyes off him, he fascinates me so. His face is a strange combination of severe dignity and genuine goodness." [3]

He was a man of great simplicity, living with his cathedral clergy in the rectory on Union Park Street; driving himself about on visitations in his buggy (he liked a fast horse); often answering his heavy correspondence by a couple of sentences scrawled on the original letter, returned to the sender. He believed in walking gently, peaceably, while building for the future. He was one of the founders of Catholic University; he sent his most promising candidates to the North American College in Rome; he founded St. John's Seminary in Brighton and brought his old teachers, the Sulpicians, to staff it.

Bostonians who despised Catholics and hated Catholicism on general terms, distinguished between their hatred and the personality of Archbishop John Williams. For his Golden Jubilee reception May 16-17, 1895 at old Music Hall, Julia Ward Howe, author of *The Battle Hymn of the Republic* in Civil War days, turned out a flattering ode. Governor Greenhalge, the Lowell ex-mayor, sat on the platform with Protestant Episcopal Bishop William Lawrence of Massachusetts and the famed Unitarian Edward Everett Hale, author of *The Man Without a Country*.

Cardinal Gibbons summed it all up when he said: "We have learned to admire and love you for your sterling honesty of purpose, for your candor and straightforwardness of character. . . .

There is no prelate of the American Church in whose judgment we have placed more reliance than in yours." [4]

Archbishop Williams from the first had sensed O'Connell's teaching ability and tried to steer him to a professorship. He recommended him to Father Charles Rex, S.S., rector of St. John's; [5] and, also, as trustee of Catholic University, twice would have released O'Connell to teach there in Washington. Invariably, O'Connell declined. He was not inclined to the regular routine of classroom lecturing; he liked better the unpredictable variety of parish work under the easy-going Vicar-General, Father Byrne; the itinerant preaching with the Temperance Band, the warming response of crowded congregations to sermons; the cameraderie of the little group of curates in the old rectory on Allen Street; occasional dinners with the laymen friends he was making at the University Club.

Francesco Satolli was only twenty years older than O'Connell. He was born July 21, 1839 in the beautiful old hill city of Perugia in Tuscany, entered the ancient seminary there and after ordination on June 14, 1862 by Cardinal Pecci (the future Leo XIII) began a brilliant career as scholar and teacher of the Scholastic philosophy of St. Thomas Aquinas. First at Perugia, then for five years at the famous Benedictine Abbey of Monte Cassino, then back to Perugia, his life was dedicated to teaching fundamental principles of human learning in the light of Catholic faith. Leo XIII, the Pope who restored Scholastic philosophy to first place in Catholic education, watched and furthered Satolli's progress with affectionate appreciation. Leo had called Satolli to Rome, as professor at the Urban College of Propaganda Fidei only the year before O'Connell became a student. In 1886, Satolli became president of the Academy of Noble Ecclesiastics in Rome, in 1888 was made Archbishop of Lepanto, and, in 1889 began his diplomatic missions, representing the Holy Father at the inauguration of Catholic University in Washington, D.C. It was during his stay at the University in 1892 that he became first Apostolic Delegate to the United States.

A seminarian from Baltimore, John M. Cooper [1885-1949],

himself to become a noted priest-anthropologist, in a letter to his mother wrote that Satolli was the best speaker he had ever heard.[6]

"Fluent, earnest, fiery, his words sweep everything before him. He throws himself into his oratory with all the force of a strong character and the whole man is manifest to you at once. As a diplomat and executive he may have been a failure (as Apostolic Delegate in the United States) but as a thinker and orator, he is a giant.

"When he used to lecture at Propaganda (Urban College) all ecclesiastical Rome would flock to hear him. His daily audience was between four hundred and six hundred and only kept at this by lack of space. They had never heard his equal before as philosopher, dogmatist, moralist. His grasp of the great leading doctrines, and even the most abstruse, was firm, clear, powerful; and the living force of his argument and the current of his oratory crushed all objections brought against him.

"He was par excellence the philosopher and theologian of his age, with a masculine force of intellect and depth of penetration to which no truth comprehensible to the human mind is too broad or too subtle. He must be put on a par with men like Bismarck and Gladstone." [7]

As Apostolic Delegate, Archbishop Satolli came to Boston for the dedication, April 22, 1894, of the great red brick Church of St. Cecelia in the Back Bay, Father Richard J. Barry, pastor.[8]

For Satolli's visit in 1894, the curate of St. Joseph's in the West End was one of a small number of Boston clergy invited to have a personal visit with him.

"Father Barry is nothing if not spectacular," observed O'Connell. "So when Monsignor Satolli arrived at the station, Father Barry escorted him to an open barouche drawn by four white horses . . . the cortege proceeded through the crowded business part of the city, to the evident amazement of some and amusement of others in this old stronghold of the Puritans. A bystander playfully remarked that all that was needed was a band to make it equal to Barnum's. I am sure Father B. would have added the band if he had thought of it in time." [9]

O'Connell was waiting at the rectory to receive his old professor, who embraced him heartily. To O'Connell, remembering Satolli in cassock and cloak and shovel hat of clerical garb in Rome, the first glimpse brought a little shock.

"He is a sight to behold in secular clothes. Angular and nervous, he never seems to know what to do with the long-tailed coat and long trousers, and, to add to the picturesqueness, his tailor is a pretty bad one. However, as soon as he got into his soutane, he was himself and he sat for a good hour, chatting with me, recalling the old days at Propaganda." [10]

To Satolli, who had not yet mastered English, it must have been a relief to lapse comfortably into his own Italian tongue which O'Connell spoke so fluently. To O'Connell, it was inexpressible consolation to tell this admired mentor the sad and mystical story of his mother's death, six months earlier.

In September of 1893, for the annual vacation Monsignor Byrne gave his curates, O'Connell went to visit the Columbian Exposition at Chicago. All the world was talking of that celebration of fourth centenary of Columbus' discovery of America with the beautiful buildings on the lagoon by Lake Michigan, the marvelous exhibits from every country. Henry Adams had just spent a fortnight there and "revelled in all the fakes and frauds (of the Midway Plaisance), all its wickedness that seemed not to be understood by our innocent natives (and) labored solemnly through all the great buildings and looked like an owl at the dynamos." [11] Later, in *The Education of Henry Adams,* from that visit would stem his brilliant parallel between the influence of the Blessed Virgin in the Middle Ages and that of the dynamo on modern materialism.

William O'Connell spent only a few days visiting the exhibits.[12] "Dear Mama . . . We have walked upwards of five hours a day since Wednesday and it is only begun. It is simply marvelous in size, beauty and wealth," he wrote. One night he was so haunted by an impression of trouble at home that he could not sleep. Early the next morning he took the train home and journeyed straight to Lowell. There the mother to whom he had said goodbye a fortnight earlier, in her usual health, lay dying.

"Thank God you came at last" she whispered. She died in his arms on the twenty-sixth of September, 1893. Seventy-five years old, she had not seen her beloved Ireland for half a century. Widowed, she had had on her slender shoulders the burden of bringing up eleven children. She had sacrificed her savings to educate one of them for God's service; and God did not forget her. She died with the priestly blessing of her son, thanks to what appeared an angelic summons.

Satolli's sympathy was balm to O'Connell's sore heart and gave to the rest of the Apostolic Delegate's visit in Boston a radiant intimacy for the young curate. O'Connell was Deacon at the Pontifical Mass celebrated by Satolli on Sunday morning; but, as a very junior curate, was not at the dinner for the clergy of the archdiocese with Archbishop Williams and Satolli at Mechanics Building that afternoon.

"I don't think our venerable Archbishop and the Delegate exchanged ten words during the whole meal. At the close the Delegate spoke in Latin, as usual, with wonderful precision of thought and enunciation. He was perfectly correct in his response to the somewhat cool presentation (by Archbishop Williams) . . . at the end of his wonderful speech there was a pandemonium of applause . . . I went for a moment to congratulate him. He was trembling from head to foot with the emotion of the hour. . . . He wrote me a letter after his return to Washington and every line was filled with gratitude and happiness." [13]

To all sons, the loss of a mother is an experience that goes deeper than any other. To a priest-son, with no human companionship of wife or children to mitigate the blank loss, it goes even deeper. A year later, Father William O'Connell was on the verge of another physical breakdown, recognized by his pastor, his gentle Archbishop and his friend-physician, Doctor Dunn. They packed him off to Rome (was there any other place in the world he wanted to go?) with a "tonic" in the form of an assignment to prepare a series of lectures on the Early History of the Church for the new Catholic Summer School that would meet at Plattsburg, New York, that year of 1895. They must have done it with tactful conspiracy for again young O'Connell failed to recognize the understanding and kindness of the older men.

"My health is always good but of late I seem to have lost taste for everything," he wrote ingenuously. "The authorities were very kind about it and I am given a good long leave of absence with permission to go anywhere I like. . . . I am leaving January tenth . . . for Rome . . . to prepare my lectures for the Summer School." [14]

Preparations of sermons or lectures were a duty that Father O'Connell took very seriously. In the ten years at St. Joseph's, he would spend a fortnight composing a ten-minute sermon, making a meditation on the subject chosen; writing it out in full and, finally, committing the "points" to memory so that he could deliver it without a manuscript. With youth's frank self-confidence, he bragged about the results.

"I have no hesitation in saying very frankly that I know I am considered rather a good preacher. I see no reason why, with proper modesty, I should not say that I know many people come to St. Joseph's when it is my turn to preach." [15]

Naturally, he enjoyed his rising reputation and did not let it disturb him when friends criticized him for "trying to do too much by adding lectures and addresses to my busy enough routine." [16] It was flattering to be asked to repeat in Horticultural Hall, Boston, the glowing talk on Daniel O'Connell, Irish patriot, which he had first given in Medford; or to deliver the Baccalaureate sermon at Boston College Commencement in June of 1894.

Some of his sermons might not have been too pleasing to Boss Martin Lomasney of Ward Eight, since the young preacher declared roundly, perhaps with the thought of the "fine-tooth comb" in mind;

"For us, as Catholic citizens . . . the religion of a candidate for office is rarely considered. . . . Most cases seem to prove that between a broad-minded capable Protestant and a Catholic of even doubtful ability, the odds will be in favor of the former. . . . The Catholic man who . . . hopes to win Catholic votes . . . ought to be made to feel that his hopes are vain unless he is a Catholic in more than name. . . . The good name of our Holy Church has often suffered at the hands of the so-called Catholic politician."

The influence of his Jesuit teachers at Boston College, his Jesuit confessor, Fr. Mazzella, in Rome, is seen in his discourse on St. Aloysius Gonzaga, patron of youth; and on St. John the Baptist, when after pointing out the virtues of self-denial and humility typified by the Precursor, O'Connell's peroration was the *Suscipe* of Ignatius Loyola.

Confession, the Sacrament of Penance, was a theme on which he loved to preach—and no wonder, seeing the souls around him in the West End, beset by seductive temptation, driven by poverty to desperate straits; stealing in to kneel at the back of the church for Mass, but hesitating to come to the Sacraments because they dared not give up the unsavory professions by which they lived.

The young Boston priest delivered a series of five lectures at Plattsburg, covering the first three centuries of the history of the Church. He divided the topic into: Christ, the Builder; the Apostles, the Foundation; the Nations, the Building; the Persecutions, the Storm; and the Catacombs, the Shelter. The lectures were so well received that one auditor, W. H. Moffitt of Brooklyn, insisted on paying to have them printed.

"My dear Friend," wrote Rector Denis O'Connell from Grottoferrata, "There is nothing in the Church in America to compare with them and they combine a vast amount of new reliable and valuable matter put forth in clear, direct style that the simplest can understand and retain. . . . You must bring them out again with more care. You owe it to the vast amount of labor that you have evidently expended . . . But why did you say that Peter and Paul died in the persecution of Nero? Of Peter it is doubtful and of Paul it is certain that he did not. . . . But you have done good work, and introduced a freshness in America in an old subject. Hearty Congratulations." [17] It was true that O'Connell had a talent, reinforced by clearness and charm of delivery which brought the lore of scholars or definitions of theologians agreeably to the level of audiences.

His first lecture, for instance, in eighty-five hundred words, narrated the Life of Christ, set against a picture of His days in Palestine. No greater challenge could be given a lecturer to an audience of convinced Catholics than to re-tell a story familiar to all, handled over centuries by so many great writers. Yet O'Connell brought it off with a clarity and sincerity that, even today, in cold print, holds the reader. O'Connell himself said:

"I had not got through many sentences before I began to feel that everybody before me was with me and deep in the subject. A little further on there was a burst of applause." [17] "After the lecture Monsignor (John) Farley (to be created Cardinal in 1911 with O'Connell) came to speak to me. He was most amiable and complimentary."

In that summer of 1895 events far beyond his ken, circumstances shaped by men above his lowly horizon, were drawing to present a dramatic, unforeseen change in the life of the thirty-five-year-old curate at St. Joseph's.

Father Robert Fulton, S.J., had educated him for it; Archbishop John Williams had fostered him for it; Archbishop Francesco Satolli would choose him for it. Yet William O'Connell deserves credit, too. Had he not worked hard as a student, as a curate, as a preacher, such men would not have had high regard for him. They had had the vision to appraise his latent abilities; they also had seen the industrious application, the strong sense of duty which were his own accomplishment.

His world was still in a humdrum routine of peace; a narrow world bounded by the hoof-beats of horses for transportation; hand-written letters for correspondence; conversation as recreation. In 1895 the telephone was in its infancy; automobiles, radio, airplanes, television all in the shrouded future. The Panama Canal was a dream in a French engineer's mind. No American soldier had ever served outside the continent. Americans had little thought for international issues.

A new era was about to be born, although few glimpsed it. William O'Connell was suddenly to become part of that era.

CHAPTER NINE

WINNING ADVANCEMENT

O gente umana per volar su nata
Perche a poco vento cosi cadi?
Dante: Purgatorio,
Canto xii, 1 95-96

*(O human folk, born to fly upward, why at
a breath of wind thus fall ye down?)*
Okey, tr.

THE UNSOUGHT, unpredicted promotion to Rome which plucked a junior curate from Boston, from among thousands of American priests, arose from the failure of a brilliant confrere to give satisfaction. A situation which brought joy to William O'Connell gave heartache to several of his seniors.

James Cardinal Gibbons, for instance, after attending the golden jubilee of Archbishop Williams in Boston, on May sixteenth, 1895, sailed immediately for Rome; and was saddened on arrival to learn that Pope Leo XIII had just relieved of his duties the rector of the North American College, Monsignor Denis O'Connell.

From the day in 1868 when Gibbons, newly named a bishop, met Denis O'Connell of Richmond, Virginia, as a seminarian at his own alma mater, St. Charles' College (where William O'Connell would be a student ten years later), a life-long friendship began. Gibbons sent Denis to the North American College for five years.

At his ordination in May, 1877, Roman ecclesiastics pronounced his talent "remarkable" and predicted that "he will be a most useful member of the Church." [1] On the death of Monsignor Hostlot in 1884, it was Gibbons who procured the appointment of his protege as rector in Rome with an extra financial allowance for acting as liaison representative at the Vatican of the American hierarchy. There had been some feeling at the time over Gibbons' insistence, as the Congregation of Propagation of the Faith favored Rev. August Schulte, first friend of William O'Connell at the college, who had borne the burden of acting rector during Hostlot's illness and the year's interregnum.

William O'Connell first met Denis of the same surname at the North American College in late 1883 when the American archbishops were staying there, consulting with the Roman Curia in preparation for the Plenary Council to be held at Baltimore the next year. "Doctor O'Connell of Richmond is with Archbishop Gibbons," he wrote his mother, "as bright, intelligent, happy a face as you could see anywhere. He was one of our best students here. Doctor Ubaldi tells me he was a wonder in his way." [2] He had met him again, in the Spring of 1895 during research in Rome for his lectures on the Early Church. He had even, admiringly, dedicated the first published edition of his motet *Juravit Dominus* "To Rt. Rev. D. J. O'Connell." [3]

Denis O'Connell hitched his wagon to the rising star of Archbishop John Ireland of St. Paul, Minnesota. He became a passionate partisan of Ireland's ideas and, from his vantage post in Rome, by voluminous confidential correspondence, directed what became a close-knit group in the Church in America.

For twenty years this group, comprised of Cardinal Gibbons, Archbishop Ireland, Archbishop John J. Keane and Bishop Thomas O'Gorman, with Denis O'Connell promoted their own sincere ideas. The internal dissension they aroused probably influenced Rome to establish in Washington an Apostolic Delegation (with William O'Connell's old professor Satolli as first incumbent). In the end, their activities had provoked two admonitory Briefs from the Holy Father; demotion of Denis O'Connell as rector in

Rome and of Keane as rector of Catholic University; and lost to Ireland the red hat he desired.

It is an interesting and instructive chapter in the history of the Church in America. It is only seventy years later that in retrospect and result, the wisdom of Rome is evident in not accepting *in toto* their partisan ideas.

Archbishop Ireland, whom O'Connell in later years character-ized as "patriot and publicist" [4] because of his constant use of pul-pit, press and postage stamps for voluminous correspondence, was the dynamic propagandist of his ideas. Those were the days of a flood-tide of immigration; and Ireland spearheaded opposition to the natural tendency of various nationalities for priests who spoke or preached in their own language and parochial schools where their children, along with English, retained the parents' tongue.

The new immigrants in Minnesota were not wealthy, and Ireland dreamed up a plan of having school boards rent parochial schools and pay all the expenses while nuns taught and priests said Mass and gave catechism instructions before and after regular classes in secular subjects. He put it in practice at Faribault, Minnesota, and soon had the rest of the American hierarchy about his ears and the whole of America buzzing about separation of Church and State; insidious infiltration by Rome and all the other time-honored accusations and discussions. It turned out a tempest in a teapot, for less than two years later, just as Rome made an official ruling that the Faribault plan "might be tolerated" but parochial schools were better, the Faribault school board ended the arrangement on its own hook.

What led directly to the ousting of Denis O'Connell in Rome in 1895 was a third iron that the group had in the fire—appointment of an American as Apostolic Delegate and a red hat for John Ire-land. Although the United States until 1908 was still "mission territory," administered in ecclesiastical questions by the Sacred Congregation of the Propagation of the Faith in Rome, the Amer-ican bishops felt they were managing their dioceses quite compe-tently. Their Third Plenary Council, to legislate on ecclesiastical affairs, had been held in Baltimore in 1884 and the Holy Father had graciously named Archbishop James Gibbons to represent him. On the death of the first native-born American cardinal, John Mc-Closkey of New York, in 1885, Rome had quite promptly elevated Gibbons to the purple.

Now, in 1895, ten years had elapsed without naming another American cardinal, and, in 1892, Leo XIII had established Arch-bishop Francesco Satolli at Washington as first Apostolic Delegate to the United States. It would appear, from the evidence, that the Holy See realized that Denis O'Connell, perhaps unconsciously, in his capacity as liaison for the American hierarchy, was represent-ing only the ideas of his admired friends, Gibbons and Ireland. "Unfortunately there are two parties in the United States," said Cardinal Rampolla in 1891, "and the Holy See cannot favor either." [5]

Relations became strained between Ireland's group and Satolli. William O'Connell, years later, said of Satolli "brilliant, impetuous, orator of the first order and teacher first of the best; he forgave his enemies." [6] The last clause is significant. Satolli had quite a lot to forgive, including some unkind remarks which Denis O'Connell imprudently let drop within earshot of the Vatican. Leo XIII had known Satolli from seminary days; had brought him to Rome from his own diocese of Perugia; had chosen him for the difficult and delicate task of establishing the Apostolic Delegation in Washing-ton. He felt bound to uphold his dignity and authority. The non-cooperating rectors, Denis O'Connell in Rome and Keane in Wash-ington, were asked for their resignations. Satolli was promoted. William O'Connell's elation at his nomination as rector in Rome was doubled by the joy of learning, about the same time, that Francesco Satolli had been named a cardinal. [7]

In Boston, during his ten years as curate, William O'Connell had had the pacific example of Archbishop Williams who met bigotry with charity and prayer; resolutely forbade his clergy to engage in temporal politics.

The times were divisive and Boston not free from bigotry. By 1893, there were estimated to be in Massachusetts seventy-five thousand members of the anti-Catholic American Protestant Asso-

ciation. Mysterious fires had damaged four Catholic churches of
the archdiocese. One man of a Catholic contingent in a Fourth of
July parade in East Boston was fatally shot and others wounded
in a street riot with A.P.A. members. A malicious rumor was current that on September fifth, Catholics intended to rise and take
over the country. The case of a Boston school teacher who persisted
in proclaiming anti-Catholic misinformation to his pupils filled
columns in the newspapers.

Through all the insults and provocation, Archbishop Williams
enjoined on his clergy, his people and the Catholic press absolute
silence, patience and calm. His leadership prevailed. The fifth of
September came and went without incident in 1893. As passions
cooled, people became a bit ashamed of heated words and bitter
suspicions. On his Silver Jubilee, Archbishop Williams could say
"I am proud of the Catholics of Boston . . . it is only because we
have something stronger than mere sentiment that we restrained
ourselves." On his Golden Jubilee, in May of 1895, young William
O'Connell, watching highest officials of state and city, and the
most respected Protestants of Boston on the platform to honor a
Catholic prelate, could meditate on the happy influence of Archbishop Williams' rectitude and imitation of the meekness of Christ
under provocation.[8]

During October, the American Archbishops, as board of trustees
of the American College, had forwarded to Rome, as customary,
a *terna,* a list of three candidates proposed for the vacancy. Archbishop Ryan of Philadelphia favored Rev. Thomas J. Kennedy
of his diocesan seminary faculty (who had to wait six years, to
follow William O'Connell in the post). Corrigan of New York was
for Monsignor Joseph F. Mooney (later Administrator of the New
York archdiocese). It had been said that the third name on the list
originally was that of Rev. Thomas J. Conaty of Worcester (who
succeeded Keane a year later as rector of Catholic University). All
the time, Satolli was urging on Rome the name of William O'Connell. Leo XIII made the appointment on November 21, 1895.

O'Connell always maintained that he had not had the slightest
hint that he was being considered for the post.

So Satolli's finger had pointed to the destiny of William O'Connell, and, from the bell-jangling, slum-crowded life of a parish assistant at St. Joseph's in Boston's West End, he found himself in the isolated, burden-weighted post of Rector of the American College. Ten short years earlier, he had been a student there.

CHAPTER TEN

RECTOR IN ROME

Taciti, soli, senza compagnia
N'andavam. . . .
> Dante: Inferno,
> Canto xxiii; 1 1-2

> *(Silently, lonely, unaccompanied*
> *We went. . . .)*
>
> Cary, tr.

L IKE THE captain of a ship, any man assuming direction of an
organization, responsible for the discipline or rules requisite
to cooperation among those under him, imposes on himself a certain reserve, a little aloofness.

For William O'Connell, settling into the rector's apartment on
the second floor of the ancient Dominican convent at Via dell'
Umilta, 30, in January of 1896, there was the problem of getting
the North American College running smoothly and of winning back
the confidence of disgruntled bishops in America, for the enrollment had dropped to sixty-eight students.

"It is a novel sensation to sit in the headplace in the chapel and
refectory, to wander all over the great rambling place as master of
it all," wrote O'Connell to his brother in Lowell. "Much as I loved
it as a student, I feel every day more and more in some mysterious
way that we belong to each other. Did we not come into existence

on the same identical day? And now here we are bound by this wonderful relationship." [1]

In the 1890's, men kept a horse and carriage as naturally as those of a later age would have an automobile. Rector O'Connell's first equipage after settling in Rome was a coupe drawn by a large bay horse named Newport. The horse had been retired from the stables of the Queen of Italy, but was still serviceable for the Rector's many errands to the Vatican or drives about Rome.

The Rector's first duty call was on Miecislas Cardinal Ledochowski who directed the mission provinces of the world, including the North American College, as head of the Sacred Congregation of the Propagation of the Faith. Tall, white-haired, this noble-born Pole when Archbishop of Posen had been imprisoned for two years under Bismarck's intensive Kulturkampf, like the tortured Mindszenty of Hungary. Like Stepinac of Yugoslavia in mid-Twentieth Century, Ledochowski had been created a Cardinal while in prison, by Pius IX. Released and exiled from Prussia in 1876, his work had since been in Rome.

Leo XIII had not been well, so O'Connell had to wait a fortnight to be received by the Holy Father on Candlemas Day, February second, with the Rectors of the other Roman colleges.

Kneeling before the frail pontiff, nearing his eighty-sixth birthday, O'Connell reported that he had taken over the administration of the American college, with sixty-eight students.

"You must make it grow," the Holy Father said. "I bless you. It is a great task for one so young, but courage—with God's help you will do well."

Life, education, experience had refined the character of William O'Connell. Fifteen years earlier, he had impetuously broken ranks with his *camerata* to intercept this Pope in procession to kiss his ring so boisterously that guards had frowned.

Now he could not find words to answer the kindly admonition. "I rose, bowed and went out of his presence, half-dazed, scarcely knowing where I was walking." [2]

To Leo XIII the giving of audiences was an old story. He, with his luminous dark eyes, could survey, size up the men who knelt before him. A few months later, when Father O'Connell was performing the routine responsibility of the Rectorship, of presenting some two hundred pilgrims from America in an audience, Leo gave the full-bodied young rector some practical sympathy.

O'Connell, sweating in his heavy cassock and mantle under the hot Italian sky, had shepherded the pilgrims through the stifling heat, the blazing sun of the vast piazza outside St. Peter's, up the majestic marble stairways, through the interminable corridors of the Vatican and was now presenting pilgrims, one by one to the Holy Father. For the tenth or twelfth time, he mopped his face and neck with a large American handkerchief.

"You find it hot, Father?" queried Leo XIII softly in Italian. "Well, I feel very cool. Observe thus that there are compensations for age and thinness!"

The visitors and pilgrims came in droves and all applied to the rector of the North American College to arrange an audience with the Pope—almost all. One day it might be an American admiral and a hundred blue-jackets from the flagship *San Francisco,* in port at Naples; the next Buffalo Bill Cody with his cowpunchers and his devoutly Catholic redskins from the Wild West. One Bostonian who did not request an audience, however, was Bishop William Lawrence of the Protestant Episcopal diocese of Massachusetts. He was in Rome most of the month of March, 1901; but O'Connell was not to meet him and make friends until he himself was Catholic Archbishop of Boston.

Distractions from tourists and pilgrims did not swerve O'Connell from the task he had set himself to re-organize the spirit, discipline and spiritual life of the college. His ordination motet *Juravit Dominus* was still sung; now he composed a hymn to the Blessed Virgin, *Praeclara Custos,* which became another tradition. He inaugurated the custom for seminarians starting each day with the invocation "Immaculate Virgin, be our aid!" he liberalized the diet and permitted smoking on the walks outside the city, which won the hearts of his students.

For the first year, it was a life as lonely as a sea captain's for the new rector and the only other member of his staff, Rev. John P.

Farrelly, an alumnus of the college little older than O'Connell, later to be Bishop of Cleveland, Ohio. Farrelly was spiritual director of the college and proved congenial and a valuable aide to the rector.

O'Connell, his students remembered for many years, began the custom of Sunday morning talks to the students on the Rule for a priestly life. He sat, in cassock, at a small table covered with green baize and bearing a small olive-oil brass lamp; laid his biretta on the table; said a short prayer, read a couple of paragraphs, and then expatiated for an hour on the trials, the tests, the opportunities of life as a parish priest. He drew homely examples from his ten years' experience in Boston that caught their interest, and then progressed to an inspirational plane that all testified later, had been of great value to them.

Often, too, he accompanied them on their walks and visits to the Blessed Sacrament, sharing with them his love of the history, traditions and art of the different churches.

Something of the ideals he held up to his students may be gathered from his address on The Influence of Rome in the formation of the American Clergy, which he delivered in Italian at the Golden Jubilee of the American College in 1909, coinciding with his own Silver Jubilee of his priesthood:

"Glance at the civilized nations. To whom do they owe those principles of law, those concepts of order which form the foundation of their constitution and life? . . . It was the missionaries who in the name of Rome, caused the sun of civilization to shine on them, who made the Christian moral virtues, the elements of greatness and strength spring and blossom among them. It was the holy monks with their institution of the religious community, who taught them a method of government. It was the bishops and abbots who revealed to warriors and conquerors the secret of founding a civilized state. . . .

"The greater the distance from the center, the greater the diminution of centripetal force. Thus, studying and living far from the center of the Faith, there arises the danger of lapsing from the sound traditions of sacred teaching. . . . The foundation of an American College on Roman soil . . . reaches a sublime ideal; it becomes . . . the link which unites the clergy of America to the Holy See. . . .

"Here the American better understands the Catholicity of the religion of Christ; has a better idea of the universality of the Church; his nationality is no longer . . . something isolated and privileged but takes the place that belongs to it in the bosom of the universal Church. . . .

"The son of America, having completed in Rome his scientific and moral novitiate, returns to his own country a cosmopolitan in mind and heart, in thought and sentiment; he brings with him as a choice gift to his nation the spirit of universal solidarity which he has acquired in Rome. Sincere and firm attachment to the Vicar of Christ . . . for Americans . . . is what the sun is for nature, what the compass is for the ship; it is the animating force. . . . The alumni of this College leave Rome carrying the torch of ecclesiastical science; but they carry, too, the flame that burns for the Papacy and with this flame they kindle love in men's breasts for him who represents God on earth." [3]

The summer heat and the scourge of malaria, its connection with mosquitoes undiscovered in 1896, had caused the Roman colleges to maintain villas in the hills. In O'Connell's student days, the Americans had had an inadequate summer palace in Grottoferrata. Denis O'Connell, in nearly ten years as rector, had made no change. William O'Connell made it one of his first projects. In two years he had found the ideal place, and the funds with which to purchase it, not far from the old palace in Castel Gandolfo which, since 1933, has been again the summer residence of the Popes.

It was Villa Caterina, on the northwestern slope of the Alban hills, south of Rome, on the old Appian Way, that, in the days of Peter and Paul, led to Pompeii. Below the lovely garden is spread to the eye the vista of the Roman Campagna, in the 1890's still a desolate expanse of malaria-ridden marsh.

Roman ruins in the extensive garden attest that from the First Century A.D. the site was favored by the Roman Emperors, from Tiberius to Constantine, as a summer palace. Here, according to archaeologists, are pillars remaining from the temple of Bona Dea where Clodius was killed, in his fight with Milo, for which Cicero, as schoolboys know, became Milo's advocate. In the Middle Ages, the sunny, protected hillside was famed as a grove of olives.

In 1830, the property was acquired by Don Domenico Orsini, whose wife, Maria Luisa, was of the noted Torlonia family. The Orsini built the beautiful villa with four-storied façade, frescoed halls and salons; and laid out the terraced gardens with fountains, palms, umbrella pines, box hedges, chestnut and olive trees. The name Caterina was kept in honor of St. Catherine, patroness of millers, to whom the olive-press in the grove had been dedicated.

Like many noble Roman families devoted to the Church and the Pope, the Orsini and Torlonia fortunes had been impaired at the suppression of the Papal States in the unification of Italy. Rector O'Connell's friends let him know that Prince Orsini was in dire need of ready cash. In the spring of 1899, O'Connell bought the villa and estate for $26,000.00. With his customary energetic zeal, interior changes were promptly carried out, and the seminarians moved out from Rome to the villa in July.

An oil painting of O'Connell, by Scifoni, hanging today (1953) in the library of the villa, shows the rector as he looked at the age of forty years. He is wearing the purple of a Monsignor, set off by the sweep of thick black hair, and the level gaze of dark brown eyes. He is shown seated in an armchair, with St. Peter's dome visible through the window at his side. This vista seems to have been symbolic on the part of the artist, as neither from the rector's study at Via dell' Umilta, nor from Villa Caterina, is the dome within eyesight.

The jut of the jaw, the resolute cock of the head, the inclusion of St. Peter's dome in the portrait, however, are evidence that the percipient in the Rome of 1900, recognized the force of character, the ability, the ambition to excel that marked William O'Connell already as a man destined to rise high in the service of the Church to which he had dedicated his life.

Removal of the seminarians to Villa Caterina took place the

first week in July, after the examinations at the Urban College were finished.

The new Rector from Boston found, virtually on his doorstep at the North American College, a contemporary problem in the controversy of the Eighteen Nineties that has been styled "Americanism." It was a burning issue which had played a part in the resignations of Denis O'Connell as rector of the North American College and of Archbishop John J. Keane as rector of Catholic University in Washington, D. C. Cardinal Gibbons had salved the wound to his friend by naming Denis O'Connell vicar of his Titular Church of S. Maria in Trastavere in Rome; and Keane soon settled in Rome also. Both were popular with the American colony there, while William O'Connell was as yet a stranger. At the farewell dinner for United States Ambassador Wayne MacVeagh in March of 1897, it was not the Rector of the North American College, but Archbishop Keane who represented the Catholics. He spoke, together with the Methodist Bishop Goodsell and Dr. Nevin of the (Protestant) American Church.[4] Monsignor Denis O'Connell, in the opinion of Maria Longworth Storer, had stayed for revenge in Rome and she wrote to Governor-General William Howard Taft in Manila "I believe his course roused all the antagonism to 'Americanism.' "[5]

This heated controversy arose, innocently enough, from a book published in 1891. It was a biography of Father Isaac Thomas Hecker, convert-priest and founder of the American society of clerics commonly known as the Paulists. Written by Reverend Walter Elliott, its first edition carried an enthusiastic Introduction by Archbishop John Ireland of St. Paul, Minnesota. In 1897, it was translated into French, edited and published with a Preface in French by Abbe Felix Klein, a warm friend of both Denis O'Connell and Keane.

Monsignor Denis O'Connell wrote an article in praise of the French version for *La Quinzaine* and personally read a paper on it in August, 1897 at the Fourth International Congress of Catholic Savants at Fribourg. This paper, which used the term "Americanism" was entitled "A New Idea in the Life of Father Hecker" and provoked a lively controversy.[6]

Into the pot, before it stopped boiling, were stirred not only allegations of Hecker's views, such as that laymen did not need spiritual directors, or that religious need no longer be bound by the traditional vow of obedience; but the views of Archbishop Ireland on public and/or parochial schools; on total abstinence; and on politics. Orders, such as the Dominicans, Benedictines, Jesuits and Redemptorists were stirred to feel that their way of life had been aspersed.

Foreign politics entered into the brew. French ecclesiastics, struggling with the rising anti-clerical spirit in the French government, recalled that Ireland, who spoke French fluently, in 1892 had given a speech in Paris citing the American way of separation of Church and State as a model for France's new Third Republic. When the Spanish-American war broke out, Denis O'Connell wrote to Abbe Klein:

"The present war is really entirely on the lines of our ideas and when, in the end, America triumphs, Americanism must triumph, too. When the center of the world's influence is transplanted by victory and alliance beyond the confines of continental Europe, when Spain will be crippled forever and Italy disabled with internal strife, the Church, to march with the times and control them . . . will be compelled to greater acknowledgment to Americanism . . . Spain's power of influencing Europe is at an end and the future belongs to Anglo Saxon ideas." [7]

A generation which heard the broadcasts of Adolf Hitler and suffered horror let loose around the globe by such fanaticism can understand that Leo XIII had to take action, and only marvel at the gentleness with which he dealt rebuke to fiery natures, without naming individuals, while doing justice to the good in their ideas in his letter on "Americanism," *Testem Benevolentiae*.[8]

Once the Pope had spoken, all the disputants calmed down and, half a century later, only research in dusty tomes and correspondence brings out what it was all about. But William O'Connell, at the North American College in Rome, had to live through three difficult years. He had to steer a clear course between both factions, guarding his every word, and even his facial expression in public. To his everlasting credit, he realized that the men on both sides were loyal churchmen, all intent on guarding the seamless robe of Christ even though, in the heat of the fray, they sometimes came close to rending it between them.

In those lonely days, with history in the making under his eyes, and time for contemplation, he forged the judgment on which he would act for the rest of his life and make future contribution to the welfare of Catholicism in his own country. He saw that while it was dangerous to the Church to be under domination of a civil government as in some European countries, it was equally dangerous for the Church, in the United States, to espouse the cause of any political party. He said little at the time, however.

"I am constantly being asked what Americanism is, and I frankly and honestly answer that I don't know—I doubt if anyone in America does.[9] . . . Some of these books like *The Life of Father Hecker* are pretty hard to understand. . . . Father Hecker was certainly a good and holy priest. But there can be no doubt that he never was sufficiently grounded in Catholic Philosophy or even in History to be able to write without blundering fearfully about principles clear as water. His heart was all right but . . . he retained undoubtedly, if certainly unconsciously and unwillingly, a lot of the old leaven of German mysticism, all mixed up with Yankee Brook Farm religious sentimentalism. . . . Father Hecker will not suffer. Everybody knows his good faith and good work . . . this book, good in intention and interesting as a biography, yet leaving an opening for a merciless censor, will be the innocent occasion of a good deal of arousing." [10]

At the height of the controversy, in 1898, he had told Archbishop Williams:

"I have kept to my original plan of absolute neutrality. . . . I found . . . I was not merely in exile, I was in utter seclusion for two whole years. . . . I refused to become involved. . . . This was a supreme test—either we must come out triumphant, or the College would be closed up. . . . Well, it will not be closed up now.

The house is crowded to its fullest capacity, the discipline and order and scholarship are publicly proclaimed unsurpassed in the city; and financially we are sounder than ever in the history of the institution, so much so that I have nearly concluded negotiations for the purchase of the finest villa within fifty miles of Rome." [11]

The Archdiocese of St. Paul which had sent six students to Rome in the ten years that Denis O'Connell was rector, significantly sent not a single student while William O'Connell held the post. The heaviest contributors to the increased enrollment were Archbishop Williams of Boston as well as Archbishop Corrigan of New York. Every time Monsignor O'Connell turned from the Corso into the narrow Street called Humility, the shabby church of San Marcellus on the corner silently preached a lesson. Marcellus was Pope just after the persecutions and martyrdoms of the Roman Emperor Diocletian. He was a mild and charitable man and holier-than-thou Christians raised a rumpus when he gave absolution to some who had apostatized, in terror of Diocletian's cruelties, and later repented. The co-Emperor Maxentius made this controversy an excuse for punishing the Pope. Tradition says that Maxentius delivered the home and oratory of Marcellus over as a stable for the draught-horses of the city and sentenced Pope Marcellus to tend the horses. He died, about 310, exhausted by his sorrows and the hard labor imposed on him, little knowing that, only two years later, the first Christian Roman Emperor Constantine would come with his banner "In Hoc Signo Vince."

Maxentius was drowned in the river Tiber in the last battle when Constantine triumphed.[12] Pope Marcellus was already dead, in ignominy in the eyes of the world, his body placed in the Catacombs by devout Christians, when Constantine built the first Basilica of St. Peter on the Vatican hill, and Marcellus' successor, Pope St. Sylvester I, consecrated it.

The Church of Marcellus on the Corso was re-built, too, and his body brought to lie under the high altar.

As rector, O'Connell had frequently to confer with Cardinal Rampolla who "receives in his apartment in the Vatican, on the third story. I usually go over in the evening and the huge antechamber is full of all sorts of people . . . (who) occupy huge armchairs around the large room and carry on conversation in whispers. The rooms are lit by old-fashioned oil lamps which only dimly illumine the apartment . . . when your turn comes and you are in the inner sanctum seated on the red sofa, His Eminence at the other end, the atmosphere is still formal but the frost has gone out of it. Rampolla is a Sicilian, very tall and dark . . . dignified . . . but cordial. He has a fascinating smile and gesticulates with large wide sweeps of his arms." [13]

There were others whose names would be famous in later years, whom William O'Connell knew, such as the Pacelli family. O'Connell was in Rome in March, 1895 when a slender, dark-haired seminarian of the oldest college in Rome, the Almo Collegio Capranica, took the leading part in a sort of morality play of which Cardinal Rampolla was the author. As rector of the North American College, O'Connell was a guest at the extraordinary event of the one hundredth birthday of the young seminarian's grandfather; and he was in Rome when the newly ordained Eugenio Pacelli said his First Mass in the beautiful Pauline chapel of Santa Maria Maggiore, April 3, 1899.

"I remember still very clearly," O'Connell said in later years, "the impression that the young man made upon me at the time. His slight but manly figure was clothed in the simple black soutane of the Roman cleric. The expression of his face was highly intellectual and during our brief conversation, I caught a glimpse of the energy and marvelous activity that have characterized his life ever since. His manner, while modest, was nevertheless stamped with a genuine dignity and his friendly smile and quick wit were evidences of the keen intelligence of which he has given so many distinct proofs in his later life." [14]

This grandfather of the future Pope was Marcantonio Pacelli, a nephew of Cardinal Caterini; a civil assistant under Popes Gregory XVI and Pius IX, and founder in 1861 of the journal Osservatore Romano. His long life lasted until 1902. Young Eugenio Pacelli, born March 2, 1876, had been ordained in Rome on Easter Sunday, 1899. His family's home was at 34, Via degli Orsini.

O'Connell, however, did not have the gift of prophecy. The Pacellis to the young Rector were just one of the charming Italian families whom he visited and, now and then, entertained at a Sunday afternoon musicale in his salon at the American College. The Rector was fortunate in that two of his students were outstandingly musical. Michael J. Scanlan, a Georgetown graduate, living at the American College while pursuing four years of studies at Gregorian University, had been director of music already at Georgetown, and a convert-student, Stuart Chambers, had a fine baritone voice. The Rector pressed them into service as soloists at his musicales for Roman society.

The seminarians, boy-like, were a little scornful of the musicales. They called the tapestries with which the Rector covered the ancient stone walls of his quarters, "moth-eaten" and they never even knew that the piano on which the Rector or Di Luca, the college music director, played for the guests, had once been owned by Abbé Liszt, gifted pianist and composer who, it was said, took minor orders to block a beautiful German Princess who, infatuated, wanted to marry him. The students, though, would have appreciated Liszt's practical joke on the avid lion-hunter who, asking him to tea, placed the grand piano in the middle of the room and asked all her friends to hear Liszt play. The shrewd little Abbé spotted the piano and understood at once that his hostess had planned to get a "free" concert.

"Où est votre piano, madame?" he asked, peering about.

"Here, here, maestro," palpitated the baroness.

"Ah, bien, je voulais y poser mon chapeau," said Liszt blandly, and gravely put his black clerical hat on top of the piano and retired to a corner to drink his tea.[15]

Liszt's piano passed into the possession of Gustavus Cardinal Hohenlohe at the Villa d'Este; and, at the latter's death, Monsignor O'Connell bought it and installed it at the American College.

A friendship that would enrich O'Connell's life for the next thirty-five years began when he met one of the four *Camerieri Segreti,* private secretaries to Leo XIII. This was the brilliant son of an English mother and the Spanish Ambassador, thirty-one-year-old Rafael Merry del Val. Educated at the Jesuit College of Ushaw, Merry del Val spoke English, Spanish, Latin, Italian, German and French fluently. Destined for high office and heavy diplomatic responsibilities, his personal absorption was in the club for working boys he had founded in Trastevere, one of Rome's worst slums and would support to his death. Noble-born, accustomed to palaces and the glittering society of courts, his ascetic and simple interior life dictated the sentence, in his own handwriting, kept on his desk and found after his death:

"I have promised with His grace not to begin any action without remembering that He performs it with me and gives me the means to do it; never to conclude without the same thought, offering it to Him as belonging to Him; and, in the course of the action whenever the same thought shall occur, to stop for a moment and renew the desire of pleasing Him."

Merry del Val came often to the American College. He played tennis with the seminarians at their summer villa; and winter afternoons he would walk out with Father O'Connell to watch them playing baseball in the grounds at Villa Borghese. A mischievous hoax at one of those games led to a paragraph in Spalding's Baseball Guide describing how well "Roman monks" played the American game. The writer, visiting in Rome, saw becassocked seminarians hitting out flies or running bases, spoke to them and got only a blank stare and a torrent of Italian. The *camerata* laughed all the way home to Via Umilta that day at their little joke on the tourists.

In 1897, Merry del Val spent nine months in Canada on a Papal assignment, and on his return was consecrated Bishop and made president of the Pontificia Accademia dei Nobili Ecclesiastici, which tightened the bond with the Rector of the American College, through similar duties and problems. Through him, O'Connell would be often at the Palace of the Spanish Embassy to the Holy See opposite the splendid sweep of the Spanish Stairs, mounting from Piazzo di Spagna to the towering Church of Trinita dei Monti.

Archbishop John J. Williams of Boston made a visit to Rome that spring of 1897, his stay lengthened by an attack of illness. As he was living at the American College, he and O'Connell had the opportunity to become well acquainted, driving together after-noons and chatting evenings, with the older man telling his mem-ories of the Vatican Council of 1870. Pleased at the progress visible in the college, and at the good reports he heard of Rome's judgment of the young Rector, the Archbishop, without telling him, requested an honor for him from the Pope. For his farewell audience, the Archbishop asked O'Connell to accompany him to the Vatican, leaving him to wait in an anteroom. Presently he was sent for and, as he knelt before the Pope, with the Archbishop smiling, Leo XIII patted O'Connell on the shoulder, praised his work at the college and announced his appointment to the title of Monsignor. Henceforth there would be red piping on his soutane, and a glow of happiness in his heart.

His first opportunity to wear the purple was at a garden party for Cardinal Schoenberg, Archbishop of Prague, at Villa Mattei in Rome. Baron and Baroness Schoenberg were friends in Rome of O'Connell, the Baroness being an American, of the Ward fam-ily of Boston. Their sister, Baroness von Hoffman, owned Villa Mattei. Their niece, later to be Mrs. Charles Perkins of Boston, lived with them. Describing the affair for the Cardinal, O'Connell wrote home, "The great avenues, bordered on either side by ancient ilex trees were filled with the wonderful kaleidoscope of cardinals in their gorgeous red feriuolas, prelates in purple, diplomats in uni-form and ladies in varied costumes . . . among such a number of . . . reds and purples, my brand-new feriuola passed unnoticed (but) it would be affectation to conceal that it felt good to be a part in the picture." [16]

Rightfully then on Candlemas Day, 1897, when, by custom, the rectors of all the houses of study gave decorated candles to the Pope, had Leo XIII publicly praised the young American.

"The Holy Father, abandoning his reserve in such matters, said to me, before his whole Court, "I know well the immense progress of the American College in the past year, and I wish to say pub-licly that I have the most complete confidence in you." [17]

The Rector was accompanied that day by one of his students from Boston, who was to be ordained in June, Michael J. Splaine. The fact that Splaine had thus witnessed the proudest moment of his life became the foundation for a friendship that lasted until O'Connell's death almost half a century later.

CHAPTER ELEVEN

OLD DAYS IN ROME

Alma Roma . . . u siede il successor del
maggior Piero.
> Dante: Inferno, Canto ii, 1.20-24

> *(Beloved Rome . . . where sits the successor
> of great Peter.)*
> > Carlyle, tr.

ROME, at the turn of the century, was not only the spiritual center for Catholics of the world, but also the rendezvous of scholars, writers, artists, musicians; and the cosmopolitan center for wealthy, cultured men and women of all nations.

Monsignor William O'Connell, after his two years of isolation, reorganizing the North American College, began to mingle with Roman society. He was specifically advised to do so by Cardinal Ledochowski of Propaganda and Cardinal Rampolla, Papal Secretary of State, who had decided together that a little social polish would be the thing for the young American.

"We had our eyes on you as a possible member of our diplomatic corps," Rampolla told him, years later, "so I advised you to be less of a hermit." [1]

Rampolla himself was, by birth, Count Mariano del Tindaro of Sicily; but had chosen priesthood. Tall, with jet-black hair, he was in his fifties when William O'Connell first knew him. He had been

Papal Nuncio to Spain but, ascetic by nature, was about to retire from the world as a Benedictine monk when Leo XIII called him to thirteen arduous years as Papal Secretary of State. To O'Connell, he typified the best in ecclesiastical devotion: "I think Roman prelates and they alone by a miracle of God's grace, are the only ones capable of undergoing day in and day out this wearing routine without the slightest sign of irritability or fatigue. . . . The hermit in his cell is allowed the luxury of peace with his solitude, but the life of an official of the Curia in Rome . . . deserves an eternal reward for its self-sacrifice and complete self-abnegation. With little genial companionship and literally no recreation, he devotes himself entirely to the service of the Church of God." [2]

Sceptics or non-believers could never know the spiritual exaltation that William O'Connell felt on Christmas Eve of 1899, kneeling beside the great composer Puccini in the portico of the basilica of St. Peter's as Leo XIII, with mallet of gold and ivory, struck thrice on the Porta Santa marked with the Cross, to inaugurate the Jubilee Year of 1900.

It was the first time in seventy-five years that the great door had been opened. Troublous times in Italy had made pilgrimage to Rome too difficult in 1850 or 1875 for carrying out the pious custom inaugurated first by Boniface VIII in 1300 A.D. The ceremony so moved William O'Connell that, a quarter of a century later, when Boston reporters interviewed him, "slowly and still more slowly the words came . . . his voice quivered . . . tears glistening in his eyes, he broke off: 'I think we had better stop here' he said." [3]

He was thinking of the frail pontiff, whiter than his papal robes, bowed under the heavy tiara in his ninetieth year, who had talked of seeing the Holy Year of 1825 as a boy of fifteen, saying, "We ever seem to see in our mind's eye . . . the multitudes who in processional order went from church to church." [4] O'Connell had heard the multitudes in procession in 1900, visiting the seven basilicas and chanting St. Philip Neri's old hymn: *Vanita di vanita; alla morte che sara? Ogni cosa e vanita.* (Vanity of vanities; at our death what will it be? All is vanity.)

It was not only of Rome that William O'Connell accumulated memories. Summer, when the seminarians were on vacation at the villa in the Alban hills, the rector could take his own vacation in journeys to Switzerland, to Oberammergau for the Passion Play, to Munich to visit his friends, Prince Ludwig and his family, at Nymphenburg; and to the Italian cities. Year after year he made such journeys, except in 1897 when the illness of his brother Richard called him to Lowell for priestly offices at a deathbed.

One of O'Connell's favorite short vacations was by train to the shore opposite Venice. No place inhabited by man on the globe imparts the peace to be found in the profound silence of the city in the sea. The spell steals gratefully over harassed ears with the first sweep of the gondolier's long single oar, away from the stone landing steps. The calm green surface of the canals, the brooding beauty of marble palaces and stuccoed houses, bowered with vines and flowers on every balconied window; the gracious curves of great church domes and stark towers of campanili lifting against the sky, say to the traveler: Here is rest; here time for meditation; here beauty.

Venice is a prayerful city. Early and late her sonorous bells ring out the call to Matins, to Mass, for the Angelus, for Vespers. Here are not Rome's mementoes of a pagan past; but only the ancient shrines of a Christian Faith, preserved by valorous arms against onslaughts of barbarians from the North or infidels from the East. Her churches, her art galleries, her proud palaces are filled with stories from the Bible; traditions and history of the Church in mosaic or oil masterpieces. Here the Bellinis, Veronese, Titian, Tintoretto, Tiepolo, Giorgione devoted their God-given talents to the glory of God.

After a morning of studying such works, in the Palace of the Doges, or the Accademia, or one of the historic churches, O'Connell could sit at a café table in the sunny silence of the vast square, broken by the throbbing thunder of bells overhead ringing the Angelus, and the whirring sweep of hundreds of startled pigeons. At little tables around him, sat the Venetians, eating a frugal roll and fresh fruit, sipping a small glass of the mild local wine. Above

the cathedral's looming façade, gleamed in the sun the four im-
mense bronze horses, made before Christ's birth in the time of the
Greek Emperor Alexander; brought home from Constantinople in
A.D. 1204 by victorious Venetians, during the Fourth Crusade.

In dreamy hours like this, in the city where Catholic faith and
Catholic art were part of the poorest citizen's life, William O'Connell contrasted life as he had lived it, for the previous decade, in
the sweated, crowded, unbeautiful streets of St. Joseph's parish in
the West End of Boston. In such hours, he forged his dream of a
Catholicism that should know the blessing of sunshine, the beauty
of art and architecture, the peace of devout living, in his native
America.

He could not know then, how or when the opportunity would
come, but the ideal was built in his mind, the purpose formed in
his will. In God's good time, the lessons learned in Italy would
bring forth their fruit in accomplishment.

He contrasted in his mind, when invited to give the Epiphany
sermon at San Andrea dell Valle in Rome, in 1898, the sermons
he had preached in Boston's West End slum to a congregation of
humble Irish Catholic servants and day-laborers. Pius IX in 1847
had set the custom of a sermon in a different foreign language on
each day of the Octave of the Epiphany. Over the years, it had
become the fashionable attraction in Rome with society thronging
in sable or sealskin, real lace mantillas and real pearls. The cream
of Rome turned out to listen to a sermon by Willy O'Connell from
Lowell, standing in the high carved pulpit on the middle pier of
the nave. He had some vanity about the placard at the church
door announcing that "the preacher will be the Most Illustrious
and Most Reverend Lord, His Excellency Monsignor William
O'Connell, Domestic Prelate of His Holiness and Rector of the
Pontifical College of the United States of North America." [5]

His work of re-organizing the American College was virtually
completed by the end of 1900. Villa Caterina was remodelled, paid
for, and a sinking fund of twenty thousand francs set aside from
sale of the old property at Grottoferrata.[6]

The Holy Father had publicly commended O'Connell for the

new spirit of scholarship and of religious devotion permeating the
growing student body. Rector O'Connell was completely happy
and contented at the end of five years and would have liked to
live forever in Rome. With the Psalmist, he could say: "The lines
are fallen unto me in goodly places." [7] He should have been remembering St. Philip Neri's song *Vanita di vanita*. He was about
to leave Rome, on a far journey, and it was Satolli's finger again
that had pointed the way.

On April twenty-second, 1901, just as Rome was most beautiful
with blooming anemones, mimosa, roses, the Holy See announced
that the new Bishop of Portland, Maine was William Henry O'Connell. On May nineteenth he was consecrated at St. John Lateran,
scene of his ordination seventeen years earlier, the rich interior of
which made an incomparable setting for the vestments of officiating
clerics, the glittering uniforms and colorful costumes of diplomats, nobles and society ladies of Rome, set off by the massed
black of the American College seminarians. After the ceremonies,
the invited guests moved up the aisle to a little door giving on
the twelfth century Benedictine cloister. It made a perfect setting
for the *colazione* served by deft waiters as the guests moved about
in the great four-sided arcade around a garden where fragrant box
bushes lined the walks.

A vivid description by an eye-witness of Bishop O'Connell's
consecration has been preserved in the letters of one of his students, later the distinguished anthropologist and professor at Catholic University, Reverend John Montgomery Cooper.

"Our Rector was consecrated Bishop of Portland on Sunday,"
wrote young Cooper to his mother,[8] "by Cardinal Satolli, Bishop
Stonor and Merry de (sic) Val assisting. The ceremony was held
in the Corsini Chapel of the Lateran, one of the richest family
chapels in the city. The place was crowded with the boys and the
friends of the college, together with the Rector's personal friends.
Among those present was (sic) Archbishop (Placide) Chappelle and
the American and Austrian Ambassadors (George von L. Meyer of
Boston and Baron Schoenberg).

"About twenty of us (students) were on ceremonies of which we had scarcely the least idea on going over. But everything in these larger Roman churches is under the direction of the master of ceremonies, usually a monsignor. He is master of all he surveys and even the Pope himself when on ceremonies, is bound to do what he says, right or wrong, under pain of mortal sin and if anybody but the Pope disobeys, he would be excommunicated. The arrangement does away with confusion. . . ."

(Seminarian Cooper did not give his authority for these stern instructions—perhaps some older student had been "having him on.")

"Well, anyway, the affair started at 10 A.M.," continued Cooper. "The rites were very solemn. First Cardinal Satolli, after a series of interrogations on the Faith of the Bishop-Elect, and delivery of two oaths of office, began Mass. Next comes the pronunciation of 'Receive the Holy Spirit' which is followed by the anointing with chrism of forehead and hands. Then ring, crozier and other insignia are delivered and gilded casks of wine and two loaves of bread are given. . . . The Canon of the Mass is said together by the Cardinal and the newly consecrated Bishop. After Mass, the latter in full pontificals, passes in procession around the Church, giving the episcopal blessing for the first time to the people . . .

"It was gotten through within an hour and a half in all. Being right in the sanctuary, we could get a good look at Satolli and Merry de (sic) Val.[9]

"The latter, whom it is rumored may be our next Nuncio, is a rather young man, certainly not over thirty-five, with a rather thin face, compressed lips, large straight nose, brilliant black eyes and broad high forehead. His general appearance gives you at once the idea of a learned, refined and saintly character and such he is. Scarcely a prelate in Rome is held in such general esteem and he is the Pope's (Leo XIII) most intimate friend. He lives at the Vatican in an apartment next to the Pope."

Since 1870, no Pope had been able to leave the Vatican to visit the historic basilica, cathedral of the Bishop of Rome from 312 A.D. In the old days, newly elected Popes had come in procession, riding a white mule, with Kings and Princes walking by their side. In

1901, the Pope was still the Prisoner of the Vatican. No wonder that Leo XIII, receiving the new Bishop in audience the next day, questioned him about every detail, and heard with nostalgia of the scene in the Corsini Chapel and the happy congratulations in the cloister garden. In his youth, the aged Pope had often visited St. John Lateran and it was an abiding sorrow that the turn of history had debarred him from stepping over its threshold for thirty years.

"Leo XIII . . . the following morning when I went to the Vatican," said O'Connell, "amazed me by his knowledge of the ceremony, who were present, how beautifully it had gone, even the colazione in the cortile had not escaped him.

"Frail, his face the color of old ivory, his eyes still bright and penetrating, his mind alert . . . leaning over me as I knelt, he whispered: 'Have no fear. It is a hard task for one so young but I am always here; come when you need me. . . .' Smiling, he slipped a great ring on my finger and hung a jeweled cross on my breast . . . how could I remain unmoved? 'You will come back to Rome,' he said, 'but I will not be here; when you hear of my death, will you remember me in your prayers and say a great funeral Mass for the repose of my soul? O'Connell, io mio fido di voi (I have confidence in you).' " [10]

CHAPTER TWELVE

BISHOP OF PORTLAND

Nel mezzo del cammin di nostra vita
mi ritrovai per una selva oscura.

Dante: Inferno, Canto i, 1 1-2

*(In the middle of the journey of our life
I found myself in a dark wood.)*

Carlyle, tr.

THE STATE of Maine, most northeasterly territory of the United States and largest of the six New England states, because of its vast extent of forest lands, is often called the Pine Tree State.

William O'Connell, third bishop of the Diocese of Portland, would understand that at first-hand experience in his long journeys by train or horse-drawn carriage to administer Confirmation in far-flung country parishes.

Figuratively, too, he would find himself in a dark wood of perplexity over diocesan problems. One hundred priests, most of them in charge of isolated parishes for many years, a number older than he in the service of God, were far different to rule than the same number of youths in a seminary. A hundred thousand American Catholics, who felt proprietary pride in the churches their donations had built and supported, were a different type from the tenement dwellers he had known as a curate in the Boston slums. The Yankee eighty-five percent of Maine's population bore no resemblance in language, customs or temperament to the blithe Catholic Italians who had surrounded him for the past six years.

O'Connell, exchanging the palm, olive and cypress of Italy for the pines, oak and elms of Maine, found the climate as cool as the welcome waiting for him. It was no secret that the Maine priests had passionately wanted one of their own as bishop; they were acquiescent but not pleased that Rome had disregarded the three names proposed by the Maine clergy.

Their new bishop, unintentionally, created an impression of arrogance by arriving with a suite of Italian retainers in a city where New England housewives took pride in domestic duties. O'Connell, fortunately for his own peace of mind, never heard what was said in Portland about his Italian valet Peppino, the latter's wife and curly-headed bambinos; his coachman, Pio; and his music master "Count" Pio DeLuca. In Rome, everyone had a household staff, and no prelate drove his own carriage; but in Portland the bishop's victoria, with liveried "dago" driving the brown and grey horse through Deering Woods of an afternoon was a sight discussed at a hundred supper tables.

The diocese had had two months to speculate about the new bishop, after the appointment was announced on April twenty-second, 1901. He had landed in Boston on June twenty-eighth and the newspapers whetted anticipation with glowing accounts of a reception July first at Lowell . . . "a purse of several thousand dollars presented" [1] . . . ; and a dinner in Boston on July second. . . . "a purse of $3,200 presented" [2] . . . and a reception at the Boston Catholic Union.

A man more familiar with the folkways of Maine might have hesitated to compete for attendance with the festivities of the holiday celebration of the one hundred and twenty-fifth anniversary of the Declaration of Independence. It was a point of honor in old Maine for enthusiastic youths to ring the bells in every church steeple from midnight to dawn; and for small boys to fire off enormous quantities of "cannon-crackers" and "six-inch salutes" as well as incalculable strings of small Chinese fire-crackers and torpedoes from daybreak until their ammunition gave out. By ten o'clock on the Fourth, when the clergy of the diocese started their procession at the Cathedral of the Immaculate Conception on Cumberland Street in Portland, another procession, enlivened with brass bands and drum-and-bugle corps, was starting the Fourth-of-July parade a couple of blocks away.

However, "the sun never shone on a fairer day . . . delightfully cool after blistering heat," [3] when the hundred clergy, preceded by fifty acolytes in red cassocks, and including Bishops Dennis M. Bradley of Manchester and Matthew F. Harkins of Providence, marched from the sacristy, through the chapel and out around the cathedral to the entrance to greet Bishop William Henry O'Connell.

The diocesan Administrator, Rev. M. C. O'Brion of Bangor, presented holy water and incense and the procession then conducted the new bishop to the throne in the sanctuary, the people in the packed cathedral falling to their knees for his blessing as he progressed up the aisle.

"There was no chance of mistaking the bishop. His stalwart figure . . . combined the bearing of a leader with all the ceremonial circumstance of his office. . . . He wore a black soutane, an alb of white lace, over all the cappa magna of purple silk, its long train borne by two acolytes," wrote a Yankee newsman,[4] scribbling fast while O'Connell, crozier in hand, stood before the altar for the singing of the *Te Deum*.

Then, seated on the throne, the Bishop received obeisance of the clergy, advancing two by two to kiss his ring; pontificated at the solemn high mass; and listened to the laudatory sermon by Bishop Bradley. Bishop Harkins spoke at the "sumptuous banquet" served in the adjoining parochial school, Kavanagh Hall, at noon.

"Bishop O'Connell found after the ceremonies were over yesterday that he had need of a short rest. Since landing from the steamer last week, he has been constantly responding to the demands of some ceremony and found that his strength had been severely taxed," the diocese learned next day.[5]

It was not his physical strength that was over-taxed, but his emotions. "No one realizes the trepidation in the heart of a new

Bishop," he confessed years later. "A new Bishop who knows his own littleness and his great responsibility." [6]

He was taking up the reins with no experience in the administration of a diocese, after a hiatus of a year since the death of the beloved Bishop James A. Healy [7] during which time the Administrator could make only temporary appointments, only time-marking solution of pressing problems. He found a large proportion of his clergy and his flock speaking a language in which he was never fluent, and speaking it in the Canadian patois rather than Parisian French.

From the modest three-room suite as rector in the old convent building in Rome, he was now moving into an immense red brick "palace" with forty bedrooms. Bishop David W. Bacon had built it like that to provide accommodations for the annual retreat of the diocesan clergy in the predominantly non-Catholic diocese. Its style harmonized with the French Gothic of the great red brick cathedral also built by Bishop Bacon. The house fronted on Congress Street, Portland's main thoroughfare, a wrought-iron fence separating the lawn from the busy sidewalk and traffic. This irked O'Connell, accustomed to the walled seclusion of Italian residences with their inner courtyards.

He offended, unconsciously, the Catholics of Portland by having a monumental Pieta in the garden removed and building in its site a vine-covered arbor in which he could walk, to read his breviary, or to smoke his cigar. This seclusion struck the Portlandites as "snobbish." When they heard he had accepted an invitation to join the exclusive Yankee Cumberland Club, their distrust rankled deeper. To O'Connell, after Rome, it seemed only natural that leading citizens and State officials should honor his office. He had been away from America so long that when Governor John F. Hill tendered him a reception at the State House in Augusta or Senator Eugene Hale and Tom Reed, Speaker of the House of Representatives were friendly, he did not realize how strongly the Republicans were courting the Catholic vote. However, his eyes were opened "when President Theodore Roosevelt came to Portland for a brief stay. . . . Speaker Tom Reed sent me the first invitation to meet the President at his house." [8] On the death of President William McKinley, by an assassin's hand,[9] one of Bishop O'Connell's first public appearances in Maine had been as invited orator at the State memorial service.

The people of Maine were too newly acquainted with their Bishop to know the blow he sustained only a fortnight after his installation at the cathedral. On July twentieth, at Lowell, his oldest sister, Miss Julia, died. She was sixty-three years old, the first-born, a native of Enagh in Ireland. From the death of the father, in William O'Connell's sixth year, she had shared with her mother the upbringing of the younger children. Since the mother's death in 1893, she had maintained the family home at 64 Fay Street, Lowell, taking over the care of the orphaned children of the brother Richard in 1897. She and William were particularly close in affection. All through his years in Rome, where his living was provided in the North American College, he had regularly sent his entire salary of one thousand dollars for the support of Julia and nephews and nieces.[10] All the years he was in Portland, he was to continue this family responsibility, paying for the education of two nephews. In the end both brought heartbreak to him, even as he had, in a moment of pessimism, half-foreseen when, in June of 1899 he wrote to Julia from Rome: "I have always been worrying too much about home. Everyone in the world has some load to carry. . . . When I look back on my own life, it has been one constant strain of hard, hard work but very little assistance. Perhaps if I had an uncle I would never be anything! I think, after studying the question all over, that uncles do more harm than good. Young people ought to be taught to depend on themselves." The mood passed, however, and he continued his aid and affection as an uncle throughout his long life, towards his kin. Aunt Sarah Fay's last years were lovingly passed under the care of Julia.[11] In 1903, the Bishop bought a house at 43 Addington Road, Brookline, Massachusetts for a home for his sister, Mrs. Bridget Hatch [12] and visited her there often. When the brother Richard died, in 1897, O'Connell had said: "The one comforting thing in the whole tragedy was the perfect fortitude of dear Julia. What a wonderful character she is, and how like dear mother!" [13] After Julia's death, Lowell never seemed to him like home. He let the property pass to his brothers and their children. Throughout the Portland years, he took a cottage each summer at Old Orchard Beach, and had his kin spend their vacations there with him.

The Diocese of Portland, to which Cardinal Satolli's finger had directed O'Connell for his first bishopric, was hardly older than the bishop himself. When separated from the Boston diocese and including, at first, New Hampshire as well as all Maine, in 1855 it had numbered but twenty-four Catholic churches in the two adjoining states. Its first bishop was Most Reverend David W. Bacon from New York, consecrated after another appointee had declined to accept the burden. It took real heroism for Bishop Bacon to accept. Only six months before, at Ellsworth, Maine, a Jesuit missionary to the Catholic Indians of Northern Maine, Father John Bapst, S.J., had been assaulted by an anti-Papist mob of Yankees. On October fourteenth, 1854, the priest was attacked, stripped, plastered with tar and feathers, ridden on a rail out of the town and left to die, unconscious. The Catholic chapel at Ellsworth was burned down by incendiaries.

Bishop O'Connell would have been very familiar with that story, because Father Bapst survived to be the first president of Boston College, 1860-69, and his death occurred while O'Connell was a student there.

However, as often happens, the memory of such deeds of violence and hatred produced its own revulsion in the hearts of Maine people and by O'Connell's day, Catholics constituted about fifteen percent of the population, living in harmony, with their neighbors.

Kavanagh Hall, where the installation banquet was held for Bishop O'Connell, had its name from an early Catholic Governor of Maine, Edward Kavanagh (1795-1844), whose sister, Winifred, donated funds to build the school. Kavanagh is said to have been the first Catholic in New England to win election to a Yankee town school committee.[14] He was elected governor in 1843, after having served four years in Congress and in diplomatic posts.

An Irish priest touring America in 1870 reported that Bishop
Bacon was "a very gentlemanly, middle-aged man with regular
round features, bald head and white hair on his poll. His dress is
that of a layman . . . except the large ring on the fourth finger of
his right hand." [15] Times were so hard for the Catholic diocese of
Portland, that Bishop Bacon forbade the Irish priest to take a
collection for the cathedral back in Cork. "The Catholic population
of Portland (1870) is only six thousand and they are poor." [16]
Bishop James A. Healy became the second Ordinary of the
diocese in 1875, a bright star in the history of the Catholic Church
in America since, technically, he had been born a Negro slave in
Georgia in 1839. He was one of three brilliant brothers, born to a
slave mother and an Irish immigrant father. The father deserves
credit for the responsibility he manifested towards his children, all
sent North to be educated in Catholic schools. Two sisters became
nuns. One brother, Patrick, became a Jesuit and was president of
Georgetown University. James and a third brother, A. Sherwood,
educated at Holy Cross College in Worcester, both were named
bishops, although Father Sherwood Healy, pastor of St. James'
Church, Boston, died before he could be consecrated Bishop of
Hartford, Connecticut. Father James Healy, trained for the priesthood by the Sulpicians in Montreal and France, was the first Chancellor of the Boston diocese under Bishop Fitzpatrick,[17] later pastor
of St. James' Church in Boston. There, by inviting the Redemptorists to preach their first mission in Boston, he was instrumental
in eventually bringing to Mission Hill the great shrine of Our Lady
of Perpetual Help. He also built the edifice of St. James' Church,
now (1953) the downtown Eucharistic Shrine of Boston. There was
never any concealment of their Negro blood yet all three priest-
brothers were widely loved, respected and honored for the quiet
dignity with which they manifested the best traits of Negro and
Celtic heritage in their dedicated lives. Bishop James Healy, Portland loved to remember, used to ride horseback around the city
and countryside unattended, his saddle-bags filled with food for
the poor.

O'Connell had met Bishop James Healy only once, on the oc-

casion of his *ad limina* visit to Rome when he dined at the North
American College. As they rose from table to join the procession
of students to the chapel, Bishop Healy politely motioned to the
Rector to lead the way. Punctiliously, O'Connell bowed, saying,
"Oh, no; after you, Bishop."

"After me?" said Bishop Healy quickly. "So that is in the future.
You are coming after me." [18]

Father Michael McDonough, who had accompanied his Bishop
to Rome and thus heard the conversation, told O'Connell later
that, on his death bed, Bishop Healy had again mentioned what
he called his little prophecy, fulfilled in 1901.

Physically the task ahead of Bishop O'Connell was a taxing
ordeal. In the year since Bishop Healy's death, Confirmations were
in arrears, many local problems pressing for solution. Visitation
of the distant parishes called for overnight train or boat journeys
to the north and east; poor Pio Zappa's teeth were to chatter many
a time driving the Bishop around Portland in that first winter away
from sunny Italy.

There were two Indian reservations in the diocese, one at Old
Town, the other at Eastport, of aboriginal Catholic Americans descended from the first converts of heroic Jesuit missioners. Their
education, in O'Connell's day, was in the hands of the Sisters of
Mercy. The new Bishop was deeply impressed by the musical
chanting by the Indians of the hymns at Benediction, and the deep
reverence with which, when the chief asked for the episcopal
blessing, the entire group knelt, bowing their foreheads to the
ground.

The bucolic lives of the French-speaking habitants in the northern farming regions interested him, also. "I was conscious of the
contrast between my life in the Eternal City with its superb
churches, its glorious processions, its grand ceremonies; and these
hidden-away portions of my flock, ennobled by the faith, manifested under the shingled roofs of their little chapels. . . . The
priests and people in these villages felt, perhaps, more than those
richly endowed, the Real Presence of Christ in home-made taber-
nacles on the rude altars of their simple wooden churches.

"Those long journeys through the northern wilderness of Maine, with its great rivers, lakes and immense virgin forests were immensely beneficial to me by the life in the great open spaces, away from petty cares of office and petty formalities of urban life." [19]

He was at his best, actually, on such visits, coming down from his room in stocking feet for a friendly chat with the village pastor, or popping out into the kitchen to assure the cook not to fuss over the supper, because he preferred a simple meal. In Portland or Augusta his manner became what the Maine folks considered "pompous," through insistence on the formality he deemed due his rank. The Catholics of his day did not realize how this very dignity was winning recognition for them from Yankees in high office. When Leo XIII died, the Governor of Maine and his staff came formally from Augusta to attend the memorial Mass at which O'Connell preached the eulogy in the Portland cathedral.[20] Many non-Catholics contributed generously to the twenty-thousand dollar clubhouse for the Workingmen's Club established by O'Connell for the longshoremen and railroad employes of Portland. He also opened an Ozanam Club for young men of the city to provide healthful recreation.

The old cathedral, too, was renovated and O'Connell obtained an outstanding series of stained glass windows, executed in Germany, portraying the events of the life of the Blessed Virgin. Various donors cooperated in this project, but the Bishop personally paid for the window above the high altar, a lovely design showing Our Lady of the Immaculate Conception, in whose name the cathedral is dedicated. The patronal feast of the cathedral thus came on December 8, the same date as Bishop O'Connell's birthday.

Along with the re-decoration of the cathedral, Bishop O'Connell carried on re-organization of the diocese along the lines of the Roman Curia. He issued pastoral letters urging priests who spoke their language to hear confessions and administer the Sacraments for immigrants [21] and emphasizing the need of harmony and unity in the Faith for his flock, diverse in racial origins.[22] The French-Canadian element was historically large in Maine; O'Connell spoke of the new waves of immigration from Italy, Austria-Hungary, the Orient. All, he said, were children of the same Church, becoming citizens of their one new republic.

His people, accustomed to the simple lives led by Bishop Bacon and Bishop Healy, were surprised by the new Bishop's frequent comings and goings. In October, 1901, he was off to Boston to dedicate a shrine at the Working Boys Home for his classmate, Father John F. Ford. On May 10, 1903, he preached in Lowell at the dedication of new St. Peter's, the parish of his own baptism. They could even take pride when, of all the hierarchy of the United States, he was the speaker at the laying of the cornerstone of the Monastery of the Dominicans at Catholic University in Washington, D. C. Making the point that the Apostolic Delegate, Archbishop Diomede Falconio, O.F.M., who blessed the new building, was a Franciscan, O'Connell delivered a masterly treatise on the variety of religious orders and their function in the Church.

Men of today have forgotten old dissensions and arguments, but at the turn of the century an anti-clerical as well as an anti-Catholic spirit was rampant. Even among Catholic hierarchy and laity were those who opposed the monastic, the religious way of life as outmoded. O'Connell spoke in defense of, in praise of the Orders, bidding them "grow and prosper in the harmony of the house of God in which there is plenty of room for all; the only sentiment here, the blessed rivalry and emulation of kindling more fires of the charity of Christ." [23]

Summers at Old Orchard Beach, Maine's famed resort, were easy for the people to approve, especially when clerical friends like Chancellor (later Bishop) John Delaney of Manchester, N. H., or the Roman alumnus Rev. Patrick Supple of Boston, shared the vacation. Not so complimentary to Maine's climate was O'Connell's bronchial affliction that led him to Florida in the winters.

CHAPTER THIRTEEN

MANILA OR NOT?

.... ed in infamia tutto il monte gira. . . .
Dante: Purgatorio, Canto xx, 114

(And all the mount doth circle in infamy.)
Okey, tr.

NOTHING IS more difficult than for human beings to understand one another truly through the medium of speech; particularly when the spoken word is passed on by different hearers over a lapse of time. The whole course of William O'Connell's life was changed in 1903 by a mistaken report of something he had said five years earlier.

The episode began by receipt in Portland of a rather garbled cablegram in Italian which read: "It Santo Padre offre a Mons. W. O'Connell, Vesco di Portland la sede metropolitan di Manilla fidando specialement nel suo zelo conoscente e suo attaccamento alla Santo Sede. Rampolla." [1]

Mariano Cardinal Rampolla was the brilliant Secretary of State to Leo XIII whom O'Connell had known well in Rome. Now he was telling the Bishop of Portland that he could be appointed Archbishop of Manila. The Philippine Islands had been bought for twenty million dollars by the United States after winning the war with Spain. The Filipinos were not happy about it but the United

States Army had succeeded in "pacifying" native objectors and William Howard Taft was head of the first American government of the Philippines, 1900-1904. Taft had been in Rome in 1902, for negotiations to reimburse Catholic missionaries for confiscated property built up during the four hundred years that the islands had been a Spanish colony. The proviso insisted upon by the government at Washington, was that the Spanish friars be replaced by American bishops and priests.

Keeping his own counsel, O'Connell set out at once for Washington. President Theodore Roosevelt had left the capital on April first for a Western tour of hunting and speech-making that kept him away until the middle of June. However, O'Connell found as chief of the Insular Bureau in Washington, an old friend, Army Colonel Clarence R. Edwards who, a decade later would be earning fame in Boston in command of the Yankee Division from Massachusetts in France during World War I. Edwards had thorough knowledge of political and Army matters in the Philippines, as well as in Washington.

The Apostolic Delegate, Sebastiano Martinelli, just named a Cardinal, could give O'Connell the ecclesiastical view. He himself was an Augustinian; and the retiring Archbishop of Manila was one of the Spanish Augustinians who had suffered from the hostility of non-Catholic Americans and dissident Filipinos.

As background to Rampolla's cable, it should be recalled that there were many reasons why O'Connell would be considered for the post and might be happy to accept it. He had been studying Spanish, the language of the Philippines, for ten years and, in Portland, had acquired one of the new phonographs with wax cylinders of recitations in Spanish. The climate would not dismay him, for he had enjoyed the ten summers he had spent in the heat of Italy and had fled to Florida during the severe Maine winters. Also he was known in the Church as a friend of the religious Orders such as the Jesuits under whom he had studied; the Oblates in Lowell and the Augustinians in nearby Lawrence. Only lately he had preached for the Dominicans, at the laying of the cornerstone of their house of studies at the Catholic University of America in Washington.

This, he soon perceived, might cause a little difficulty, as the Roosevelt Administration saw eye to eye with Cardinal Gibbons and Archbishop Ireland in a policy of installing secular clergy to replace the Friars.

There was another difficulty in the political question. O'Connell was not sympathetic to the new policy of imperialistic adventure which had marked those days for the United States. Theodore Roosevelt, who as the ebullient assistant Secretary of the Navy had issued the orders under which Admiral George Dewey took Manila in the beginning of the Spanish-American War, had no idea of handing over the Philippines to the Filipinos. Roosevelt had also been embroiled by his close friends, Bellamy Storer, Minister to Spain, and his wife, Maria Longworth Storer, in the project of seeing Archbishop John Ireland made a Cardinal. Control of the Church in the Philippines and a red hat for Ireland were inextricably mixed in the motives of the group which included Denis O'Connell, whom William O'Connell had superseded as rector in Rome and who now was in Washington as rector of the Catholic University of America.

Roosevelt, whose friendship for Archbishop Ireland had a practical political angle of attracting the Catholic vote for his candidacy as President in 1904, had actually prevailed on Cardinal Gibbons to suggest to the Vatican a different candidate for Archbishop of Manila, namely, Thomas A. Hendrick of the Diocese of Rochester.

Rampolla's cable to William O'Connell thus was evidence that the Vatican was well informed and had no intention of seeing the spiritual welfare of Filipino Catholics made a pawn of Republican politics in the United States. The Vatican did not concede to Theodore Roosevelt any "right of investiture" in respect to naming either Bishops or Cardinals.

Roosevelt seems to have had hazy notions about the Catholic Church and its prelates. The first time he met Gibbons, in 1891, he had described him as a "cultivated Jesuit with rather kindly emotions and a thorough knowledge that his Church must become

Republicanized and Americanized to retain its hold here." [2] Roosevelt's mother-in-law, incidentally, was a convert-Catholic residing in Rome, where O'Connell had known her. It was her custom annually to bring to the college church on Via dell' Umilta the flowers for the Repository on Holy Thursday. Some American Republicans took rather an airy view of Leo XIII himself. William Howard Taft, on his mission to Rome in 1902, when the ninety-two-year-old pontiff exerted himself to grant a private audience, wrote: "The old boy is quite bubbling with humor. He is lively as a cricket." [3] Roosevelt had plans concerning the Church. During the Spanish-American War, he had written to Mrs. Storer in Madrid: "I absolutely agree with you about Archbishop Ireland. It will be a fortunate thing to have him made a Cardinal especially in view of what must occur in the Philippines." [4]

Into these hopeful plans of putting the Church in the Philippines into the hands of American clergy; of making Hendrick Archbishop of Manila; of seeing Ireland a Cardinal, suddenly fell the swift-running rumor that the Vatican had offered the metropolitan See of Manila to William Henry O'Connell.

Fortunately, if fortuitously for the Republicans, there existed at the time in Washington certain gossip that could block the Bishop of Portland. Everywhere he went in the city, he heard a dismaying, and (because untrue) a maddening story impugning his American patriotism and loyalty. He could not pin it down. In the end, it was more than a year before he traced it to its source.

The gist of this widely-spread gossip was that he, William O'Connell, in 1898, had supported, in Rome, the Spanish cause against that of the United States. It was one of those character-assassinations familiar to later generations in periods when wars had raised emotions to high pitch. Yet it was as difficult to disprove as is any negative. It gained color from his long friendship with young Monsignor Merry del Val whose father had been Spanish Ambassador to the Vatican.

Obviously, even a whisper that a man had disapproved the war with Spain would irretrievably blacken a man in the eyes of the former Colonel of the Rough Riders who now sat in the White

House. Roosevelt had written to Mrs. Storer: "If any man, clerical
or lay, Bishop, Archbishop, priest or civilian, was in any way
guilty of treasonable practices with Spain during our war, he should
be shot or hung and it is an outrage on justice that he should be
at large." [5]

William O'Connell's conscience was clear; but he was realistic.
Putting loyalty above personal advancement, he went back to
Portland; cabled to decline the appointment; and wrote a candid
report. His motive for declining the proffered See of Manila, he
wrote was that "inasmuch as he had not concealed from the beginning of the Spanish-American War, his sympathy for Spain
and had openly stated the war was unjust, he had been openly
criticized as lacking in patriotism. As a result his nomination to
Manila would without doubt give rise to considerable comment
and would arouse suspicion on the part of the civil officials, and
this would certainly, sooner or later, be the cause of grave difficulties." [6]

The Vatican was realistic, too. O'Connell's candor was appreciated; his reasoning accepted. But the Republican Administration's
candidate was not accepted, either. Eventually, the man who became Archbishop of Manila in the summer of 1903 was Jeremiah
J. Harty, a priest of the Archdiocese of St. Louis.

Three months after William O'Connell, inwardly chafing over
the vicious gossip, but stoically silent outwardly, had foregone the
Manila post, came the turn in events that, unpredictably, brought
reward to him. Leo XIII died on July 20, 1903. His lingering last
illness gave Cardinal Gibbons time to sail for Rome, and to participate in the conclave which elected Giuseppe Cardinal Sarto,
Patriarch of Venice to reign as Pius X. O'Connell's close friend,
Merry del Val, soon succeeded Rampolla as Secretary of State and
was made a Cardinal. This was galling to Archbishop Ireland, who
had written to Mrs. Storer: "I am not yet totally won over to the
new Pope. I shall never be if he names Merry del Val his Secretary
of State." [7]

His friend's promotion was joy to O'Connell in Portland; and
Cardinal Satolli later supplied balm for any regrets over the Manila

affair by writing him confidentially that it looked as though a coadjutor might be named for Archbishop Williams of Boston, and
that William O'Connell was the logical choice.[8]

It was nearly a year before O'Connell succeeded in tracing the
source of the aspersions on his patriotism. He found that many of
his Boston friends had heard the gossip, but had dismissed it as
unbelievable. When it continued to circulate, a number of prominent non-Catholic Boston men signed a letter indignantly repudiating any animadversions on William O'Connell's character or
conduct; and forwarded it through Mayor Patrick A. Collins of
Boston to the new Apostolic Delegate in Washington, Archbishop
Diomede Falconio.[9]

One question still rankled in O'Connell's mind—who was responsible for the malicious gossip that linked his name with that
of Merry del Val in disloyalty to the United States? He knew, that
like many other Americans not under the sway of yellow journal-
ism or an adventurous urge for fighting, he had thought it was not
the business of the United States to interfere in the affairs of another country. He admitted, in his letter to the Holy See, that before the outbreak of hostilities, before the blowing up the U.S.S.
Maine at Havana harbor, he had said among friends that he thought
it would be unjust to force a war upon Spain. He knew, too, that
once war was declared, he had imposed on himself strict guard
over his utterances.

He looked back through his keepsakes and found the letter
Merry del Val had written him, at the very time Archbishop Ireland had rushed to Washington to negotiate (fruitlessly in the end)
with the Spanish and French ambassadors and the Congressional
leaders to effect an armistice with the revolutionaries in Cuba, and
thus to avert war with the United States.[10] Surely William O'Connell and Merry del Val's sentiments of that pre-war month were
equally pacific and humane. William O'Connell, knowing that the
Queen-regent Cristina of Spain had chosen Merry del Val to prepare the boy-king Alphonso XIII (born six months after his father's
death in 1885) for his First Holy Communion and Confirmation

had, evidently, offered a Mass and prayers for the widowed Queen in her weighty national problems. Merry answered:

"I must send you a line to say once more how deeply I have been affected by the thought and delicate feeling which were expressed in the token you sent me this morning. Many, many thanks. I wish I could express in words how much I value this action on your part. My personal acquaintance with the Queen and my knowledge of her admirable character and right-minded intentions make me naturally feel very deeply for her at this crisis. She really is a devoted child of Holy Church and a most talented woman. On the other side, my sincere friendship for so many Americans, my deep sympathy for all that concerns them and my earnest desire for the welfare of souls in the great Republic makes me feel as if I were rent in two. It is all so unholy, so unjust, so wanton, so needless, so terrible. Still, God knows best. He will draw good from evil no doubt tho' our poor blind eyes cannot see the workings of His Providence nor measure its ultimate design. Many thanks again. Yrs. Aff'ly in Xt. R. Merry del Val." [11]

No, O'Connell thought, re-reading the five-year-old letter in Portland, there had been nothing which could be called disloyal. He continued discreet inquiries and, finally, he tracked down the rumor to its original source. It shocked him, because in his letter-box he had friendly letters from ten years back from the man; because he had even dedicated his first published music to him. In 1892, Denis J. O'Connell, then rector at North American College, had written: "My dear friend. . . . My hearty thanks for the music and the compliment (of dedication) which I appreciate as much because I know your heart went with it. It is the *Juravit* they sing here nearly all the time. . . . You are our first musician in print. Talent you have and may the Lord give you industry and inclination to write more. Come over and hear it and you will find a room here. . . . Sincerely yours in dno. D. J. O'Connell." [12]

It was nearly a year before William O'Connell had the testimony he needed and asked Denis O'Connell for an explanation and retraction. He wrote Denis frankly, addressed to the rector's office at The Catholic University of America:

". . . Could you let me know from whom you learned the rumor and more precisely what was said? . . . I remember that at the time of the Santiago victory many complaints came to me . . . that our students, some few of them, were making trouble and causing discord in Propaganda (college classrooms—ed.) by a too obnoxious flaunting of their national sentiment which, in a school composed of men of every nation and every shade of opinion was certain to result in grave disorder. . . . I spoke to the students reiterating that even among our own citizens in America there was vast divergence of opinion as to the justice of this war and adding that in any event it was scarcely the part of a minister of God, the God of peace, to make too open a show of the love of war . . . that their duty would be to put out the fire of hatred, not to kindle it or fan it, once kindled.

"This was my speech in almost so many exact words. It came to me, not long after, that one of the students *had told you* that I had forbidden the students to show their patriotism and had expressed dissent from the rejoicing at the victory of Santiago. This is a *lie*, purely and maliciously a lie. . . . Here is where, if you wish, you may be of assistance in hunting down the nasty and cowardly calumny. My position as Rector, God knows, was no rosy path . . . I think you will agree with me. I shall not, without your permission, make public anything you write, shall consider it sacred as personal correspondence, as I wish my letters to be considered also." [13]

Monsignor Denis O'Connell evidently relied on the last sentence of the above letter; William O'Connell to the end of his life observed it scrupulously. Both men were dead before the correspondence came to light.[14]

The pity is that Denis O'Connell took refuge in obstinate silence. He never answered William O'Connell on the matter. The latter wrote once more from Portland: "Some three weeks ago I sent you a letter. As yet I have received no answer." There it rested. The immature plaint of a student in Rome fell on the right ground to nurture a poison-plant of malicious gossip which changed the future career of William O'Connell. Instead of becoming Archbishop of Manila, he would be a Papal Legate to Japan, Archbishop of Boston and a Cardinal of the Holy Roman Catholic Church.

Many would think that both Ireland and Denis O'Connell had greater natural talents, more magnetic personalities than the boy who was born William Henry O'Connell of Lowell. Certainly, two Presidents of the United States, McKinley and Theodore Roosevelt, reputedly had asked the Pope to give a red hat to Ireland, as well as other prominent Americans who admired the Archbishop of St. Paul.

The turning point, in the view of the Vatican, apparently came over the affair of the Archbishopric of Manila. The candor with which William O'Connell sacrificed his own advancement, and the scrupulous silence he observed in public, soon brought their own reward. In April, 1903 Archbishop Williams of Boston broached to a meeting of the New England bishops, the idea of a coadjutor with right of succession in the See of Boston. Rome moved deliberately. It was April 4, 1904 before Richard Neagle, as secretary, would send formal notification to Portland (O'Connell at the time being in Europe) that the three names to be balloted upon for coadjutor were Bishop Matthew Harkins of Providence, Rhode Island; Auxiliary Bishop John J. Brady of Boston; and Vicar-General William Byrne of Boston.[15]

However, six months earlier, that ever vigilant and beneficent friend, Cardinal Satolli, had written to O'Connell in Portland that the Holy See recognized the need of a coadjutor in Boston, although he doubted if the *terna* from Boston clergy would be considered in Rome as satisfactory but that he hoped that a "wise choice" would be made in Rome.[16]

William Howard Taft and William O'Connell were on friendly, informal terms. There was no ceremony when Taft lunched at the Cardinal's residence in Boston. They went into the dining-room together and John Riedi brought in the soup. The two, Taft and O'Connell, were similar in height and build, with Taft having the edge in avoirdupois.

Taft picked up his soup spoon and looked quizzically down his façade towards the soup-plate. O'Connell beamed at him, with twinkling eyes.

"By the way," he remarked significantly, "do you—er—er?"

Taft's infectious chuckle responded.

"I do!" he said genially.

Whereupon the prelate and the ex-President, with no further ado, each tucked a corner of a big damask napkin into his collar and enjoyed the soup, confident that no untoward accident would spot their garments.

That luncheon was far in the future, however, in 1904. Instead it was time for William O'Connell to make his first *ad limina* visit to Rome, the formal report that every bishop is expected to render in person at least once in five years.

He had a creditable report to render on the condition of the Portland diocese but the chief delight to him, back in the beloved Eternal City, was to have his friend Merry del Val, now wearing the purple of a cardinal, introduce him warmly to the new Pope. O'Connell would mourn the fatherly kindness of Leo XIII whom he had known for twenty years; but he was immediately captivated by the saintly personality of Pius X.[17]

"The difference, both in appearance and in temperament of the two Pontiffs could scarcely be wider apart. Leo was emaciated, colorless, detached, aloof, philosophic, speculative; Pius hearty, florid, solid, amiable, practical, intimate." [18] Pius X was sixty-nine years old at the time with "the keen and practical outlook which had come to him as a busy parish priest and an overworked bishop in a very active city (Venice)" as O'Connell put it.[19] Theodore Roosevelt gave the worldling's view when he wrote that Pius "was a worthy, narrowly limited parish priest, completely under the control of his Secretary of State Merry del Val, who is a polished man of much ability in a very narrow line, but a furiously bigoted reactionary." [20] Roosevelt was not the only American to underestimate the rosy little "parish priest." The American embassy had to caution the rector of the American (Protestant) Church in Rome after he publicly referred to "my friend Joseph Tailor across the Tiber," punning on a translation of the Italian name Sarto.[21]

O'Connell found changes at the Vatican. Piux X, chafing at the rigorous isolation of being "the prisoner of the Vatican" had moved up to the top floor where, at least, he had a view out over the countryside to the distant gleam of the sea by which, in Venice, he had so long been surrounded. Merry del Val, as Secretary of State, was ensconced in the former private apartment of the frail Leo XIII on the first floor.

O'Connell had a wonderful winter at Rome in 1904-05. Cardinal Satolli, who had visited him in Portland in October, was back, living at the Lateran palace. His good friends, Fathers E. J. Moriarty and John Cummings of Boston and Dr. William Dunn had sailed for Rome with him on the S.S. *Canopic* on November 19. Monsignor Edward F. Hurley was functioning capably as Vicar-General in Portland and Chancellor Charles Collins was reporting reassuringly by every mail.

It was the last carefree and happy period that O'Connell would know, while he had youth and vigor to enjoy it all, and he was staying strictly out of the squabbles back in New England over the question of a coadjutor to the Archbishop of Boston. Of course, his enemies for the rest of his life would whisper that he spent the winter in Rome playing politics to get the appointment. That is a matter of opinion. O'Connell himself always said that "never once had I sought, in the slightest way, any of the posts or positions to which I was named. . . . They had all come, as it were, out of a blue sky." [22]

A post "out of the blue sky" was in the offing, little as any could guess it, when he had his farewell audience with Pius X in February, 1905. "He gave me a precious gift, a sacred relic of the True Cross in an exquisite reliquary of gold and enamel. 'You are young and strong,' he said to me, 'and we shall have work for you to do soon.' I little dreamed what the Holy Father had in mind." [23]

CHAPTER FOURTEEN

PAPAL LEGATE TO JAPAN

Per correr miglior acqua alza le vele
omai la navicella del mio ingegno . . .
Dante: Purgatorio, Canto i, 1, 1

*(To course o'er better waters now hoists sail
the little bark of my wit.)*

Okey, tr.

IN 1905, fighting on the Yalu River in Asia had unsuspected repercussions on the other side of the globe, in Portland, Maine, sending William O'Connell on a voyage around the world.

Contributing to issuance of the Papal letter which started Bishop O'Connell off to Japan, were several factors under consideration by Pius X and his Secretary of State, Cardinal Merry del Val.

One problem, inherited from Leo XIII's time and soon to culminate in rupture of the Concordat with France, was the mounting anti-clerical policy of the French Administration. Another was the upsetting of the world's "balance of power" by Japan's surprising victory in the field over the vast empire of the Tsar with its huge population. Yet a third factor was the report after a survey, covering three years among Asiatic peoples, made by the Jesuit Orientalist, Father Joseph Dahlmann.

It was as obvious to Merry del Val, as to Theodore Roosevelt, that Japan would emerge from the war with a new status in the

115

congress of nations. Roosevelt and John Hay, his Secretary of State, fearing that prolongation of the conflict might ruin Russia where revolution had broken out in January, 1905, and upset the balance of power in Europe and Asia, intervened in June to negotiate peace. Peace parleys opened at Portsmouth, New Hampshire on August ninth and the peace treaty was signed there on August twenty-third.

The Papal Secretary of State had to think, not of political treaties but of spiritual concerns in the Japanese Empire, re-opened to Christian missionaries a scant half-century earlier.

He knew, of course, of the glorious mission of St. Francis Xavier, who first brought the Catholic faith to Japan on August fifteenth, 1549. He recalled that Japan, in 1582, had sent to Rome the first native Catholic envoys of any Oriental nation, representing some three hundred thousand Japanese who had eagerly embraced the Faith. He remembered how the Tokugawa Shoguns, military dictators, mewed up the Emperor in his Kyoto palace and ruthlessly grasped power, and persecuted native Christians. The Tokugawas did not want divine honors for themselves, like the old Roman Emperors; but, in the merchants of Spain and Portugal and England who flocked to Japan in the wake of the missionaries, they dreaded conquest by Western nations, such as they saw in the Philippines, India, the Dutch East Indies.[1]

By 1636, the Tokugawa Shoguns had exterminated all the Christian confessors they could find, exiled or martyred foreign priests and decreed absolute isolation of the empire. For the next two centuries, their laws forbade Japanese to leave the country or foreigners to enter, except for the single Dutch trading ship permitted to touch at Nagasaki yearly.

Merry del Val knew, also, the heroic story of the Japanese Christians, who, under penalty of death, had secretly preserved their faith, baptizing children liturgically, teaching them the Creed and Pater Noster and the Ave Maria for ten generations, although deprived of priests and sacraments. Pius IX had made the seventeenth of March a feast of the Church, commemorating that day in 1865 when loyal crypto-Christians had revealed themselves to the first Catholic missionaries permitted to take up residence in Nagasaki, after Commodore Matthew Perry's American warships, in 1854, re-opened Japan to the rest of the world.

Those first Catholic missioners to re-enter Japan were priests of the Foreign Missionary Society of Paris and for the last half of the Nineteenth Century, French missionaries had been in charge of the field in Japan. Now Merry del Val and Pius X saw two dangers ahead.

One was political—the danger that the Japanese in their new flush of victory might resent monopoly by one Western country of the missions, schools, hospitals and orphanages where the Catholic Faith was exemplified. The Holy See had no wish to have the Japanese think that Catholicism was a French religion only. The other danger was spiritual—the possibility that the anti-clerical and Modernist spirit rampant in France might affect French priests and their Japanese congregations in the Land of the Rising Sun.

So, when Father Joseph Dahlmann, S.J., reached Rome, after three years of journeying throughout China and Japan, he found Merry del Val anxious to hear all the facts and observations he had gathered in the Orient.

"The friendly reception which I had from His Eminence immediately on my return from China in 1905 convinced me that the Cardinal-Secretary of State was already well informed, and that the preparatory stages had reached a point of decision, bringing the founding of a university (in Japan) one step nearer," wrote Fr. Dahlmann.[2]

Father Dahlmann had spent most of the year 1903 in Japan. In 1905, while he was making his long way home through China and India, the Holy Father had received a petition, signed by a number of native Japanese priests of the Nagasaki diocese, asking, as descendants of the Sixteenth Century martyrs, that the Jesuits, the first missionaries at Nagasaki, might be sent them again.

All these considerations, therefore, were in the mind of Pius X when, on July 3, 1905, he summoned Father Dahlmann in a private audience and told him: "Et tu redibis in Japoniam. Ego volo ut Societas Jesu in Japoniam redeat et magnum collegium aperiat."[3]

(You shall go back to Japan. I wish to see the Jesuits established again in Japan and opening a Catholic university there.)

That Pius X and Merry del Val had been considering O'Connell for this mission for sometime is indicated by the pontiff's hint in February, "We shall have work for you soon." [4] Even Pius X, however, could not have guessed in February that the Russo-Japanese peace parleys initiated in June by Theodore Roosevelt would take place in the very diocese of Bishop O'Connell. To find a hotel large enough for the two delegations, the sessions were held at Wentworth-by-the-Sea in Portsmouth, New Hampshire, but the official conference was designated at Kittery, across the river; and Kittery is in Maine, in the diocese of Portland.

This geographical coincidence may have salved the pride of Archbishop John Ireland of St. Paul,[5] whom Theodore Roosevelt would have preferred for the Papal Envoy.

It would seem that the mission to Japan was in the nature of "a trial run" for O'Connell, before Rome decided on a coadjutor for the Archdiocese of Boston. Two years earlier, when the failing health of Archbishop Williams led to public speculation about naming of a coadjutor, the press had proposed Bishop O'Connell of Portland as a leading candidate.[6] Bishops, however, are chosen in the Vatican, not in newspaper offices, and in 1905, Rome had not yet named any coadjutor for Boston. Selection of an American prelate as Special Envoy to the Emperor of Japan was logical enough in view of the role of the United States as peacemaker; but the general public might have expected the choice to fall on some internationally known figure, like Cardinal Gibbons, or the brilliant Archbishop Ireland or Bishop O'Gorman who had accompanied William Howard Taft to Rome in 1902 to confer at the Vatican on the question of the confiscated "Friars Lands" in the Philippines. Instead, the man named was a Bishop from the northeast corner of the land, from a diocese not noted for numbers or influence of Catholics; a Bishop comparatively unknown in his own country.

The Russians and Japanese were drawing near conclusion of their Peace Conference when the Holy Father's letter, delayed in the mails, arrived at Portland on August thirty-first. With airplanes not yet in the picture, the journey to Japan was necessarily a long one. Bishop O'Connell lost no time in setting out.

Only fourteen days after learning of his mission, the Bishop had arranged for the interim administration of diocesan affairs, gotten together the ceremonial robes he would need, and secured reservations for his party, by Canadian Pacific railroad and the Pacific Mail steamer *Korea,* sailing October fourteenth from San Francisco.

As secretary-chaplains, he took with him the chancellor of his Portland diocese, Rev. Charles W. Collins, and an alumnus of the North American College at Rome, Rev. Patrick Supple. Father Supple was one of three brilliant priest-brothers from Hopkinton, in the Boston archdiocese. In 1905 he was an assistant in St. Peter's parish, Cambridge, whose pastor was Father Edward J. Moriarty, former fellow-curate of O'Connell at old St. Joseph's. The Bishop of Portland, when business took him to Boston, generally stayed at Father Moriarty's rectory in Cambridge.

On this journey, O'Connell began another lifelong habit, of including in his baggage a small trunk filled with books he wanted to read. The trunk this time was crammed with books treating of this land of alien culture, civilization and language which he so unexpectedly was to visit. The works he found most interesting were romantic and poetic descriptions of Japan by Lafcadio Hearn. As the exotic name betrays, Hearn was the son of a Greek mother and Irish father, one-time journalist in New Orleans, but for many years a schoolteacher in Japan. He had married a Japanese woman, and acquired Japanese citizenship for the sake of their children.

Professor of English Literature at the Japanese Imperial University in Tokyo, Hearn had died a year before O'Connell went to Japan. His description of a foreigner's first day in Yokohama sums up what O'Connell saw:

"Charm unutterable in the morning air cool . . . with the wind-waves from the snowy cone of Fuji. . . . Elfish everything seems; for everything as well as everybody is small and queer and mysterious: the little houses under their blue roofs, the little shop-fronts hung with blue and the smiling little people in their blue costumes. The illusion is only broken by the occasional passing of a tall foreigner. . . . Each building seems to have a fantastic prettiness of its own . . . low, light, queerly-gabled wooden houses, unpainted, with their first stories all open to the street, their matted floors well raised above street level. . . . You notice the dresses of the laborers are lettered with the same wonderful lettering as the shop draperies . . . these ideographs have a speaking symmetry . . . the picturesqueness of these streets is due to the profusion of Japanese characters in white, black, blue or gold, decorating everything, even doorposts and paper screens . . . everything Japanese is delicate, exquisite, admirable, even a pair of common wooden chopsticks . . . even the little sky-blue towel with design of flying sparrows . . . the bankbills, the commonest copper coins are things of beauty. . . . Fujiyama's white witchery overhanging the whole city and bay and the mountains begirdling it . . . all Japan with its cities and towns and temples, and forty millions of the most lovable people in the universe." [7]

It is only justice to recall, after the war of 1941-45 colored American thoughts of Japan, that before the Western world set Japan on the path to industrialization, old Japan as Bishop O'Connell was fortunate to see her, had a unique charm and beauty and her people were lovable. They were poor but hard-working, toiling in the terraced rice-paddies, golden with harvest; hauling loads on small carts by man power and cobbling clogs out of wood because lack of pasturage denied them draft-animals or hides for leather; cheerfully smiling on a meagre diet of rice, vegetables, seaweed, occasional fish. For want of bricks and glass, their low cottages were of wood with paper screens, drawn back to admit the sun for light and heat. They left their wooden clogs at the doorstep to keep immaculate the padded rice-straw cushions (tatami) that floored their rooms, serving as seats by day; as bed at night. The poorest house had its carefully tended garden; and flowers growing on the ridge of its thatched roof; or designs carved in the blue-grey tiles. They had a genius for making beauty out of lack. Men and women wore silk kimonos because need of cultivating every foot of ground to feed the pressing population forbade pasturing sheep for wool; silkworms could be raised in woven wicker trays and fed on mulberry leaves. They drank tea because intensive fertilization with human waste required to raise enough crops on their scanty arable land rendered water undrinkable without boiling; but they made of tea-drinking a ceremonious rite of hospitality.

When O'Connell visited Japan, it was just fifty years since Commodore Matthew Perry's warships had broken down two centuries of isolation from the rest of the world; only fifteen years since the Emperor Mutsuhito had promulgated the law that changed Japan from a feudal empire to a constitutional monarchy with the ballot, a bi-cameral Parliament, and universal, compulsory schooling.

The first American Minister to Japan, Townshend Harris, arriving in 1856, had found a country with no railroads, an army equipped with bows and arrows, spears and swords. The American Minister of 1905, Lloyd Griscom, had witnessed mobilization of a Japanese Army and Navy so modern, so powerful that it defeated the huge forces of Russia; and was negotiating with Japan's modern and excellent railway administration about a projected deal with the American rail magnate, E. H. Harriman.

History shows no parallel for the extraordinary intelligence and energy with which the Japanese people, in fifty short years, had made their own all the mechanical inventions and political institutions of Western civilization. No other country of Asia had so mastered the Westerners' own weapons and ways to meet the white men on an equal footing and to avoid imperialistic domination. It was to the leader of this tremendous national undertaking, the Emperor Mutsuhito, that O'Connell was bringing a personal greeting from Pope Pius X.

The emperor, like his people, lived in a "palace" with sliding walls of paper screens, floored with the thick straw mats, unheated save for pots of glowing charcoal. Minister Griscom teased the heavy-built Bishop about the pangs of kneeling for hours, like the Japanese, with stockinged feet tucked under. "I tried doing this in my room at the hotel and I must say the operation was a painful one," confessed O'Connell. "I could manage to get down on my heels but to remain in that position . . . was torture . . . and after a few minutes in that posture, I found it absolutely impossible to rise without the assistance of my two secretaries each pulling either hand." [8]

It turned out that Griscom had been teasing the Bishop. The suite at the Imperial Hotel in Tokyo was as comfortable as any in Rome or America; it had only recently been built on the designs of the American architect Frank Lloyd Wright. The Imperial Palace, and the homes and offices of Cabinet ministers or wealthy Japanese families who entertained the Bishop, all had apartments with European furniture, specially maintained for receiving foreign visitors.

"It was quite clear to me that in the brief visit . . . there was small chance of my being able to penetrate the mysteries of Japanese life and customs . . . so, from the start, I decided my mission would be best accomplished by dealing with the great men of the Empire," O'Connell had resolved.[9]

O'Connell had three distinct objectives in his mission. The first was diplomatic, to deliver the Pope's letter to the Emperor and win good will; the second, educational, to secure cooperation in reestablishment of a Jesuit university in Japan; the third, ecclesiastical, to survey the Catholic mission field in the country. At the same time, he wished to avoid appearance of any political color to his mission.

This was important because, just as the O'Connell party reached Japan, certain events had stirred up popular feeling against America to the point of riots outside the American Embassy. Harriman, coming to Tokyo in July, had virtually concluded a deal to acquire Russia's share in the South Manchurian railway linking it into a globe-girdling system of Harriman-controlled railroads and steamships, dividing the profits with Japan. However, Theodore Roosevelt, bitter foe of Harriman's financial monopoly, told the secret in Washington to Japanese peace conferees Komura and Kaneko, persuading them to rush back to Tokyo and get the agreement with Harriman canceled. Roosevelt was so provoked on learning that Griscom had facilitated Harriman's negotiations, that he transferred the Minister to Brazil. Griscom was packing up to leave Japan when O'Connell arrived.

Roosevelt himself had been conducting some secret diplomacy that summer through William Howard Taft, charged with intimating to the Japanese Premier, Count Katsura, that Korea should be maintained as a buffer-state to restrain Russia's desire for a warmwater outlet on the Pacific. The President's eldest daughter, Alice Roosevelt, was traveling with the Taft party and, incidentally, became engaged to Congressman Nicholas Longworth, also of the party, under the chaperonage of Mrs. Griscom at the U. S. Embassy in Tokyo.[10]

The Taft mission, which coincided with similar ideas on the part of Great Britain, showed its effect when Russia was required to recognize Japan's interest as "advisor" to Korea in the Portsmouth Peace Treaty in September. Five years later, Taft, as President of the United States, would recognize the annexation, in 1910, of Korea by Japan. In 1950, American forces would be fighting in Korea to check Russian aspirations again. Unhappy Korea was only a pawn of larger nations.

The bitterest anti-American feeling shortly before O'Connell's arrival on October twenty-ninth was provoked by publication of the Peace Treaty terms in which the Japanese commissioners at Portsmouth had been persuaded to forego any cash indemnity from Russia.

Bishop O'Connell's method of making clear that his was a Papal mission, entirely separate from any American connection, was to make his first official call, on reaching Tokyo, on the Japanese Foreign Minister.

"Immediately after my visit to the (Japanese) I called on our own American Minister, Mr. Lloyd Griscom. His charming wife's . . . cousin had married young Prince Rospigliosi, I had known them well in Rome while I was Rector of the American College. . . . Mr. Griscom, to my surprise, informed me that a few days before, he had received a letter from the President (Roosevelt) . . . instructing him to exercise toward me every civility." [11]

Cousin or no cousin, Minister Griscom in his sprightly memoirs, makes no mention of Bishop O'Connell being in Tokyo; and Bishop O'Connell was too polite to mention that the Princess Rospigliosi's marriage was recognized through his investigation and report to Rome of the circumstances of her previous marriage and divorce from a non-Catholic resident of the Portland diocese.[12]

Bishop O'Connell did not forget to write, in his own hand, from Rome to President Roosevelt:

"Mr. President, I beg leave, on the occasion of the marriage of your daughter Miss Alice, to offer to you, the Father of the Nation, the hope that your distinguished daughter may find happiness and prosperity in her new state of life. No American can remain indifferent to whatever concerns your welfare or that of those near and dear to you; and, from the Eternal City, I join my 'vota' to those of my countrymen at home.

"I feel that you will be glad to learn that I was received by His Majesty the Emperor of Japan with every mark of respect and courtesy; and that the Minister of the United States, as well as the consul, were most kind to me. I cannot sufficiently thank you for your great goodness to me on all occasions but I do pray God to bless and keep you in vigor and energy and vitality and to give you every blessing your heart desires." [13]

Indeed, Emperor Mutsuhito had shown every mark of courtesy to the Envoy of Pius X, sending, for the audience on November tenth, an Imperial coach, with gold chrysanthemum crests on its panels, drawn by six white horses, with liveried servants, to fetch Bishop O'Connell at the Imperial Hotel.

All the Japanese in the streets bowed respectfully to the equipage as the horses trotted by the green expanse of Hibiya Park, by the wide moat with pine branches picturesque above its sloping stone wall, and over the drawbridge, where sentries saluted.

Premier Katsura was waiting at the palace to conduct the envoy of Christ's Vicar on earth into the presence of the monarch whose ancestry, Japanese were taught, stemmed direct from the Sun goddess.

Whatever the facts of the Emperor's ancestry, the occasion was truly historic, the first meeting of the two oldest institutions existing in the world of today. The Papacy stretches in unbroken descent from St. Peter, first Vicar of Christ's Church. The Japanese Imperial family's line has occupied the throne of the Empire of the Rising Sun for twenty-six hundred years.

William O'Connell, born in Lowell, Bishop of Portland, linked the two for the first time.[14]

The Emperor, a short man not yet sixty, with black hair, mustache and beard, wearing a dark blue uniform as generalissimo of the army, was seated on a throne of gold lacquer. He received the Bishop, rising as O'Connell bowed, and, "with a pleasant smile on his rather mysterious countenance, offered me his hand." [15] Presentation of the Pope's letter and brief addresses were conducted by interpreters. The Emperor concluded the interview by again extending his hand, and O'Connell, well used to protocol in Rome, backed ceremoniously from the room.

Then came an interview with the Empress, arrayed for the occasion in Parisian foreign dress. Afterwards the coach was waiting to drive the envoy back to the hotel. This marked courtesy on the part of the Emperor set the mood for the rest of O'Connell's visit.

"From that moment until the end of my stay, I scarcely had a moment I could call my own," he remembered.[16]

O'Connell, with good judgment, politely declined most of the invitations showered upon him, to make time for conferences with key officials, Catholic missionaries and native clergy. He found the Japanese as disturbed as the Vatican at the virtual monopoly France enjoyed of sending missionaries. Those in the field were devoted and hard-working; but the attitude of the radical, anticlerical government in power in France in 1905, offered scant guarantee of continued support or new recruits; while Japanese diplomats frankly feared the sympathies of the French government with Russia, their recent foe.

The trouble, O'Connell soon found, was that "the cathedral was called, not the Catholic Church, but l'eglise française . . . they were exemplary ecclesiastics but . . . in their schools and academies the French language had predominant place. . . . Add to this that in the late war with Russia, it was known that France was a close ally with Russia." [17]

O'Connell, at Catholic church functions, was deeply impressed by the fervor and piety of Japanese Catholics. "The influence of their gentle Christian lives was far out of proportion to their numbers. They knelt most of the time during the divine service in an attitude of prayer. . . . They had learned to sing quite well the plain chant of the Mass. . . . In true Japanese fashion they left their wooden shoes outside . . . and as the floor of the cathedral was covered with a grass matting, one was glad to notice the absence of all noise of shuffling feet. The stillness in the church, during Mass, even when the congregation filled the edifice to the doors conduced very much to the feeling of religious awe in the presence of God. . . . Before I left Tokyo, the Japanese . . . gave me a most delightful reception on Sunday, November nineteenth in the pretty garden of the cathedral. . . . The men and women in their kimonos of varied hue and texture formed a beautiful picture." [18]

"I took occasion, in conversations with Prince (sic) Katsura, the premier,[19] to launch the idea of a Catholic University in Tokyo. . . . In developing the idea, I stressed the point that the Jesuits, the order to which (Xavier) belonged, were distinctly international in their constitutions and . . . the projected university might well be entrusted to them. To all this, Prince Katsura gave a very enthusiastic assent." [20]

Here, then, was the beginning of Jochi Dai Gaku or Sophia University (Sophia being the Greek term for Wisdom) which, opened in 1912 and placed under the Jesuits by Pius X, has taught thousands of Japanese, Catholic and non-Catholic, and continues to offer a flourishing medium for the exchange of culture between East and West.

The German Jesuits, in the years to come, were to find themselves in the same position as O'Connell had found the French. While they, in exile from their native country, dedicated themselves to educational and spiritual labors, the wars in Europe of Emperor Wilhelm II and of Adolf Hitler aroused prejudice against their nationality and cut off financial support from home. However, the

German Jesuits, by their correct conduct and deep scholarship won the hearts of the Japanese, so that their teaching was never interrupted and the University grew steadily until, after 1946, the American Jesuits were able to reinforce their numbers and American generosity aided in support. When the first atomic bomb was dropped on Hiroshima, August sixth, 1945, the Jesuits, Father Hugo Lassalle, Father Felix Kleinsorge and Father Hubert Schiffer, were victims, wounded and disabled for many months by atomic radiation, in the rectory of the mission church they served at Hiroshima; and the other Jesuits, on summer vacation at their novitiate in the hills above Hiroshima, were heroes of the rescue work in the stricken city. In appreciation, the Japanese officials and Buddhist abbots aided in erection of the beautiful new Church of Our Lady of the Assumption in Hiroshima, where American Franciscan nuns maintain perpetual adoration and recitation of the rosary for world peace today.

William O'Connell did not live to see this monument of fraternal charity and shrine of prayer for Peace, but his was the initial impetus that led to its building.

Another fruit of the O'Connell mission of 1905 was the action of the Japanese Government in sending an envoy to the Papal Court, after the Lateran Treaties of 1929 opened the way to establishment of the Vatican State in Rome.

A Japanese friend with whom Cardinal O'Connell would correspond the rest of his life was a man of highest standing and a devout Catholic. This was Admiral Shinjiro Yamamoto, who in 1919 was tutor of the present Emperor Hirohito of Japan, accompanying him on his historic journey around the world, first Japanese Emperor to leave his country's limits. Admiral Yamamoto died in 1942.

The Japanese Catholics, in the time of Francis Xavier, gave the Church twenty-six canonized saints; two hundred and five Beatified victims and over two thousand martyrs for the faith. By the time of World War II, thirty-five years after O'Connell's mission, the Church in Japan had an archdiocese, five dioceses, two vicariates apostolic and seven prefectures apostolic, all presided over by a purely native Japanese hierarchy with another one hundred and fifty Japanese diocesan priests and about two thousand Japanese Sisters. Since the end of the war, two regional seminaries for education of Japanese priests have been established at Tokyo and Fukaoka.[21]

O'Connell in his conversations, opened the way for exchange of diplomatic representation between Japan and the Vatican; and also made patent to the Japanese that the Holy See was anxious to encourage education of native Japanese clergy.

It was the old, old pattern of the Church. America had been discovered under the auspices of Spain and the first missionaries were Spanish. As time passed, they came to be French. Only two years after O'Connell's visit to Japan America would cease to be a "missionary Province" because her own American clergy had been encouraged, educated and consecrated to the hierarchy. O'Connell was passing on the same torch to Japan.

O'Connell became aware of the strong desire of the Japanese to acquire Western education, to put themselves on a par as a world power, economically and diplomatically. The chief public appearance he made was at the Imperial University of Tokyo, before three thousand professors and students.

"There was the most profound, almost religious silence, and as I looked into the faces of the audience I beheld that calm, expressionless Oriental mask which betrayed no emotion, favorable or unfavorable. I had faced many an audience in my life but never one like this." [22]

The Papal Envoy delivered a eulogistic, non-committal oration in Latin.

"I explained the exalted position of the Pope as chief Pastor of Christendom; that as common Father of all the Faithful, his loving care was extended to all races and all nations . . . I went on to tell that as Francis Xavier had loved (the Japanese) to the end of his days because of the kindly traits of their character, I, too, having witnessed these same kindly, hospitable, and polite qualities, had conceived the deepest respect."

During his stay in Japan, although his daily Mass was said at a

portable altar in a room of his suite at the Imperial Hotel, each
Sunday O'Connell pontificated at High Mass in the Tokyo Cathedral, and dined, afterward, with the French Archbishop Osouf and
his clergy.

The good will of the Emperor and Cabinet officers towards the
Holy See was manifested in bestowal on Bishop O'Connell of the
grand cordon of the Imperial Order of the Sacred Treasure, while
his two secretaries were honored with the fifth class of the Order
of the Rising Sun.[23] The Premier, Count Katsura, tendered an
elaborate farewell banquet to the Special Envoy.

In four weeks, due to the receptive cordiality of the Japanese
authorities, O'Connell's mission was completed in its threefold
aim. Now it was time to report to Rome.

O'Connell's three principal recommendations were put into execution soon by the Congregation of Propaganda. Religious Orders
of other nationalities than French were encouraged to make foundations in Japan, so that fifty years later, missioners and nuns of
many nationalities, including, since World War II, great numbers
of Americans, are to be found in the field. The education of native
clergy was fostered, Japanese bishops and archbishops consecrated
and many Japanese women became members of religious orders.

The praise bestowed on Bishop O'Connell for his mission to
Japan, over the years would be well warranted. The dignity of his
conduct, the tact with which he had devoted himself entirely to
conferences with the proper Japanese authorities, the attention
with which he had discerned not only the needs of the Church but
the best interests and concerns of the Japanese, laid the foundations for what have ever since been felicitous relations between the
most advanced Oriental nation and the Holy See, even though the
proportion of Catholics among the Japanese is one of the least in
the nations of the world.

It was pleasant, for the Bishop of Portland, at his first audience
with Pius X, to find his work pronounced "a success far greater
than our highest expectations." [24]

On February twenty-first, came announcement that William

Henry O'Connell had been named coadjutor, with right of succession, to the Metropolitan See of Boston, Massachusetts.

"All these changes came with such rapidity, that . . . it seemed that my life had become almost a kaleidoscope in which I was moved rapidly from one place to another, each one more difficult than the one before." [25]

It must have been a month of prayer and patience, for Merry del Val and Satolli would have told him that the Congregation of Propaganda had recommended his name on January twenty-second; the Pope had approved it on February first; the Papal brief came to him on February eighth.

Boston was stunned at the news, released there after the Consistory on February twenty-first.

CHAPTER FIFTEEN

COADJUTOR IN BOSTON

Trova' mi stretto nelle mani il freno del governo
del regno, e tanta possa di nuovo acquisto,
e si d'amici pieno.

Dante: Purgatorio, Canto xx, 55-57

*(I found tight in my hands the reins of government and so
much power from new possessions, and so rich in friends.)*
Okey, tr.

ONE OF the seven capital sins that has a way of stealing into
human hearts is Envy. O'Connell's appointment as Coadjutor-Archbishop of Boston, with right of succession, inspired matter
for confession in many hearts. Unbridled tongues throughout New
England buzzed that the promotion was due to his "knowing the
right people." A leading Boston newspaper commented candidly:
". . . he numbered as his personal and intimate friends many
of the most influential churchmen in Rome . . . with the powerful
friendship of Cardinal Satolli. . . . Bishop O'Connell was not the
choice of the church authorities of the (Boston) archdiocese. When
the Maine bishopric became vacant, Msgr. O'Connell's name was
not among those submitted." [1]
Indisputably, O'Connell knew well some important people in
Rome,—Popes Leo XIII and Pius X; Cardinals Rampolla, Ledochowski, Satolli, Merry del Val. What his critics overlooked was

that men of such rank and calibre would not have befriended the young American had they not seen in him worthy qualities and talents useful to the Church. Every step on his ladder of promotion had been won by hard work in the grade below.

Had O'Connell, in 1881, not taken most of the honors at Boston College Commencement, Archbishop Williams would have sent him, like other candidates, to the seminary at Troy, New York, or his own alma mater in Montreal. Instead, O'Connell went to Rome. Had he not been a brilliant student in Rome, Satolli would not have remembered him, ten years later in America. If his performance as Rector at the North American College had been inept, Merry del Val would not have chosen him for a friend.

O'Connell referred to the subject on his seventieth birthday: "If some success has followed my work in life, much is due to the fact that . . . I performed what I had to do under the direction of those to whom I was responsible. Like a good soldier, all my life I have accepted orders from my superiors and obeyed them faithfully to the best of my ability. . . . No one better than myself realizes the infinitude of my unworthiness and the immense lack in my ability to realize fully my highest aspirations in word, work and deed. But I can honestly say I did my best. I preached and wrote and worked without ceasing . . . after my priesthood, every single step upward has come to me unsolicited and even without previous notice." [2]

It is easier to look back philosophically at seventy, than at forty-seven in the thick of the fray. When William O'Connell returned from Rome in 1906 as Coadjutor in Boston, he was facing covert hostility and everyone knew it.

Portland was not happy either in Rome's choice of a successor to O'Connell. Instead of one of the Maine priests whose names they had sent in, they received another man from the Boston Archdiocese, Rev. Louis S. Walsh, former supervisor of diocesan schools in Boston. Walsh himself was not happy about going to Portland; he would have preferred coadjutorship in Boston. The *terna* for Boston, sent in by the local suffragans, had named, in order, Bishop Matthew Harkins of Providence; Auxiliary Bishop

John Brady; and O'Connell's old pastor, Vicar-General William Byrne. The Chancellor, Rev. Richard Neagle, who had carried most of the burden of the archdiocese during Archbishop Williams' ill health of latter years, was not mentioned at all. O'Connell was later to appoint him pastor of the fine parish of the Immaculate Conception, Malden; but their relations were strictly icy and polite for years.

It might be speculated that Pius X had had O'Connell in mind for the Boston coadjutorship for a year or more. Was there significance in the Pope's gift, during O'Connell's *ad limina* visit as Bishop of Portland in February of 1905? It was a relic of the True Cross in a beautiful reliquary of gold and enamel. Boston's cathedral is dedicated to the Holy Cross.

The new Coadjutor landed in Boston from Naples on March thirteenth, 1906. Bishop John Delaney of Manchester, his good friend, was at the dock and so were Mayor John F. Fitzgerald of Boston and the mayors of Portland, Maine, Lowell and Medford, representing the cities in which he had previously lived. There was considerable feeling in Boston that of the two clerics who had gone to Japan with him, only the Portland chancellor, Rev. Charles W. Collins, had been made a Monsignor during their stay in Rome. Dr. Patrick Supple returned without the touch of purple. His friends resented it. Collins, too, found the green-eyed monster rampant in Portland. He left the diocese and came to Boston to serve the rest of his life under O'Connell.

There was an interval of a few months, in which O'Connell arranged matters of the Portland diocese, while waiting appointment of his successor. In Portland, it was filled with the farewell receptions that are customary for prelates. But, too, he had to keep dashing back and forth, via the Boston and Maine railroad, for welcomes staged in Boston. They gave him a civic reception at Symphony Hall on April eighteenth; Boston College alumni held an affair on May first; the American College *Romani* had a dinner for him at the Somerset Hotel May seventeenth. Such affairs were pleasant, and he could carry them off agreeably, because, on April third, he had struck the keynote, at the official assumption of his office as Coadjutor in Holy Cross Cathedral, Boston.

It was no easy task to face the old Archbishop, who had not wanted him, and five hundred archdiocesan clergy, many in open hostility, and three thousand laity who did not know yet whether they wanted him or not. He chose, dramatically, to forego the soundingboard and elevated stance of the pulpit. Father Robert J. Johnson of Gate of Heaven parish, South Boston, delivered the clergy's address of welcome. Then William O'Connell, thick-necked, dark-haired, tall, vigorous, impressive in his flowing purple and white-lace robes, strode to the centre of the sanctuary and sent his melodious voice echoing to the farthest corners of the vast cathedral.

"The priests of Boston gave me a purely religious reception in the cathedral at which the venerable Archbishop assisted on his throne," [3] was all O'Connell cared to say later of that day.

Those who heard never forgot the drama of it, the disciplined self-control with which he faced an unfriendly assembly; the mastery with which he convinced them that they could, they must, work together with him for the glory of God and the exaltation of Holy Mother Church.

"Rome has made her irrevocable decision," he began, candidly. ". . . we come here . . . to prove by act what as Catholics we believe; that ecclesiastical authority (is) derived, not from the pleasure of the people or the favor of the government; not from the vote of the clergy or the suffrage of the Bishops, but solely from the Apostolic See of Rome. . . . This is the great and high meaning of this hour, and with it, the hour goes into history, recorded, dead. The future lies before us."

It was a bold challenge. It reached through the web of human partisanships, emotions; it touched basic realities in the heart of each priest whose life had been vowed to Christ and His Church. O'Connell talked a bare twenty minutes, but each moment was packed with verities all recognized.

"I come as Coadjutor—that means not merely a helper, but a co-worker with him who governs. . . . In the work before me, I

need not only your hearts but your minds in full cooperation . . .
I claim now the right respected by all honest men; to be judged
only by my own acts, not for what others do or say. . . . Every
man placed high shudders at the publicity into which his most insignificant actions are forcibly thrust."

He then paid a heartfelt and deserved tribute to Archbishop
Williams for his thirty years of service. For the first time in twenty-
five years he opened his heart to three thousand hostile strangers,
telling the story of the Archbishop's sermon in that same cathedral
on young Father John Smith from Lowell and how it had determined his own vocation.

"That blessed influence which has been the greatest factor in my
whole life I owe . . . to the ardent words of a good man. Those
words came from the lips of Archbishop Williams . . . the debt to
Rome I can never hope to cancel, but the first instalment on that
debt I owe . . . to him who gave me to Rome twenty-five years
ago, an untrained, inexperienced youth. Today Rome gives me
back to him . . .

"In the liquidation of that first great debt, I cannot act alone. I
must have your cooperation . . . there is now only one thing required of all of us equally—to make the declining years of one
who has earned peace and rest, years of tranquility and happiness.
He who from this day breaks the sacredness of order and harmony
in this Diocese will have small claim to respect from any of us
who rule or labor in it . . . the past is dead. The future is at the
door. For strength to meet it, let us turn now to Him who will
lead . . . to Him who waits now to strengthen our weak hearts with
His holy benediction. *Procedamus in pace*. Amen." (Let us go
forward in peace.) 4

William O'Connell had gauged his men aright. Most of them responded to his candor, his sincerity and his frank offer to let
bygones be bygones. The record of accomplishment in the Archdiocese of Boston in the next fifteen years was astounding. No one
man could have done it alone. His clergy cooperated. There was a
year of interlude, in which he wound up the Portland affairs,
established his household on Union Park; traversed the archdio-

cese, for long-neglected Confirmations and made acquaintance with the pastors and curates of the outlying parishes.

"I went my rather lonely way absolutely ignoring the annoyance of others, without either fear or rancor," he recalled.[5]

By June first, 1906, for the first time, he was to experience having his own home, at 12 Union Park, near the Boston Cathedral. After years of crowded, companioned life in seminary, rectory, college, cathedral rectory, it seemed lonely. He offered for his favorite brother Edward, who had a number of children to bring up on the salary of a Lowell fire department captain, to educate a nephew, Joseph E. O'Connell. Young Joe lived with him at Union Park and attended Boston College High School. The sixteen-year-old boy chafed, evening after evening, at putting classical music records on the primitive phonograph, or listening to his uncle talk of Rome or of literature. The fare was too rich, the association too overpowering for a lad who had never been out of Lowell before. "In later years I appreciated what he had been doing for me," remembered Joe O'Connell, "but at the time I was bored. I had no vocation for a life in religion; I suppose I was disappointing to my uncle."

As a matter of fact, the nephew Joe and his sisters gave lifelong happiness to the Cardinal in warm family associations. Not so happy was his experience with three other nephews to whose support and education he had contributed at considerable sacrifice from his small salary as rector in Rome, or while Bishop of Portland. One had been with him in Rome, as a seminarian, in 1900-1901, transferring, in 1903, to the seminary of the Sulpicians in Montreal.[6] O'Connell had the pleasure of ordaining him at the Cathedral of the Holy Cross, Boston while Coadjutor. The other two entered on business careers and were not closely associated with the Cardinal in later life.

Archbishop Williams, with characteristic consideration, arranged for his Coadjutor's residence, writing to him in Portland: "While you could live here, it is perhaps better for you to get a house nearby for yourself. I will take care of the expense and you can start . . . and be recognized from the beginning as an entity apart." [7]

To Boston, it appeared an exotic entity, a household of Italians, for O'Connell brought with him the music director Pio de Luca; the coachman, Pio Zappa; and houseman, Peppino, and the latter's wife and children. O'Connell enjoyed speaking the liquid Italian with them, recalling their faithful service in Rome and in Portland; but to old Boston there was something so foreign about the household that legend grew and was embroidered. Before the Cardinal died, many Bostonians thought the Cardinal had brought from Japan his servants—maybe Koreans—anyhow, Orientals. As a matter of cold fact, O'Connell in fifty years had just six servants in his household, Peppino died in his service in Boston and the Cardinal, after pensioning his widow and sending her back to her native Italy, found a well-trained young Swiss at a hotel in 1909 and brought him to America. This was John Riedi, who with faithful Pio Zappa, served the Cardinal the rest of his life. For the kitchen and parlor-maid work, two Irish Catholic sisters, Delia and Mary Hines, replaced Peppino, and John Riedi married Mary. It cannot be a hard master who earns fifty years of devoted service from those about him.

In August, 1907, Bishop O'Connell was on Retreat with the diocesan clergy at St. John's Seminary when he was summoned to the Cathedral rectory. Archbishop Williams was dying.

"His death occurred only a few days after, on Friday, August 30, 1907. . . . At his request . . . I administered the last sacraments which he received with the most touching devotion . . . as I knelt at his bedside to say the prayers for the dying, he made the responses in a distinct, though very feeble voice, and, at the end, placing his venerable hand on my bowed head, he gave me his paternal benediction. I was shaken with unspeakable emotion, knowing that as he laid down the great burdens of his office, they were to fall on my shoulders, unworthy as I knew them to be." [8]

His first rude shock was the refusal of Cardinal Gibbons to preach the eulogy at the Archbishop's funeral. The next was the refusal of Williams' dearest friend in the hierarchy, Bishop Bernard

J. McQuaid, whom Williams had been visiting earlier that month, to preach the eulogy. McQuaid's age and grief might be an excuse. Gibbons was the man for whom Williams had petitioned Leo XIII creation as a cardinal, after refusing it for himself. Williams had been named by the Holy Father to give Gibbons his red biretta when it came over the seas. In the end, after it had been announced that O'Connell would both sing the Mass and preach the sermon, Gibbons re-considered and telegraphed that he would pontificate, but not preach, at the funeral, set for September fourth.

With all the details to be handled, arrangements to be made, letters and telegrams to be despatched, reporters to be seen, it was not until the Sunday afternoon that O'Connell could "close my doors and set to work upon the panegyric. Though . . . I was nearly overwhelmed by the fatigue and anxiety which the death naturally begot, I wrote the eulogy of my revered predecessor from beginning to end in three hours, without change of a word or a phrase." [9]

The eulogy is thirty-five hundred words of as fine prose as O'Connell ever wrote in his life. One paragraph particularly sums up the last year they had spent, side by side, in Boston.

"Many of you, most reverend Fathers, knew him longer than I . . . and had the privilege of the knowledge which only intimacy can give. But during the year that has passed, the book of his heart and mind was completely opened to me and, during his brief illness, his inner soul revealed to me . . . as hour by hour he watched the shadows gather . . . his natural and habitual reserve were replaced with a tenderness of manner and a freedom and familiarity of speech . . . in that closeness of companionship, while death was waiting at the door, he dropped like a mantle his usual manner and revealed himself . . . in all the affectionate nobility of his soul . . . his high spiritual intuition, his shrewd knowledge of men, his modesty amounting almost to shyness . . . reducible to one idea . . . ever present, constantly abiding—He lived in the presence of God . . . out of the unity of that force was developed the trinity of virtues which animated every action he performed— Justice, Charity, Sincerity. . . . It was this which gave majesty to his regime. . . . I dare ask at this solemn moment . . . in your charity when you think of the great and good Archbishop do not forget him upon whom his great burden has fallen and who still must struggle . . . through storm and tempest . . . mayhap at last to the haven of rest into which he now has passed." [10]

William Henry O'Connell was forty-seven years old when the mantle fell from the weary shoulders of Archbishop Williams onto his. Because he was Coadjutor, there was no delay, no interim in his taking up the duties of the office of Archbishop of Boston.

The pallium was conferred on him at the Cathedral of the Holy Cross on January twenty-ninth, 1908, by James Cardinal Gibbons, with Archbishop John M. Farley of New York, the New England bishops of Portland, Manchester, Burlington, Providence and Hartford, the Governor of Massachusetts, the Mayor of Boston and a throng of notables and clergy attending.

In the biography of one man—even the life of a Cardinal— there is no room for listing everything that was done during his tenure of office.

Moreover, if credit is due to Cardinal O'Connell's vision, direction and leadership, equal credit must go to the devoted clergy, religious teachers and loyal laymen and women whose efforts and support brought to fruition the institutions, the new churches, the parochial schools, the great charitable enterprises he suggested to his flock.

The Cardinal recognized this himself. One of the last acts of his long life and one that gave him much pleasure,[11] was to set his Imprimatur—the let-it-be-printed stamp—on the work he had initiated some years before, a History of the Archdiocese of Boston, by the priests Rt. Rev. Robert H. Lord, Rev. John E. Sexton and Rev. Edward T. Harrington. Dr. John Tracy Ellis, distinguished historian of Catholic University, called it "the best history of any American diocese . . . three large and scholarly volumes." The publication was the Cardinal's way of recognizing that his was only an interval in the continuing existence of the Archdiocese which, under God, was built and is maintained by the joint labors of clergy and laity.

For details of the growth in the Cardinal's era, of churches or institutions or societies, these volumes may be consulted. They constitute rewarding reading for all Catholics of the Archdiocese of Boston.

William O'Connell had, to a high degree, historical perspective. His aim—sometimes, being human, he fell short of it,—was to view his office historically, and himself objectively in relation to the office.

"The Bishop of the Church stands like a sentinel," he wrote in a Pastoral letter. "His See is a watch tower whence he scans his own peaceful camp, ever alert against aught that could work disorder in the ranks. Bishops are responsible each for his portion of the vast spiritual army whose banner floats over the whole world. And the Universal Bishop, Rome's Pontiff, higher still in his apostolic eminence, keeps vigilant watch over all.

"Thus the life-blood of Christ's mystical body circulates from the Sacred Heart of Jesus through every artery and every smallest blood vessel which reaches to the minutest division of the humblest member. . . . Such is the marvelous organization of the Church of Christ, compelling the wonder and admiration even of her enemies, because she is the design and the work of God. . . . This is our glory and our unspeakable privilege: to be partakers of the fulfillment of God's eternal plan by membership in His Church." [12]

He knew, better than those who would flatter him, that the tremendous growth in the Archdiocese of Boston, the increasing number of communicants, the beautiful new churches, the modern colleges and parochial schools, the diocesan charities, were not his singlehanded work.

They had done it. Who were they? Everyone!

Irish servant girls, housed five flights up in Beacon Street houses, contributing a dollar a week. Boston Elevated motormen, and Boston police and firemen, giving from their small pay. College graduates, in law or medicine, paying their tithes. Men rising to power in business or politics who could toss in a thousand or fifty thousand dollars. Priests in the three hundred and fifty parishes, working twelve to fifteen hours a day for their keep and a pittance a month.

From his watch tower, O'Connell saw the Catholic Church made up of individuals—saints, sinners and the mediocre; all kinds and all conditions—but linked in the bond of one Faith, nourished with the same Sacraments, acknowledging one aim, in differing degrees—to love God, glorify His habitation, help their neighbor, spread the gospel to the far places of the earth.

Sometimes, humanly, a Cardinal might feel like intervening, to ask if a working woman could afford her donation; or to fulminate at a sharp politician or tricky dealer to ask if he wanted to rob the poor and God, too. The few times he did it, headlines in the press would remind him, in the end, to leave them to God and stick to his job.

His job, primarily, was to keep burning the sanctuary lamps that denoted in each church and chapel the Real Presence of Christ Who is head of the church; the little lamps whose rays could reach into every home where God was loved; could kindle a glow in each heart to carry into street or store or office, spreading the spirit of Christ.

Born the month the American College was opened, December eighth, 1859, O'Connell pontificated in the College chapel, celebrating the Golden Jubilee of the college whose existence he had saved in the troubled days a decade earlier.

It was a good report that the Archbishop of Boston could present at Rome in 1909. In the first eighteen months of his incumbency, he could point to thirty-one new parishes established; twenty-nine priests added, nine parochial schools and a preparatory school founded; two orphan asylums opened, three religious communities invited to the archdiocese for specialized work.

At his farewell audience with Pius X, in addition to giving approval for O'Connell's project to make his diocesan seminary purely American and secular in its faculty, the Holy Father hung around his neck a beautiful gold cross, set with sapphires and diamonds.

He had earned it, with the five difficult years as rector in Rome, the hard job of unifying the Portland diocese, the mission to Japan, and the year as Coadjutor among the hostility of those who had favored other candidates. The jeweled cross, symbol of his office as archbishop and—in its choice of sapphires—in common tradition linked with the Cardinal's purple, was given him on the twenty-fifth anniversary of his ordination.

CHAPTER SIXTEEN

ARCHBISHOP IN BOSTON

Come pesa il gran manto
A chi dal fango il guarda
che piuma sembran tutte l'altre some.

Dante: Purgatorio, Canto xix, 1, 103-5

> *(How the great mantle weighs on him who*
> *keeps it from the mire, so that all*
> *other burdens seem feathers.)*

Okey, tr.

NEW BROOMS, traditionally, sweep clean. If brought into rooms where cobwebs and clutter have accumulated for several years, the clean sweep is a necessity.

William O'Connell entered upon the administration of the Archdiocese of Boston on the death of an eighty-five-year-old prelate whose last years had been passed under the cross of diminished strength and dimming eyesight. O'Connell's responsibility began on the eve of a new era for the Church in the United States. In 1908, centenary year of the Archdiocese of Boston, the American hierarchy "came of age." [1] No longer were their affairs to be administered by the Sacred Congregation of the Propagation of the Faith in Rome as mission territory, but to stand on a par with the hierarchy of older lands in relation with the Holy Father and the Roman Curia.

143

It might be providential, or again, farsighted, on the part of Pius X that the new Archbishop of Boston was the first in the hundred years of the See, to have had long training and experience in Rome. The promptness and clarity with which O'Connell put in operation various archdiocesan bureaus, institutions and regulations of Curia earned the compliment of being widely copied in many other dioceses throughout America. Fellow-bishops wrote asking for copies of his system.[2]

Simultaneously, the Archbishop commenced re-organization of charitable institutions and of parish life which his year's study, as Coadjutor, had shown to be greatly needed. With the guiding hand of Archbishop Williams losing its grip, hospitals and charitable homes for youth had run deeply into debt; and in some parishes, pastors had become virtual autocrats. The changes and reforms in administration, directed by the new Archbishop, naturally earned him enmity in some quarters, but admiration from the public, including the Protestant community, edified at his business-like methods.[3]

Illustration of the laxity that had insidiously crept in can be seen in the new regulations Archbishop O'Connell found it necessary to promulgate in the Diocesan Synod to which he called his clergy at the Cathedral in February, 1909.

"High Mass must be sung in every parish church on Sundays and Holy Days of Obligation. . . . Strict attention is called to the Statute forbidding the absence of any priest from his parish over Sunday without permission. . . . The soutane is to be worn in the house and church at all times. . . . A short instruction, rarely exceeding five minutes, must be given at all Low Masses on Sundays and Holy Days of Obligation. . . . All deeds of church and school property must be deposited in Chancery. . . . No expenditures exceeding one hundred dollars, or repairs or changes in parish property may be made without the permission in writing of the Ordinary.

"All signboards, including names and addresses of undertakers . . . are to be at once removed from church walls . . . expensive pomp and elaborate floral display should be discouraged at funerals. . . . Hereafter no eulogy will be preached at funerals without the consent of the Archbishop." [4]

Catholic education was close to O'Connell's heart. He urged that parochial schools be built wherever possible; and insisted that each pastor, in addition to Sunday School, provide an hour's instruction weekly in religious and Church matters for children attending public schools. He announced that he had bought, from private owners, the *Pilot,* a paper once edited by the Irish-Catholic hero John Boyle O'Reilly, henceforth to be the diocesan organ.[5]

Intensification of the interior life of both clergy and laity was deeply felt by O'Connell as the foundation of growth for the archdiocese. Strange as the thought is fifty years later, one of the new ordinances he found necessary was that enjoining each priest to make a retreat at least once a year. He also took steps to make the same privilege accessible to the laity.

"No one knows his neighbors," he said. "We do not know their cares, their griefs nor their sorrows; we do not know the temptations they are battling. . . . Unless one has some place to go, some haven of rest, he could not stand it. . . . Catholics know that there is One Who is always ready to listen . . . (in) that wonderful communication of heart to heart that brings peace to the soul and understanding to the mind and consolation which seems to renew life." [6]

Already, in 1907, the Archbishop had invited Father Fidelis of the Cross [7] Provincial of the Passionist Order, to open a retreat house for men in Boston. On May fourteenth, 1911, he would be able to dedicate their building on the old Nevins estate, on the hill in Brighton, named for the Passionist, Blessed Gabriel of the Seven Dolors.[8]

It was a friend of days in Rome who aided the Archbishop to establish a retreat house for laywomen in Brighton, Mrs. Charles B. Perkins. Before her marriage to the Boston architect, Mrs. Perkins' girlhood had included many visits in Rome where her uncle was Cardinal Schoenfeld and her aunt the Baroness at whose garden party O'Connell had first worn the bright robes of a Monsignor. Mrs. Perkins had made Retreats at the Newport house of the Religious of the Cenacle and it was she who acted as "straw-bidder" for the property on the hill across from St. John's seminary when it was sold at auction in 1909. A year later, on October eleventh, 1910, the Archbishop said the first Mass in the remodelled house and convent, of which Mother Alexandrina Filippi, daughter of a noble Italian family, was first Superior.[9]

Archbishop O'Connell was thoroughly in sympathy with the teachings of Pius X. On February twenty-fourth, 1911, in a Pastoral Letter urging daily attendance of the laity at Mass, frequent reception of Holy Communion, adoration of the Blessed Sacrament and early preparation of children for the Sacrament, he pointed out:

"We see on all sides the federation of inimical forces. The spirit of the time is all against Christ and His Church. . . . The greatest remedy against these deceptions is the Remedy Christ Himself has provided. The Bread of Angels alone can give us fortitude of spirit and clearness of spiritual vision." [10]

In his first years as Archbishop, O'Connell was a little like Stephen Leacock's horseman who "rode off in all directions at once."

As part of organizing the archdiocese on the model of the Roman Curia, he had purchased a house at the corner of Bay State Road and Granby Street in Boston's fashionable Back Bay. At first it served as the Archbishop's residence and the Chancery. As it became crowded, he was to transfer his own living quarters to 46 Rawson Road, Brookline, a rambling frame structure on a high terrace insuring seclusion and quiet. He named his young priest-nephew, Jimmy O'Connell, as Chancellor.

At Granby Street, a handsome granite mansion, he could receive and entertain the Boston Brahmins, many of whom had known him in Rome. Here he could give, in his turn, the dinners that membership entailed in exclusive Bostonian societies of learned men like the Winter's Night or Thursday Evening clubs.[11]

During his quiet year as coadjutor, O'Connell had been studying the position of Catholics in Boston. After Rome, where kings and queens, princes, scholars, university professors were proud to be known as Catholics, the situation at home distressed him. It was time, he thought, for the Church in Boston to come out of the catacombs.

He tackled the problem with characteristic frankness, at the Centenary exercises of the Archdiocese in 1908, speaking in the cathedral. First he sketched the historical background.

Referring to creation of the diocese by a brief of Pius VII, April 8, 1808, O'Connell recalled "in one hundred years the missionary district with its four priests, two churches and population of a thousand . . . has grown . . . into a province . . . with seven bishops, over eleven hundred churches and more than two million people.[12]

"Between the Puritan and the Catholic in the beginning lay a dreadful gulf . . . the Puritan distrusted the Anglican; he frankly hated the Catholic . . . he had been persistently taught that the Pope was AntiChrist, the Mass abominable idolatry. . . . So, as a result of political hate, religious strife and simple ignorance of facts . . . the Catholic . . . was to be exiled first and, on returning, to be hanged. . . .

"The French and Irish Catholic . . . entered silently, hunted, exiles . . . but . . . human beings with a right to live. The Englishman and the Puritan stood for the first time face to face with the Catholic and Irishman. . . . Who could wonder a century must pass before their children's children in our day would begin to see one another not as enemies, but as friends at last in the great brotherhood of a common citizenship?

"What of the future? No lover of New England will stand passive in this problem. There are rents enough growing in the social fabric without perpetuating those made by our fathers. . . . What care I what Tudor flatterers or Stuart courtiers did to set brother against brother? My life is here and now.

"In 1800 it was only a struggle between two races. In 1900 the offspring of a dozen races and nations occupy the scene. To seek to force upon any one of them the distinctive blood-traits of another would be labor in vain. That was the mistake of the Puritan who would perforce change Celtic enthusiasm into British coldness, the wealth of Catholic ritual into the frigidity of Puritan observance. . . .

"Two great problems must today be met frankly and faced courageously. First, the difference between race and race must be changed into confidence by fraternal love. Second, faith showing forth clearly God's commands, must reveal also the higher duty which new responsibilities and higher place impose on us all . . .

"The Catholic Faith changeless and undying; Christian Hope in the fulfillment of a great destiny for our country; Charity, uncooled and unquenchable for all—these are the torches we kindle afresh today at the tombs of those good men whose ashes have mingled with New England soil. . . . They did their duty well—and now, for ours!" [13]

In that sermon, which by its frankness, its keen analysis of dangers in the body politic, its clarion call to fraternal charity and civic responsibility startled Boston fifty years ago, William Henry O'Connell set forth his own American credo. For the rest of his life he would preach and practise it, in Boston, and throughout America. He made himself a watchman on the ramparts, equally sensitive to discern rot or decay within the walls, as to sense danger from without.

As the proportion of Catholics waxed ever greater in America, he became more vocal, more determined that Catholics must be good citizens. As prosperity, higher education, political office improved their status, he was equally concerned that they keep their Catholic faith and ideals untarnished, uncorrupted.

In his first year in charge of the Archdiocese of Boston, he had sounded his keynote:

"If there is any form of government which needs for its permanence and prosperity the conserving force of right moral Christian sentiment, it is a republic. . . . It is idle to imagine that philanthropy will . . . stem the tide which infidelity and irreligion have started. It is mere folly to attempt to supplant faith by humanitarianism. . . .

"We Catholics have . . . done our own duty to our own under

circumstances which have proved our sincerity; for while our
people are among the poorest of this country in material goods
. . . out of their slender means they have erected, at the cost of
millions and millions of dollars, schools and institutions wherein
their children might be taught that there is a God to whom all men
must be responsible, that all authority is from God, that civil rulers
are sacred in that authority, that the law of the land is to be obeyed
. . . that the rights of property are sacred." [14]

O'Connell inherited the results of a bad guess made sixty years
earlier when Bishop Fitzpatrick persuaded the Jesuits that the
newly filled in flats of the South End of Boston would continue to
be the exclusive residential section of the city.

Neither Bishop Fitzpatrick, nor his successor Archbishop Williams, nor Father John McElroy, S.J., of Boston College, can be
blamed for what happened to the South End. Civic planners of
their day laid out the broad streets and delightful squares and parks
with high hopes for a City Beautiful. Prosperous citizens erected
handsome bow-fronted brick mansions and put carved lions on
their doorsteps.

Briefly, the story was that a rival set of city planners and land
speculators underwrote more land-filling in the Back Bay and the
tide of fashion flowed down from Beacon Hill to occupy it. George
Santayana in *Persons and Places* describes the 1870's when fashionable folks lived on Beacon Street but still drove or walked over
to the Cathedral on Washington Street or the Immaculate Conception Church of the Jesuits on Harrison Avenue at East Concord
Street.

By 1907, the South End was in low ebb. Holy Cross Cathedral,
begun in 1866, when twenty Boston men in ten minutes subscribed
thirty thousand dollars for the start, stood in all its Gothic glory
amid a dreary welter of saloons, livery stables, slatternly tenement
houses.

Its façade was overshadowed by the iron uprights of an elevated railroad; its organ and chant drowned by the strident squeal
of elevated trains roaring by at three-minute intervals on Washington Street. As an engineering proposition, the Elevated might have

been run down Tremont Street or Albany Street, equally well. A community that would put the Elevated underground to favor the Old South Church and the department stores on lower Washington Street, was perfectly willing to put the Cathedral of the Holy Cross "in the shade." Had Bishop Fitzpatrick waited ten years to buy his new cathedral site, he might have had for Boston a situation as lovely as that of the Arlington Street Unitarian Church, overlooking the gracious green expanse of the Public Garden.

Instead, William O'Connell found most of the Catholic institutions submerged in a squalid environment, inconvenient of access from the newer residential sections and seriously diminished in real estate value. They included St. Elizabeth's Hospital on Brookline Street; the Home for Destitute Catholic Children and Boston College on Harrison Avenue at East Concord Street; various diocesan offices in run-down brick houses around Union Park, near the Cathedral at Washington and Waltham Streets. The Elevated had not even cared to plan a station near the cathedral. Catholics must walk down from Northampton Street or up from Dover Street picking their steps through garbage-strewn purlieus or avoiding staggering drunks and tramps who infested the district.

So O'Connell dreamed a dream—a magnificent, virtually incredible dream—held fast to it and fitted each step into its plan for years.

His dream was to take the Catholic Church in Boston out of the catacombs, by building on the hilltops around Boston a little Rome, such as he remembered on the seven hills of Peter's city. Hills were an integral part of his vision. Like the Psalmist he said to himself, "I have lifted up my eyes to the mountains from whence help shall come to me." [15]

CHAPTER SEVENTEEN

CREATED A CARDINAL

Che, seggendo in piuma
in fama non si vien.
> Dante: Inferno,
> Canto xxiv, 1, 47-48

*(Not by sitting on feather (cushions) does one
come to fame . . .)*
> Carlyle, tr.

IN THE autumn of 1911, William O'Connell had a tremendous secret to keep locked tight behind his firm lips and jutting, cleft chin. The Holy Father had enquired whether he would accept a Cardinal's red hat.

A man may decline to serve as a cardinal. Archbishop Williams was said to have twice declined, through modesty. A cardinal may resign his office. To most men, however, creation as a cardinal represents a distinction and a responsibility to be cherished the remainder of their lives.

There are ninety-six United States senators; but only seventy Cardinals in the whole world at one time. Cardinals are appointed by the reigning Pope, not elected like senators. On the other hand, senators cannot elect a president; but the cardinals are the

Church's organ for expressing the will of God in election of a Pope.

Sapphires are by tradition gems for ring or pectoral cross of a Cardinal. William O'Connell may have dared hope the honor was intended for him when Pius X presented him with a cross set with sapphires. At any rate, he had received the confidential inquiry whether he would accept the sacred purple, with all its responsibilities, in time to prepare his Pastoral Letter, published on November first, 1911, after the public announcement. In it some of the jubilation of his spirit shines through the words. Elation was justified, for he had not yet reached his fifty-second birthday; he had been a Bishop but ten short years; Archbishop of a Metropolitan See only four years.

"To be ranked among the princes of the Church; to be exalted to the sublime Senate of the Pope; to take station among those great and holy men chosen from historic Sees and selected from among the most pious and learned in the whole Christian Commonwealth; to partake of the historic glory of those who, in centuries past, have kept the gates of the City of God; to be chosen an elector of the oldest and most potent throne in all the world:—" he wrote, "That is the meaning of the overwhelming honor to which your own undeserving spiritual father of this Diocese has been raised. . . .

"To me it has come only through your merits and your works— yours and those, too, of our fathers in the faith and the flesh, holy prelates, zealous priests and saintly parents . . . who in their tears and suffering and labor, reared the fold which today is lifted up . . . to highest honor . . . the oldest monarchy takes the young western republic into the very intimacy of her noble family and into her centuries-old council and government." [1]

There had to be confidential advance notice, because of the elaborate ceremony with which new cardinals are invested with office. Measurements had to be taken and directions forwarded to an ecclesiastical tailor in Rome for cardinal's robes to fit William O'Connell's imposing figure. His calendar had to be cleared and arrangements made for administration of the archdiocese during his absence. Reservations must be secured for the voyage to Rome in time for the secret consistory set for November twenty-seventh.

The news of imminent naming of new cardinals was announced in Rome on October twenty-eighth. It was released in Boston by receipt of a personal cable from Cardinal Merry del Val to Archbishop O'Connell. The Sunday newspapers were filled with the news. It so happened that Mondays were the Archbishop's days for receiving the general public without appointment at Granby Street. The house was jammed with flowers and a stream of callers poured through all day. Mayor John F. Fitzgerald enthusiastically cabled to Merry del Val Boston's joy at the honor.

O'Connell, who had only returned from the Eucharistic Congress at Madrid in early September of that year, sailed on November eleventh from East Boston on the same steamer with Farley and Falconio. Thousands lined the dock, chanting the Te Deum and hymns.

Both O'Connell and Farley had studied at the North American College and the ex-Apostolic Delegate Falconio chose to receive there with them, the *biglietto,* or official announcement.

Ancient ceremony requires that formal creation of new cardinals take place at a secret consistory in the Vatican, at which those to be named are not present. The waiting at the American College seemed interminable to everyone. The three Americans stood in the salon with the rector, Archbishop Thomas Kennedy, all in purple robes. With them was a Vatican official, solemnly holding a paper-knife. They were waiting for the Papal messenger, in a carriage drawn by the famous Vatican black horses. Finally was heard the clatter of hoofs. A gentleman appeared at the door.

"I beg to inform Your Excellency that there is a messenger from the Papal Secretary of State."

"I will receive him," said the archbishop.

More waiting, and then entered the messenger, accompanied by gentlemen-in-waiting, and bearing a large white envelope. The rector, slitting the envelope and drawing out a heavy sheet of white paper, bowed and read the message aloud:

"The Holy Father is pleased to create you a cardinal of the Holy Roman Church."

There were speeches—of thanks—of congratulation—and, of course, a dinner.

Two days later, at a private consistory in the Vatican, the Holy Father presented each of the new cardinals with the scarlet biretta. Finally, on November thirtieth, the great public consistory, thronged by cardinals, bishops, clerics and the public, took place in St. Peter's basilica, brilliantly lighted and hung with the festive red draperies. Pius X placed on the head of each new cardinal the *galero*.

The ceremony, because of the number of new cardinals created, was held in the Hall of Benedictions, above the vestibule of St. Peter's, crowded with clergy, diplomats, friends. The Sistine Choir rendered the music. Pius X, on the throne, received the new cardinals, filing in from the Sistine Chapel, where they had taken the oath, and to which they retired after the ceremony for singing of the Te Deum. A little later, at another secret consistory, attended by the older cardinals in the Vatican, took place the ceremony of sealing, then opening the mouths of the new cardinals. This represents their fidelity and confidential office to the Holy Father. At this consistory each new cardinal learned the name of his Titular Church. To every cardinal in his life-time, is assigned as "Title" one of the ancient, historic churches of Rome, signalizing his closeness to the person of the Pope, the Bishop of Rome, whose Title is the basilica of St. John Lateran.

O'Connell's titular church was that of San Clemente. He took possession of it formally on the eighth of December. During his stay in Rome, he sat for the Austrian sculptor Dora Ohlsen, whose bust of him appears on the medal commemorating his elevation.[2] On December nineteenth, he had his farewell audience with Pius X; and, late in January, returned to an enthusiastic welcome in Boston.

Despite the cold and driving snow, crowds estimated at one hundred thousand welcomed the new Cardinal as he landed at Long Wharf, Boston, and was escorted across the city to his

Granby Street residence by marching detachments of Catholic societies. Buildings along the route were decorated, and the thronged
receptions that followed, day after day in February, testified to
Boston's pride and appreciation of the honor that Rome had paid
her Archbishop. Twenty-five of the leading non-Catholic citizens
presented him with a gold casket and scroll, containing twenty-five
thousand dollars.

The truest manifestation of joy took place at the solemn pontifical High Mass in the Cathedral of the Holy Cross the morning
after the Cardinal's return, when, for the first time in his gorgeous
robes, he took his place on the throne on the Gospel side of the
high altar. The cathedral, hung with red and gold and elaborately
adorned with evergreens, was filled to capacity when Pio drove the
carriage to the front entrance and the stately figure took place in
the procession which passed between saluting swords of the Fourth
Degree Knights of Columbus.

William O'Connell's personal code was so simple that it could
be put in two sentences. In fact, he so phrased it, at the first sermon he delivered as Cardinal, in the Cathedral of the Holy Cross
on his return from receiving his red hat in Rome.

"My American citizenship I prize as one of God's choicest gifts
to me—mine to honor with the best that is in me and to defend
with my last breath. My Roman priesthood, the dignity of Bishop
and Cardinal, my Roman faith, demand my devoted attachment,
while life lasts, to Peter's See.

"Of those who would quibble about divided affection, I would
ask, when was it forbidden to any good son to love, according to
their merits, with all the fullness of his heart's love, both mother
and father." [3]

Thus he stated and re-confirmed the principles which he had
formed twenty years earlier when the controversies on the twin
questions of Americanism and the French view of Heckerism had
created the situation that sent young Father O'Connell to Rome in
1895 as rector of the North American College.

All through the Roman years, the Portland years and the first
years in Boston, he had kept his own counsel, eschewing contro-

versy or partisanship. Now, in the elation natural to being named
one of the seventy cardinals of all the world, he spoke out to his
clergy at the banquet with which they welcomed him home. He
said very frankly that he viewed his red hat as "the highest possible
approbation upon his work given unstintedly by the Vicar of Christ
himself." Then he went on to explain the principle on which his
work had been founded—"the one mainspring which has guided
me . . . to model my regime as a Christian bishop along the lines
of his (Peter's Successor) slightest wish in whatever concerned faith
or morals, or the discipline of ecclesiastical life." He referred indirectly to past history, saying: "That any Bishop of the Church
should assume a merely parochial, or provincial, or national attitude is a most glaring contradiction of terms . . . that he should
dare to assume a position of self-sufficiency is so repugnant to
common sense that it is unworthy of argument."

"A bishop's . . . office is so momentous, so fraught with such
enormous consequences not merely for the present, but, in a certain sense for all time, that his own opinion or judgment of what
he does or does not do is relatively insignificant. For the flock is
not his, but Christ's, and neither his mind nor his heart, nor conscience can rest tranquilly unless he feels in perfect union, absolute
concord with the mind and heart of Him who rules the whole
Church.

"The mere suspicion of any other sentiment in the mind or
heart of a bishop is criminal . . . and the presence of such a dis-
jointed and egoistic vanity in the regime of any Catholic prelate
has often wrought havoc. . . . The very universality of the Church
demands the most absolute unity; and no bishop, whatever the
apparent holiness of his life, can be other than a renegade and
traitor to his office who harbors, even for a day, the conceit that
he is independent in his rule or, indeed, that he may with im-
punity, toy with the cord which binds every See in the Christian
world to Rome, the center of all spiritual authority.

"I am well enough acquainted with men and events to realize
that in every Christian land, there are those who seem incapable
of beholding anything but a bogy in Rome's influence . . . and I

know that this unwarranted fear and unfounded alarm is not confined to the enemies of the Church. . . . What sort of logic or what particular species of faith can engender such an irreconcilable attitude is a thing beyond my comprehension as a Catholic . . ." [4]

The Cardinal did not contemplate building a new cathedral for the Boston Archdiocese. "To those who ask me if I intend to build a new cathedral in Boston, decidedly no," he said.

"What this rushing age, this restless atmosphere of America needs, is the beauty of a tradition, which it almost entirely lacks.

"To me, the Cathedral of the Holy Cross, built by the sacrifice of a generation past and by a saintly bishop who has gone to his reward, is a doubly sacred thing. I love every stone in it and I never enter it without thinking of those whose sacrifice and labors built it.

"What do present surroundings matter? These will change as all modern cities change, but in the midst of constant changes will be that one perpetual reminder of the faith and fidelity of a people and a bishop whose prayers and aspirations have woven themselves into the very fabric of the edifice. Let us keep our old churches as we keep our old friends." [5]

Cardinal O'Connell, from boyhood, had never suffered from shyness or timidity. As authority was vested in him, he came to speak authoritatively, with an assurance that those who did not like him sometimes considered to be arrogance.

"Thank God, I do not know what fear means when there is a clear duty to perform," said the Cardinal once, "either in reprimand, rebuke, or resistance to the evil influences of self-made leaders, whose sole purpose it is, no matter what their unctuous pretensions, to weaken discipline and utterly destroy Catholic unity. While I have a voice to raise, it will be lifted loud and strong against such interlopers and disturbers of the peace of God's House and Kingdom." [6]

The Cardinal had a very keen distinction between humor and vulgarity; the one he enjoyed, the other he would not tolerate. A really brilliant priest once lost a coveted appointment at the last moment because the Cardinal overheard him make a joke about

another man's physique. The Cardinal also could distinguish un-
erringly between honest candor and ill-bred rudeness.

In 1906, a young college graduate, much troubled as to his
vocation and confused by many varying counsels, rang the doorbell
of the new Archbishop-coadjutor, O'Connell. Overcome with shyness and his own perplexity, to his horror he heard himself blurting
out the thought that had been in his mind.

"You can be nobody's fool if the Holy Father appointed you to
this job," he stammered, "so I wanted to ask you what I should
do."

O'Connell, far from taking offense, discussed the question pa-
tiently and advised the youth to apply for the American College in
Rome and devote his life to service in the Boston archdiocese. On
ordination, the young priest found that the Cardinal had kept him
in mind, following his progress, and immediately put him to work
in responsible administrative posts.

It was not only a young seminarian or priest whom the Cardinal
would help. While he was living on Union Park not far from the
Cathedral, he bought his newspaper every day from a "newsie" on
the corner and chatted so kindly to the boy that he learned that he
was soon to enlist in the Army.

"Now," said the Bishop, the next day, "here is a letter to my
own doctor. He won't charge you anything. I want you to go see
him."

Years later, the man said that the interview had started him on
what proved an honorable career in the service and good livelihood
on his retirement. His own home was underprivileged and his upbringing neglected. The physician, on reading the letter of introduction, gave the boy a fatherly instruction in hygiene, moral and
physical, that kept him straight through hazards and temptations.

"But what helped me most, and what I have never forgotten, was
the Cardinal's own words to me, of farewell. He said 'struggle always to keep your self-respect and never lose your dignity.' A short
sentence, but it stuck by me and I owe my success in life to it,"
said the man, on the Cardinal's death.

The Cardinal could appreciate a joke on himself. He liked to tell close friends of making an unheralded visit to a parochial school, on his way home from a Confirmation. He appeared, all two hundred and forty pounds of him, in full scarlet robes and biretta, at the door of a First Grade room. The flustered little nun cried out, hopefully,

"Children dear, who is this?"

"The Little Flower," piped a six-year-old, his mind stuffed with the recent publicity on the canonization of St. Therese of Lisieux in 1925.

The Cardinal was amused, too, at the young girl at a convent boarding school who, as she kissed his ring after his elevation to the purple, greeted him nervously as "Your Innocence."

The weight of flesh which accumulated on his tall and erect frame was not due to over-indulgence. His meals were spartan-light, at home, unless he was entertaining. He liked a finger of good whiskey in a glass of water, at bedtime, but suddenly deciding it was unnecessary, gave it up, without regret. He kept a cellar of good vintage wines, but the operative word was kept; they were for entertaining, not for table beverage. In his latter years, when diabetes developed, he voluntarily chose a near-starvation diet rather than be dependent on insulin. His reason—church ceremonies could not be interrupted because it was time for an insulin shot.

His self-discipline was tremendous. He actually gave up the greatest personal pleasure he enjoyed, because he felt it a duty. This was membership in the exclusive clubs of old Boston society.

His years as Rector in Rome had led to friendships with many prominent Bostonians, as Rome in those days had a large colony of Americans from New England. It was natural that when he came to Boston, in 1906, the acquaintance was continued and widened and he was invited to become a member of two highly intellectual dining clubs. Such men as Judge Robert Grant, William Roscoe Thayer, James Ford Rhodes, Alexander Agassiz, President Francis A. Walker of Massachusetts Institute of Technology, James Jackson Storrow, Jr., who would give Boston the beautiful Esplanade on the Charles River, Professor Charles S. Sargent, were among the circle of fifteen in the Winter's Night Club, for instance.

Once a month, in rotation, they met at some member's house for dinner. Judge Grant, in his autobiography, noted that "Cardinal O'Connell . . . was a gracious host and gave excellent dinners." The Judge, however, did not know the secret of the Cardinal's cuisine. For such special occasions, the Cardinal invoked the expert aid of his friend Emil Coulon, experienced manager of the Hotel Westminster. The conversation skimmed the cream of what Judge Grant calls "the Brahmin mind of Boston," since all were highly educated, widely traveled and reared in a tradition of literature and art.

Yet one day a tale-bearer carried to the Cardinal a comment he had heard that His Eminence was way above his own flock in penetrating doors never before opened to an Irish Catholic. Rather than arouse envy or ill-feeling among his own, the Cardinal, giving as polite excuse the pressure of his duties, resigned from the clubs that had been his rare relaxation.

"His was the only resignation in my time, except for invalidism," commented Judge Grant, wonderingly.[7]

The Cardinal, while always dignified, adapted himself with charm and affability to the preponderance of non-Catholic society in old Boston. It required tact and forbearance after Rome, where a host and hostess, inviting a Cardinal to tea, would meet him at the door, carrying lighted tapers, kiss his ring on bended knee, and reserve a throne-chair upholstered in Cardinal red, for his exclusive occupancy.

An example was the tea at Granby Street residence which the Cardinal gave when Maréchal Joffre of France was in Boston. Most of the distinguished officers escorting Joffre were not Catholics. One Catholic American general, automatically dropping to one knee and pressing his lips to the hand extended, was embarrassed to find flesh instead of jewel. The Cardinal had left off his ring purposely, so that the Protestants would feel no compulsion to kiss it.

A little misunderstanding on the part of the Protestant visitors that day greatly embarrassed the Cardinal, however. He had arranged, as signal to the caterer, that he would clap his hands when ready for refreshments to be served. The escort party proved larger than anticipated, so that quite a crowd was standing in the anteroom and hall. When the Cardinal clapped his hands, the crowd assumed that some speech they could not hear, had been concluded, and set up dutiful applause, confusing the waiters. The Cardinal and the Maréchal never did get any tea!

Another story about the Cardinal's ring began with a paragraph in the Boston newspapers that the Cardinal was confined to the house by a severe cold. As a matter of fact, His Eminence had given a polite excuse for not accepting an invitation. He went for his walk as usual that afternoon, with secretary, choosing a location where he would not be likely to meet people who knew him. However, a little group of urchins hailed him.

"Hi, Cardinal! Heard you was sick."

"Oh, thank you, boys, thank you. I am better now."

"Kin we kiss yer ring?" shrilled the biggest boy.

The Cardinal stripping off his glove, benevolently extended his hand and the boys lined up, except for one who hung back.

"Come on, sonny," said the Cardinal. "You can kiss my ring, too."

"Like heck he kin!" protested the leader. "He's nuttin' but a black Protestant!"

The newsmen and photographers, who covered the Cardinal on orders from their editors, sometimes caught the rough side of the Cardinal's tongue. They complained that he would keep them waiting an hour for one of the birthday interviews that were traditional each year. He said it was because they kept straggling in and expecting him to repeat what he had said earlier.

One of the best newspapermen in Boston chanced to weigh even more than the Cardinal. He was sent out one year, arriving as the group were being ushered into the audience-room.

"Be seated, gentlemen," said the Cardinal graciously.

The unfortunate fat man found only one chair left. It was a gilt antique. It collapsed in splinters under his impact, leaving him sprawling on the floor.

"Why didn't you bring an axe?" snapped the Cardinal.

The Cardinal was very anxious that his clergy keep a high standard in their sermons. He, himself, rarely preached over ten minutes, but packed plenty of meat into what he said. When microphones were first coming into use, a priest noted for being long-winded, was to preach at a Cathedral service. Already nervous at preaching in the presence of His Eminence, the man was still more upset at having to deal with the new-fangled contrivance. He fumbled with the buttons, muttering desperate inquiries—Which makes it louder?—Which makes it softer?

"Is there any button that makes it *shorter?*" came the Cardinal's carrying voice from the throne.

One of the most revealing stories was of the old Irish widow who was so proud that a man of Irish descent was Boston's first cardinal, that whenever his name was mentioned, tears would come in her eyes as she ejaculated, "God bless him!" Her son, introduced to the Cardinal at some parish function, mentioned this. The Cardinal inquired the mother's name and address.

"Wonderful," he said. "I always wanted people to like me and I am afraid most of them don't."

Soon after, an autographed photograph of His Eminence was delivered at the address, which he had memorized in the midst of a crowded function.

The Cardinal had a retentive memory for everything except dates. One day, as he stepped out of his Lake Street residence, he spied a certain priest with an armful of books, on his way to the library.

"Set down your books, Father, and take a little stroll with me," he invited.

They strolled in silence for some distance through the Seminary grounds and suddenly the Cardinal pointed.

"How beautiful the song of that little robin yonder."

"Not a robin, Your Eminence," contradicted the priest, who was an amateur ornithologist. "It is a Baltimore oriole."

"Yes?" said the Cardinal. "Good afternoon, Father!"

Twelve years went by. Young Father John J. Wright was ordained in Rome and became secretary to His Eminence. He was walking with the Cardinal in the garden when a bird flew towards them, perching on a branch close at hand.

"What bird is that, Father?" asked the Cardinal.

"Your Eminence, my native habitat is Copley Square," replied the young secretary honestly. "Of nine hundred priests in your archdiocese, you have chosen the least competent to answer your question. If I must hazard a reply, however, I will venture that it might be a partridge."

"Hm!" sniffed the Cardinal. "I should have Father X— here!"

For twelve years he had recalled that expert correction!

CHAPTER EIGHTEEN

SS. COLUMBAN AND CLEMENT

... Vagliami il lungo studio e il grande amore.
Dante: Inferno, Canto i, 83

(I studied long and with great love.)
Carlyle, tr.

Two saints, one of his own choosing, the other appointed by the Holy See, commanded respect and devotion to their ancient shrines from Cardinal O'Connell.

One was of Roman birth, Saint Clement, third successor to Saint Peter as Pope in the First Century. The other, born in Ireland, Saint Columban, brought the learning, culture and Faith from Irish monasteries to France and Italy in the Sixth Century.

"The more experts study the obscure problems of the Middle Ages," wrote the Vatican librarian who became Pius XI, "the clearer it becomes that the renaissance of Christian learning in France, Germany and Italy is due to the work and zeal of St. Columban. This shows the merit which Catholic Ireland has acquired in the world." [1]

When O'Connell became Archbishop of Boston the shrines in Italy of both saints were threatened with ruin. He became the link between Boston in the United States and two monuments in Italy valued by archaeologists and scholars for their treasures of history

164

and art; revered by Catholics for their associations with the early days of the Church.

Seven years later it would be said of O'Connell: "For twenty-five years this Oratory (of St. Clement's in Rome) had been closed, alike to the pious pilgrim and the studious archaeologist, owing to the vast quantity of water by which it was inundated. Today our tune is changed from lamentation to exultation, thanks to the princely munificence of the present great Cardinal Titular of San Clemente whose love for art and archaeology and his appreciation of the historic value . . . are only equalled by his generosity." [2]

And, as Archbishop of Boston, it was not only a pious act, but a friendly fraternal gesture to join with the hierarchy of Ireland in contributing to the restoration of the abbey at Bobbio, built by Columban.[3]

Columban's monks and their successors through the centuries, like the dedicated religious of Christendom in the so-called Dark Ages, were the teachers and guides of the people of their district. This one abbey of Bobbio, hidden in the mountain wilderness, had a library of seven hundred folios of hand-written and illuminated manuscripts. Scattered and pillaged, by the invasion of Napoleon's troops in 1797-8, these exquisite ancient books today are collectors' items, many of them acquired and preserved at the Ambrosian Library in Milan, the Vatican Library in Rome and in secular collections in Europe and America.

The monks at Bobbio did more than preserve literature. They taught the mountain inhabitants scientific agriculture. In 1910, at the restoration of the ancient abbey, by excavations beneath the Fourteenth Century upper church, was brought to light a "Farmers' Almanac" a thousand years old.

Worked in black and white mosaic, on the floor of the abbey church, where all the peasants could study it and the preaching monks expound it, is a set of twelve large panels, with the name of the month in Latin at the top, the appropriate sign of the Zodiac beneath. In each panel a farmer is depicted, employed in the type of work the well-trained agriculturist will perform in that month. Step by step, through the year, the farmer prepares his fields, sows his seed, turns his cattle out to pasture, harvests his grain and hay. In August, with the crops in, he is seen coopering little kegs for wine; and in September, he is treading out the grapes to make wine. In November, he takes his pigs into the forest and knocks down acorns with a long stick to feed them. The reward of the year's toil comes in December when, with his barns and storehouses full, he kills a pig, now well fattened, for the Christmas feast.

Such work of re-integrating the past with the present, of recovering precious historic monuments and of documenting tradition through archaeology, as seen at Bobbio, was soon to influence William O'Connell in an even greater opportunity presented to him.

This came a year later, when, at his elevation to the cardinalate, Pope Pius X named him Titular of the Church of St. Clement in Rome.

One of the new Cardinal's first public pronouncements was his talk on taking possession of this Church in Rome on December eighth, 1911, "with a deep sense of gratitude to the Holy Father for assigning me this historic church" and "great pleasure in being associated with the Irish Dominicans."

"On this very spot," said the Cardinal reverently, "stood the house of Clement, the third successor of St. Peter in the Roman Pontificate . . . it became an oratory. . . . St. Peter and St. Paul . . . stood in this very place and offered up the Holy Sacrifice."

"This hallowed spot is indissolubly bound up with the beginnings of Christianity and the inception of the world-wide jurisdiction of the See of Peter." [4]

Today's beautiful choir enclosure of carved white marble, inlaid with designs in purple and green marbles, where the Irish Dominicans of the Twentieth Century still chant their Office daily, dates from this Fourth Century church. The twin marble ambones, or raised pulpits at each side of the choir show us the early custom of reading Gospel and Epistle at Mass to the people by deacons. Gregory the Great preached one of his homilies from these ambones, and many a noted Pope or cardinal has spoken from them, up to Pius IX and William Cardinal O'Connell.

An Irishman born on St. Joseph's day, 1812, ordained in Rome and assigned to residence at San Clemente in 1847, is the hero of the next chapter of San Clemente's history. Father Joseph Mullooly, O.P., was the first man in eight centuries to guess at the Christian memorials underneath the basilica. While his contemporaries scoffed, he studied old manuscripts, made tentative diggings; in 1857, he unearthed evidence, in marble pillars of the Fourth Century basilica. The Holy Father, Pius IX, encouraged his research. Pius IX had affection for his long-ago predecessor Clement, because on the night of November twenty-fourth, 1848, fleeing would-be assassins, in disguise, he risked his life to stop at San Clemente to invoke the saint's aid. When Pius IX was able to return to Rome, to reign longer than any Pope to date except St. Peter, he felt gratitude to St. Clement.

No one was more pleased than Pius IX when removal of one hundred and fifty thousand cart-loads of rubble [5] revealed to the world the glories of the original basilica of San Clemente. No one but Father Mullooly felt more badly than Pius IX when subterranean floods concealed them again ten years later.

But the luck of the Irish is proverbial. In 1911, another Pius named as Titular of San Clemente, William Cardinal O'Connell of Boston, son of Irish parents. O'Connell, in Rome on the eighth of December, after receiving his red hat, took possession of his Titular church.

The Dominican Prior met him at the portico, to present the insignia of crucifix, holy water and incense. The procession passed through the courtyard into the upper basilica. The Cardinal paused to pray at the side-chapel of the Blessed Sacrament, and then took his seat in the ancient marble Bishop's chair in the apse behind the high altar. At San Clemente, besides preserving the position of the marble choir enclosure in the nave, just below the high altar, the ancient custom, as at the papal altar in St. Peter's, places the priest celebrating Mass facing the congregation in the church.

For his first pronouncement in his Titular church, the Boston Cardinal went, in his sweeping red robes, down the tessellated marble floor to the choir and ascended the high marble pulpit, the

Gospel ambone. He told the crowded church of his great delight in receiving as his Title the historic basilica.

The new Cardinal appointed as vicar of his Titular church, Father Louis C. Nolan, O.P., who was acting vicar, also, for the Dominican Master-General and, in 1912 was named Prior at San Clemente. Six days after taking possession of his Title, the Cardinal presided at a meeting which included the British Ambassador, Sir Rennell Rodd, and engineering experts. An appeal to the public in America and Britain for contributions to the work was authorized for publication. This appeal, probably, influenced the culture-minded Bostonians, for, on February 16, 1912, twenty-five Boston bankers and business men, all non-Catholics, called on the Cardinal at Granby Street to present a gold casket containing a check for $25,000.

"Actuated by the desire of testifying the esteem and regard which we feel towards you, we ask you to accept this little gift, small, indeed, but given most freely," read, in part, the accompanying parchment, containing an illuminated Latin address.

The Cardinal, a week earlier, had written Father Nolan in terms illustrating his direct way of getting things done: "I wish to take up the matter of the necessary work for the drainage and proper repairs and care of San Clemente. . . . I don't wish anything done by committees or anything of the kind. I wish to do this work myself in my own way and I wish you would report to me at the earliest possible moment the result of your conference with Cardinal Merry del Val, to whom I have written in this matter." [6]

The two friends had thoroughly discussed the question of San Clemente's needs during O'Connell's stay in Rome; and Merry del Val, for the next two years, despite his heavy burden of work as Secretary of State to Pius X, faithfully supervised the project in frequent consultation with Prior Nolan in behalf of his Boston confrere.

The work extended over two years, with many difficulties in driving a great tunnel, seven hundred yards long, deep under the level of old Rome, to divert the subterranean waters to the ancient

Roman sewer, the Cloaca Maxima, discharging into the River Tiber.

Cardinal O'Connell was in Rome himself, in 1913, and on May twenty-sixth, visited San Clemente, personally inspecting the work. He returned the next year for the ceremonies at its completion.

The necessary funds for this engineering project, O'Connell, with a nice delicacy of feeling, devoted from the purse presented him on his elevation, by twenty-five prominent non-Catholic Bostonians. He felt that their generosity should be used to preserve the archaeological monument appreciated by scholars, artists and cultured people of all races and all faiths.

In undertaking, in 1933, to write his Reminiscences, the Cardinal doubtless was moved by the fact that the same Boston publishing firm had brought out the memoirs of Bishop William Lawrence, whose span as head of the Protestant Episcopal diocese of Massachusetts had coincided with O'Connell's administration of the Archbishopric of Boston, including largely the same geographical territory.[7]

Unfortunately, the Cardinal's physical defects, which he bravely concealed from the public, prevented him from giving to his memoirs the painstaking review of documents and data that would have ensured accuracy in the work. The encroachments of cataract on one eye and the illness of diabetes forced him to dictate from memory and prevented him from reading the proofs and making desired corrections.

Pius XI, who as Achille Ratti had for years been the learned librarian at Milan and the Vatican, in 1934 spent an hour turning over the pages of a copy of "Recollections of Seventy Years" which Cardinal O'Connell had had bound in white for personal presentation to the Holy Father. The Pope told the Boston Cardinal that he had already noticed one of the autographed editions in the Vatican library. "I was afraid that you were forgetting the old librarian," he said, taking the white book in his hands and turning over the pages. Pausing at an illustration of O'Connell just after his ordination, he smiled. "You have changed," said the Holy Father. What pleased the Cardinal most was the Pope's comment on the picture of Brigid O'Connell. "I see there the face of a great administrator. You must have inherited your mother's traits. A good mother is a wonderful blessing." [8]

There are a number of factual errors to be found in the pages of "Reminiscences of Seventy Years," but if expert proofreaders failed to detect factual inaccuracies in O'Connell's Reminiscences, no one should blame the aging, infirm prelate for lapses of memory while dictating.

On that day Cardinal O'Connell walked in procession to the basilica, assisted by Father Lepidi, O.P., Master-General of the Sacred Palace, and Father Esser, O.P., Secretary of the Congregation of the Index. At San Clemente's entrance, he was welcomed by Father Cormier, O.P., Master-General of the Dominican Order. Father Cormier unveiled the bust of the Cardinal by the Roman sculptor Cavaliere Mauro in the lower basilica, and the procession then moved down to the pagan Mithraeum and the Roman walls. Here Cardinal O'Connell formally opened the subterranean tunnel that his funds had built to drain the waters off into the Cloaca Maxima.

The actual work on the tunnel was not completed until October of 1914, and the Cardinal transmitted from Boston the final payments for the work, on November 28, 1914, amounting to $32,-810.93. An amusing little note by Father Nolan in the Dominican archives reports that he had scrupulously given to charity the balance of over-payment, one lira and 42 centesimi—roughly, thirty cents in United States money of that day.

For forty years now, the tunnel, running from beneath the Colosseum to San Clemente, a distance of seven hundred yards, has functioned admirably to keep the ancient basilica free of water and accessible to the thousands of scholars, pilgrims and tourists who have been edified and educated by the early Christian frescoes and the old pagan temple made accessible by Cardinal O'Connell's initiative. The engineers he selected for the project were C. A. Mills, Signor Leonori and Cavaliere Luini.

Not the least credit for this noteworthy project of archaeological and religious significance, goes to the twenty-five merchants of Boston, non-Catholics all, who subscribed the original purse presented O'Connell on his elevation to the cardinalate, which made possible the undertaking.

CHAPTER NINETEEN

CONCLAVES, 1914 AND 1922

Che tu mi meni la dov' or dicesti
si ch'io vegga la porta di San Pietro.
Dante: Inferno, Canto i, 133-34

*(Lead me now where thou hast said, so that I may
see the Gate of St. Peter.)*

Carlyle, tr.

A PRINCE OF the Catholic Church is called on, in the course of his duties, to attend many functions, make many journeys. The Vatican works a seven-day week and so do the heads of far-flung diocese or mission posts throughout the world.

Cardinal O'Connell was no exception and he learned to find in journeying his best chance for a short vacation from mail, telephone or conferences. He spoke at Eucharistic Congresses in Madrid in 1909; Montreal in 1910; Chicago in 1926; Dublin in 1932. He virtually commuted between Boston and Washington for conferences of the American hierarchy or board meetings of the trustees of Catholic University. He led pilgrimages to the Holy Land in 1924 and to Rome for the Jubilee of 1925. Ecclesiastical business called him to Rome frequently. After his seventieth year, on the advice of physicians, he acquired a picturesque house in Nassau, where Patrick Cardinal Hayes [1] of New York also wintered,

172

and spent the stormy February months of Boston's bleak climate there.[2]

Two frustrating journeys to Rome were indelibly engraved in the Cardinal's memory. The first occurred in 1914.

He had sailed on April twenty-fifth, for his regular *ad limina* visit to the Holy Father. On May twentieth, he delivered an address in Italian at his titular Church of San Clemente, signaling completion of the gigantic task of diverting the subterranean waters to a sewer discharging into the Tiber.

"The heir to a great treasure," he told the congregation, "has the responsibility to guard sacredly his inheritance, to secure its safety against damage. . . . I took possession of a treasure menaced with certain decay and destruction by water. . . . As a tribute of our Christian faith, we lay this completed task, done for the glory of God and honor of St. Clement, at the feet of the successor of Peter and Clement, our beloved Holy Father, Pius X." [3]

In Rome, Cardinal O'Connell had many meetings with his close friend, Cardinal Merry del Val, but neither sensed the approaching death of Pius X. The year before, when the Pope's health had given concern, Cardinal Merry del Val had privately advised O'Connell, who, after Easter, went to New York, and stayed unobtrusively for a fortnight at the Plaza Hotel, ready to sail at a moment's notice. In 1914, however, the seventy-eight-year-old Pontiff apparently reassured both Cardinals by his seeming health, and Cardinal O'Connell left Rome for a visit with his friend, Prince Ludwig Ferdinand of Bavaria, at Nymphenburg, outside Munich; and a stay at Carlsbad, famed health resort.

The American Cardinal realized very promptly that the assassination of Archduke Francis Ferdinand of Austria at Sarajevo on June twenty-eighth was prelude to the European war. Cardinal Farley was in Europe that summer also, and made for neutral Switzerland, but Cardinal O'Connell, advancing his reservation by two weeks, boarded a steamer at Hamburg on July twenty-ninth, landing in Boston on August eighth. How often and bitterly did he regret that decision, prompted by his sense of duty to his Archdiocese at home.

On the Feast of the Assumption, American newspapers carried reports of the Holy Father celebrating Mass and afterwards receiving in audience a large group of Americans. Two days later, however, Pius X was ordered by his physicians to stay in bed and, shortly after one o'clock in the morning of August twentieth came his death.

With the startling news of the death of Pius X, William O'Connell realized that he was to perform the most solemn responsibility of a Cardinal—to participate in election of the two-hundred-and-fifty-eighth Successor to Peter.

He grieved for the dead pontiff to whom he owed so much, with almost the affection of a son, tinged with awe in recognition of the saintly nature of the man. Prophetically, O'Connell wrote in 1926: "Troubles and difficulties filled his whole pontificate . . . doubtless in the process of the canonization of that Holy Pope they will all be unfolded . . . amid difficulties and trials of every kind, the gentle Pius worked and prayed . . . when the Great War broke out, his Christlike soul entered upon its final agony. . . . I saw him only a month before his death. . . . I knelt and kissed his garment, the garment of a saint. . . . From that day to this, I have prayed to him as a friend who is a friend of God." [4]

Seven years after William O'Connell himself went to God, the Church on June 3, 1951 pronounced Pius X the eighth Pope to be declared Blessed. Archbishop Richard J. Cushing and the faithful of Boston provided the silver casket in which lay the body of Pius X, friend of Cardinal O'Connell, in St. Peter's basilica, prior to the official canonization on May 29, 1954.

O'Connell, on receiving word of the Pope's death, booked passage on the *Canopic,* due to sail from Boston that same day. However, down in Baltimore a devoted young chancellor, Father Louis Stickney was working to get his Cardinal, the eighty-year-old Gibbons, to Rome, also. He succeeded in having the *Canopic* touch at New York delaying her sailing until August twenty-third, so that Gibbons and Cardinal Begin of Quebec might embark.

The delay was fatal to the hopes of all three Cardinals, particularly to O'Connell, though he had to constrain his feelings in deference to the older prelates. At Naples he would not be further constrained to their company, but hired an automobile to speed to Rome, while the others took the train provided by the Italian Government.

The conclave, they knew from telegraphic dispatches, had opened on August thirty-first. O'Connell was eager to arrive in time to cast a ballot for his friend and hero Cardinal Merry del Val. Old Cardinal Rampolla had died the year before and Merry del Val was now arch-priest of St. Peter's in his stead, Secretary of State to Pius X since 1903, and eminently *papabile,* as the Italians say.

Only twenty miles short of Rome, the hired automobile broke down and repairs had to be made in the small village of Velletri. O'Connell heard the village church bells chiming madly.

"Is it a feast day here?" he asked.

"Non, non! The new Santa Papa, Benedict XV," came the answer.

"And who—who was elected?"

"Della Chiesa!"

In the 1890's as Rector at the American College, O'Connell had often met and knew well Genoese Giacomo Della Chiesa, young *minutante* in the Secretariat of State under Cardinal Rampolla.

Thanks to the break-down of the motor car, Gibbons and O'Connell arrived together at the Vatican on September third, and were admitted to the conclave for a brief audience with the new Pope who was just changing from his cardinal red to the white robes. They then retired to the Hotel de Russie. It was no consolation to them that Cardinal Farley, because of having been in Switzerland, had been able to participate in election of the new Pope.

Three days later, William Cardinal O'Connell had his first opportunity to witness the historic ceremonies of the coronation of a Pope. Due to the tense atmosphere on the declaration of war by England and France on Germany, the ceremony was held in the Sistine Chapel.[5]

To Merry del Val, O'Connell voiced his disappointment at the election, but the ascetic Cardinal replied only: "I am happy to be relieved of a strain which I doubt if I could further bear. I shall leave the Vatican without regret and the quiet of Santa Marta will be a welcome relief. *Non habemus hic manentem civitatem.* (We have not here an abiding place.)" [6]

In 1914, Cardinal O'Connell left Rome the day after the coronation, boarding the *Canopic* at Naples for her return voyage, arriving back in Boston on September twenty-fourth. To the reporters, as doubtless he had already said to Benedict XV in his private audiences, the Cardinal declared:

"Had the conclave been postponed a day, as (the American Cardinals) expected, they would have been in time to take part in the election . . . undoubtedly a new regulation will be made in regard to the opening of the Conclave that will enable Cardinals to reach Rome in time to participate in future elections.

"As the world now knows," the Cardinal told the Boston press on September twenty-fourth, "the Conclave resulted in the election to the Pontificate of Cardinal Della Chiesa, who assumed the name of Benedict XV. Three of the American Cardinals arrived too late to participate in the election, Cardinal Gibbons, Cardinal Begin and myself. The other two American cardinals, Cardinal Farley of New York and Cardinal Cavalcanti of Rio de Janeiro, were able to be present by the merest chance. Cardinal Farley had been detained in Switzerland on account of the war and was able to reach Rome in time. The South American Cardinal was then nearing Gibraltar on his way to Carlsbad, and thus managed to arrive in time.

"The ancient regulation . . . was made when Cardinals did not reside at such a great distance from Rome as they do now; and undoubtedly, a new regulation will be made . . . that will enable Cardinals to reach Rome in time to participate in future elections.

"Nearly twenty years ago, when I occupied the post of rectorship of the American College in Rome, I knew the present Holy Father during those years when he was connected with the secretaryship of state and then I saw his ceaseless activity and capacity for hard and important work. . . .

"As soon as my name was announced, the small room was cleared and the Holy Father fairly hurried to the door to embrace me and recalled at once our former and uninterrupted friendship. On three separate occasions during my short stay in Rome, the Holy Father received me in private conference." [7]

It is not necessary to point out, to Catholic readers, that selection of a Successor to fill Peter's Chair has nothing in common with, say, a Presidential campaign in the United States to select an occupant of the White House.

The Presidential election is a political device, derived from the consent of the governed, in order to secure an orderly administration of the civil state.

The conclave to select a Pope, is the mechanism for transmitting, uninterrupted, the rule of the Church founded by Christ and by Him promised to endure to the end of this world. Should Popes cease to be elected, the Apostolic Succession would be concluded with the death of the last Bishop consecrated by appointment of the last Pope; administration of the Sacraments of Holy Orders and Confirmation would cease to be valid; and the visible Church would no longer be manifested in the world.

The consecrating power of the Catholic Church, transmitted from St. Peter as first Head of the Church, runs from the Bishops to the priests, in the ineffable privilege of celebrating the Holy Sacrifice of the Mass in which the Real Presence of Christ is perpetuated in the Church.

Before World War I, and prior to the development of modern means of rapid global transportation, it was natural that the principal Catholic clergy from whom cardinals might be eligible, should be Europeans, for convenience of assembling in conclave when needed, and for ease of communication with the Pope.

Leo XIII, in creating two American cardinals, McCloskey and Gibbons, and a Canadian, Tachereau, had broken precedent in liberal fashion, particularly as both the United States and Canada were still missionary provinces, largely supported by and under the jurisdiction of the Sacred Congregation of the Propagation of the Faith.

The Boston Cardinal's next dash across the Atlantic for the conclave at the death of a Pope came in 1922, again undertaken suddenly on receipt of a cablegram from the Papal Secretary of State.

The abrupt cabled announcement of the death of Benedict XV on January twenty-second, had caught Cardinal Dougherty of Philadelphia on a winter cruise to Bermuda, and O'Connell with no steamer sailing until the departure of the slow cruise-ship *President Wilson* from New York on January twenty-fourth.

Benedict XV had been ill with pneumonia from January nineteenth, in a day when no penicillin, no anti-biotics had been discovered, when pneumonia for a sixty-seven-year-old man was frequently fatal. He died at six o'clock in the morning of January twenty-second, and on the morning of February second, the conclave was sealed, with fifty-three cardinals present.

It had been a hectic thirty-six hours at Rawson Road and the Granby Street Chancery office, after the news of the Pope's death arrived. John Riedi was packing multiple valises with the Roman street dress of black for a cardinal; with the purple robes of mourning, and the scarlet robes and the great flowing red cappa magna with its ermine, the white-and-gold mitre and crozier that would be needed for the coronation after the conclave. Monsignor Richard L. Haberlin, who was to go as conclavist-secretary to the Cardinal, had all his business as Chancellor to arrange and delegate. Dr. John L. Slattery, superintendent of St. Elizabeth's Hospital, who was a Knight of St. Gregory and would go to complete the Cardinal's official suite, had hospital affairs to arrange and his own packing to do.

With all their frantic dispatch, the *President Wilson* had to be held an hour and a half at the dock in New York to get them aboard on January twenty-fourth. Steamship officials were willing to delay the ship, to accommodate the Cardinal, but powerless to advance the sailing because of the solid booking of tourists for the cruise.

In life nothing escapes change and yet men live through it. By the time Cardinal O'Connell came to dictate his memoirs in 1933,

Time had softened his memories and disappointment of 1922, when he suffered this bitter disappointment.

People in 1922 were not yet generally explaining their emotions by the Russian Pavlov's experiments on reflex conditioning in dogs, nor by Freud's ideas about identification of disagreeable incidents with symbols. Yet it is easy, now, to trace Cardinal O'Connell's identification of a sharp disappointment, necessarily repressed for the sake of dignity, with a symbol as concrete as a railroad train.

It was at the end of two weeks of mounting suspense and tension that the Cardinal in 1922 boarded a train at Naples for Rome, still believing he could reach Rome in time to vote in the conclave.

As he stepped from the train to the platform of the railway station in Rome, he received a shock. A Vatican official, waiting there, announced the election of Achille Ratti as Pius XI, a scant hour earlier, while the Cardinal was still rattling toward Rome in the train. An eye-witness, an American reporter who had met the steamer and ridden in the train with the Cardinal, described the scene.

"It was one o'clock when the train pulled into the Rome station. Wearing his black cassock, bordered with red, Cardinal O'Connell descended from the train. He was smiling, happy that the great race was over. Not a word had he yet heard about the ceremony which had occurred just half an hour previously in St. Peter's Square" (when the new Pius XI gave his blessing, *urbi et orbi* from the portico to the assembled multitude for the first time in fifty-two years).

Then came the stunning news.

Cardinal O'Connell caught his breath. The smile was transformed into the gravity of vain hope. He recovered his composure. He slowly paced the platform. He called the American reporter to him.

"This is a great disappointment. It has happened twice now," he said.

He paced the platform again. Photographers took his picture. He restored the smile. The Vatican prelate asked if he wished to enter the conclave which had not yet adjourned. He was shown to a waiting automobile and driven straight to the Vatican.[8]

It was human enough that O'Connell, after that bitter moment on the railroad platform, should attribute to Cardinal Gasparri a lack of cooperation or courtesy. Gasparri was Camerlengo, charged with arrangements. He might have given earlier warning of the Pope's illness to the American Cardinals; or, possibly, he could have delayed a little the sealing of the conclave.

It was reported after the conclave that on the first ballot, of the fifty-three cardinals present, Gasparri received twenty-four votes, Merry del Val twenty-three. The presence of the two Americans might have given Merry del Val the lead. Instead, on the fourteenth ballot, Achille Ratti, a quiet little man whose life had chiefly been spent buried in dusty research in the libraries, became, literally, second choice for the new Pope.

The first elected was Cardinal Laurenti who received his red hat on the same day with Ratti. Laurenti refused the onerous honor. Only the June before, when Benedict had received Laurenti, Ratti and Tacci, elevated together to the rank of Cardinal, the Pope had prophesied: "There has been a generous distribution of red during the past few days, but soon there will be a distribution of white, and the white robes will surely fall on one of you." As a matter of fact, the choice fell on two of the three, but it was Achille Ratti who would wear the white robes as Pius XI in 1922.

What Cardinal O'Connell did was to ride through the streets of Rome to the Vatican; to knock on the double-locked doors of the conclave quarters in the Vatican palace for admission, still in his traveling costume of black cassock and shovel hat; and to stride past the saluting halberds of the Swiss Guard and bowing prelates and chamberlains.

He had something to say and there was just one man to whom he intended to say it. Gasparri was no coward. As Camerlengo in charge of the conclave, he came punctiliously to greet the infuriated Boston Cardinal.

"When I saw Cardinal Gasparri," said O'Connell a few hours later to a friend, "I did not fail to express my regret that the conclave did not wait until America was represented. As Camerlengo, he replied that he had simply followed the Apostolic Constitution and that the conclave had proceeded strictly according to precedent.

"I told him very frankly and somewhat firmly," added O'Connell, "that I did not feel that his explanation was satisfactory, since it was all a matter of interpretation. A broad interpretation would have permitted us (Cardinal Dougherty and himself) to arrive on time and would have been far more expedient as well as representative."

O'Connell was intimating that as Secretary of State, Gasparri could very well have given the American cardinals a hint a week or so before Benedict's death, that the end appeared near.

O'Connell had been wearing the sacred purple for ten years before Ratti was made a cardinal and named Archbishop of Milan June thirteenth, 1921. Ratti, only eighteen months older than the Boston prelate, had been Nuncio to war-shattered Poland during the three difficult years after World War I. He was a Cardinal but one hundred and fifty days, when the lot fell upon him in the Conclave of February, 1922. Cardinal O'Connell said of him: "Like Leo XIII his luminous mind poured a brilliant light upon the secular problems of our age, and, like Pius X, he brought a new vigor of life to the sanctuary and the schools of the young levites. . . ." [9]

Both Ratti and O'Connell had great veneration for the saintly Pius X, who had given each his promotion, Ratti in 1910 to the Vatican library, and O'Connell in 1911 to the cardinalate. At his election, Ratti said, with emotion, that he should take the name of Pius XI in memory of Pius X who had called him to Rome.

The fret, the tension, the suspense had been in vain. As in 1914, so in 1922, O'Connell had not been present to vote in the conclave.

There was no rancor and a real sense of justice in the new Pope. With all the pressure of his duties and preparations for the coronation, he granted a private interview the very next morning to the Cardinal-Archbishop of Boston, listened to O'Connell's candid statements sympathetically, and promised that he, personally, would change the Apostolic Constitution to ensure future American representation.

The promise was kept. At the first consistory called by Pius XI after his coronation, Cardinal Lucon of Rheims sponsored a proposal to prolong the interval and Pius XI promulgated the present rule by which fifteen days elapse before the opening of a conclave, and the Camerlengo is empowered, in case of need, to extend the interval to eighteen days.

His relations with Cardinal Merry del Val remained warm. When the latter died, February 26, 1930, unexpectedly, following an operation for appendicitis, it made a deep impression on O'Connell. Dr. Elliott Cutler, noted Boston surgeon, later advised the Boston Cardinal to undergo an interim appendectomy. O'Connell absolutely refused.

He would have been glad to know that, in 1953, a tribunal was set up in Rome to conduct an informative process for beatification of Raffaele Merry del Val. With the previous beatification of Pius X, that made the second of O'Connell's close friends to be proposed for the honors of the altar.

CHAPTER TWENTY

MILLIONS AT HAND

Deh: or mi di, quanto tesoro volle Nostro Signore
in prima da San Pietro . . . Certo non chiese se
non: Viemmi dietro.

> Dante: Inferno,
> Canto xix, 1, 90-91, 93

(Tell me now, pray, how much treasure did our Lord
ask of St. Peter? Surely nothing save: Follow Me.)

> Cary, tr.

THERE WERE saints of old who gave up high station, like Bernard of Clairvaux, or stripped themselves of rich inheritance to follow Lady Poverty, like Francis of Assisi.

In our own day Congressional hearings or news items have told of men so dedicated to Communist ideology that they risked high office, or put inherited wealth at the disposal of subversive forces seeking to wreck the country and government under which their capitalistic fortunes had been derived.

The case of William Henry O'Connell was different from either of these categories. He believed thoroughly in the American way and the Constitution of the United States; and labored all his life to give his flock education and inspiration as loyal, patriotic American citizens.

His vocation was not to the contemplative life of the cloister, but to the active, busy, bothered priesthood of the Holy Catholic

Church in the highways and byways of the world. He was not born to great wealth, but knew for the first fifty years of his life the economies of an average working-class family, the privations of small income, the sharing of meagre cash with those more needy.

Thus it was a surprise to him—and a nine days' wonder to Boston—when, in his fifties, he suddenly became a millionaire!

It was the result of a chance encounter in Rome twenty-five years earlier. The theatre magnate Benjamin F. Keith [1] touring Europe, called at the North American College to see about a Papal audience for his devout Catholic wife, Mary Elizabeth. Keith and O'Connell were at once congenial, and O'Connell, seeing the seminary atmosphere interesting to the theatre man, invited Keith to dinner.

Keith, whose theatres were renowned for their rich decoration, looked askance at the bare walls while O'Connell recited the history of the old convent.

"The architecture is very fine," he said, "but the walls and ceiling very bare, white-washed. Proper decoration would make it really beautiful."

William O'Connell never knew how to beg. He was too proud; his was not the Franciscan spirit. In all the years to come, when he met most of the multi-millionaires of America; when other college presidents or Anglican Bishops were frankly tackling the Morgans or George F. Baker or Stephen Harkness or the Rockefellers for surplus millions, William O'Connell would never get into the act. That night in Rome he only answered off-handedly:

"I agree entirely; but I have too many other things to do for the college just now. I am buying a country villa for the students in summer. I can't think of the refectory yet."

"Will you let me think of it?" asked Keith quietly. [2]

The beautiful frescoes of walls and ceiling of the old refectory at Via Dell' Umilta 30 in Rome today were ordered and paid for by the non-Catholic Benjamin F. Keith. After the deaths of Keith and his wife, their only son, Paul Keith, dying in 1918, bequeathed the Keith fortune in equal shares to Harvard University and William Henry O'Connell.

At last his secret daydreams could be made to come true. For all his stalwart build, his imperious, formal manner, William O'Connell had a deep strain of sentiment. He showed it, for instance, toward his native city of Lowell.

"When I was a child in Edison School and was wont to play on the Common, two landmarks of great architectural beauty were constantly before my eyes. One was the jail, which, with its towers and splendid architecture, I thought, modeled after some ancient chateau. . . . The other was the old Livingston mansion.

"It had always been in my mind to do something for my dearly beloved native city. . . . This was made possible far earlier than I expected through the generosity of Paul Keith and his beloved mother. These two landmarks are now Catholic institutions of learning, Keith Academy for boys and Keith Hall for girls. Gratitude is the loveliest flower of the human heart. I was God's instrument . . . through the generosity of the Keiths." [3]

Rome and the influence of Rome continued to occupy the Cardinal's mind. "In the Public Library of Boston we behold the noble exterior lines of a Roman palace," he told the Knights of Columbus at a 1910 banquet, "while its court is a model of that of the Chancery Office of the Roman Church. On another side of Copley Square is a belfry from pinnacle to pavement modeled after the Italian campanile of the Middle Ages. Turning again, we find in Trinity Church a fair representation of the lines and architecture of some of the finest Spanish cathedrals. In the Art Museum, the greatest of its treasures are replicas of Saints . . . and symbols that represent Catholic sentiment." [4]

Although he kept his great plan locked in his own mind for years, from the beginning of his reign as Archbishop, he worked towards its fulfillment. His long walks, trailed by Pio in carriage or automobile, were directed with an eye alert for suitable sites and an ear attuned to whispers of property that might come on the market. By 1909 he was already buying up hilltop sites in Brighton, westerly section of Boston, adjoining Brookline and Newton; and persuading the officers of Catholic institutions to build artistic structures around the nucleus of St. John's Seminary at Lake Street and Commonwealth Avenue.

The Passionists, at St. Gabriel's Monastery, the Jesuits at the new Boston College; St. Elizabeth's Hospital, moved from the South End to the Brighton hill in 1912; the Religious of the Cenacle with their retreat house for women in 1911 were all steps in his program for "getting the Catholic Church in Boston out of the catacombs." In the Back Bay, Boston's fashionable residential section, he acquired a handsome residence at the corner of Bay State Road and Granby Street, overlooking the Charles River, for the Chancery office; and a stately brownstone mansion opposite the Public Garden at Arlington and Beacon streets for the League of Catholic Women.

Very early he had almost betrayed his dream publicly, when at the blessing of the cornerstone of Blessed Sacrament Church in Jamaica Plain, he said:

"We have blessed the foundations of a church . . . which will be another beacon on the hilltop to signal the weary hearts of men toward God and Heaven. . . . Surely Boston ought to be a city of peace and order. On every hilltop now for miles around gleams the sacred sign of our redemption . . . around and about the whole city God has set up his fortresses of sacrifice and prayer." [5]

Speaking to the Italo-American population of Boston's North End in 1916, O'Connell was eloquent on the Catholic heritage summed up in the thought of Rome.

"Go out and say to all: 'I am a Catholic, a Catholic of proud and lovely Italy. Peter died up on the hills of Rome. Paul was beheaded out beyond the gates and from the soil sanctified by their sacred blood, given freely for the faith of Christ, the great Mother Church of Rome arose. . . .

"Dante and Giotto and Raphael and Michelangelo . . . received their loftiest inspirations from the very Faith which we possess. Columbus is ours and Cabot and Vespucci. They, like us, loved the great Madonna Santissima, the great Mother of God . . . whatever you have of civilization you owe to Catholics of Italy. . . . No cheerless, self-satisfied and smug respectability will ever take

the place of the glowing life and love of our Roman inheritance.
. . . The Cross, the Mass, the dear Madonna, the whole sacred
ritual and glorious graphic symbolism of our creed are dear to us
as life." [6]

When the Keith fortune came into his hands, he crowned his
plan by building a Renaissance mansion as Archdiocesan residence
for himself and successors on the Brighton hill near St. John's
Seminary, with the Chancery office at the foot of the hill, and
the mausoleum under his windows.

The Cardinal himself in later years told of his bending Father
Fidelis, C.P., to his plan for "little Rome." Typical of his influence
on other institutions—

"I chose, almost by accident, the site for St. Gabriel's monastery. . . . I happened to be passing by, turned in here and found
on the grounds a rather shattered old mansion which had once been
a beautiful residence. The proprietors had died, or moved away.
As I looked around (on) one of the most beautiful panoramas I
have ever seen . . . the thought flashed to my mind that it would
be wonderful . . . for a religious house dedicated to retreats for
Catholic laymen. . . . Finally the day arrived when we came into
possession of the property. . . . I made up my mind that the house
. . . ought to be conducted by the good Passionist Fathers. It so
happened that Father Fidelis, superior at the time, and Father
Justin came to see me. It seemed like the answer to my prayer.

". . . . There was some hesitation because the idea was a new one.
I think, too, Father Fidelis had in mind another site . . . he came
back in a few days and demurred a little about accepting this site.
In these matters, the Bishop must decide. The decision was made
and accepted. . . . The good Fathers came into possession of the
dilapidated house and the old barn . . . the work grew . . . they
built a special house for retreats. Now they have built this very
beautiful church. I thank God that He has permitted me to see the
crowning of the thought which He . . . pictured in my heart and
soul years ago. I thank God for the good work the Passionist
Fathers have done for my people." [7]

The Seminary was closest of all the many institutions and undertakings of the archdiocese whose problems occupied the Cardinal's mind, year in, year out. There were several reasons for this. The education of priests was basic to continuance of the Holy Sacrifice of the Mass which is the heart of the Church's worship. It was vital to provide ministers for the increasing number of churches and parishes required by the growth of the Catholic population.

There were personal motives, too, for the Cardinal's intense individual participation in the seminary life. From the days of the Americanism trouble, which he had watched as Rector of the American College in Rome, William O'Connell had had a firm opinion that priests for American parishes should be educated by American secular priests or laymen. He felt that men who must labor in the crowded city parishes, where white, black, and children of fifty races were mingled in the pews, and gave support by voluntary contribution, instead of State subsidy, should have priests of their own background.

With complete simplicity, he admitted this interest on a significant occasion. This was the installation of Bishop John B. Peterson at Manchester, New Hampshire, in St. Joseph's Cathedral on July 14, 1932. From 1901 to 1911, Father Peterson had been a professor at St. John's Seminary. From the summer of 1911, when the Sulpician Fathers withdrew, as Rector, he had been the instrument of the Cardinal's ideas for changes in instruction and in discipline, and/or his plans for new building. He had done a magnificent job. This is the tribute that Cardinal O'Connell paid him at his installation:

"When the time came for me to reorganize St. John's Seminary at Boston, it was perfectly clear to me that Father Peterson would carry out my plan of reorganization as devotedly as he had worked in his post of professor. And my judgment was confirmed. Under his direction, and chiefly because he acted faithfully and loyally to my direction—St. John's Seminary became (I do not say it boastfully but as a mere statement of fact) one of the finest seminaries in America. . . . Merit of that kind deserves recognition and it was my duty as well as my privilege . . . to bring it to the attention of those who could adequately reward it. And so my pleasure (in the installation) is not only official, as Metropolitan of this great Province, but personal, in my appreciation of the high character and well-deserved labors of your new bishop." [8]

In the thirty-six years that the Cardinal held to his vision and worked toward his plan, enrollment of candidates for the priesthood of Christ almost trebled, from eighty-six students in 1907 to two hundred and forty-one at the time of his death. These figures do not include the hundreds of vocations to religious Orders and Sisterhoods from the Archdiocese in the same years.

The Cardinal saw construction of new wings of Theology House (1915 and 1925); the decoration of the chapel with stained glass windows and murals (1908); the re-building of Philosophy House, after the fire of 1936, into St. William's Hall; the Library building (1928); the new gymnasium (1937); the new junior seminary, St. Clement's Hall (1940).

In forty years, St. John's Seminary would have but four Rectors, testifying at once to the Cardinal's eye for a good man, and the devotion with which his choices fulfilled the task. They were Monsignors John B. Peterson, 1911-26; Charles A. Finn, 1926-33; Joseph C. Walsh, 1933-38; Edward G. Murray, 1938-51. Monsignor Finn had been a student at the American College during the Cardinal's rectorship; Monsignor Murray, a younger man, had been sent to Rome for his studies by the Cardinal.

Meanwhile, over the years, on the opposite hill in magnificent vista, Boston College had added the Science Building, St. Mary's Hall and the beautiful Bapst Library.

The Cardinal's former residence at Rawson Road had become St. Francis' Friary, a retreat house for laymen, staffed by Franciscans. In the same twenty years, encouragement and support had been given to such splendid installations as the College of the Sacred Heart, begun as an Academy in the South End, moved to the Back Bay and enlarged in 1924—, with purchase of the Loren D. Towle estate on Centre Street, Newton; Regis College for Women, opened by the Sisters of St. Joseph on the Morrison estate in Weston in 1927, whose Science Building, added in 1938, would bear the name of Cardinal O'Connell Hall; Emmanuel College, first Catholic college for women in New England in the building the Sisters of Notre Dame had erected in 1915 in the Fenway, and Notre Dame Academy in the early Chancery building on Granby Street. An echo of the dream, was the Cardinal's gift to St. John's Seminary in 1918 of a villa, recalling Santa Caterina in the Alban Hills, a sixty-acre estate on the shores of Lake Winnepesaukee in New Hampshire, first seminary villa in the United States. He also bought the beautiful Louis K. Liggett estate, in Chestnut Hill, presenting it to Boston College.

Brick and mortar, stone foundations and gilded cross, year by year, the Cardinal saw his "little Rome" change from a dream to a solid reality. He began the work with empty hands, but God had blessed the undertaking. Providentially, the Keith millions had come to him and been dedicated to the dream; fortunately the years of his prime, his *vigor in arduis* had coincided with America's prosperity so that the generous Catholic laity could cooperate with loyal support.

For the Rectors of the Seminary, their post was hard enough when the Cardinal lived at 49 Rawson Road, Brookline, and had his offices at Granby Street in the Back Bay. From 1927, when he moved into the new house at 2101 Commonwealth Avenue, with a lawn and paths that led from his front door to the seminary, there was hardly a day when the Cardinal was in Boston, that he did not drop in at St. John's. One day he might appear in the kitchen, tasting the soup. Another day a slightly tardy professor might find the Cardinal installed in his classroom, holding class in his stead, with a basilisk stare for the belated teacher.

The Keith fortune did not fall into his hands in a lump of solid cash. Because the estate was comprised of theatre holdings, real estate and sound investments, it was nearly fifteen years before the estate was settled. In the end, however, the net cash total received from the bequest by Cardinal O'Connell amounted to a bit more than $2,270,000.

Legal requirements are scrupulously observed by American courts, in the case of such large bequests to institutions. One of the first acts of the executors and legatees, after the will had been filed, was to determine judicially the exact intent of the testator, Paul Keith. We are not here concerned with the provisions affecting Harvard University. The important ruling, for our study, was that the half of the estate left to William Henry O'Connell, had not been bequeathed to the Archbishop of Boston, nor to the Catholic Church.

The bequest was an outright gift to the individual William Henry O'Connell, his to use, or keep, or give away freely, with no strings attached.

He chose to give away every penny of it, for charitable purposes. He even declined to take for himself, and added to the charitable donations, legal fees duly allotted to him by the court in handling the estate from 1923 to 1936, amounting to $29,767.80. That sum of thirty thousand dollars, be it noted, was earned money, earned by long hours of keeping accounts for the court, managing the huge estate, supervising investments that virtually doubled the sum realized for charity. It was money ordered paid to him by the courts, the customary legal fee for such work. The Cardinal tossed the extra thirty thousand into benefactions for the poor and the Church.

Contacts through the years with O'Connell in Rome, Portland, Japan, were necessarily infrequent. After the deaths of Mr. and Mrs. Keith, Paul Keith told the Cardinal that it had been their wish for him to make a bequest ultimately to His Eminence. However, the affair was to be at the discretion of Paul Keith. It was entirely possible that he might marry, have children, form personal desires for the disposition of his wealth. The Cardinal, therefore, was truly surprised when the death of Paul Keith revealed for the first time the large amount of the gift.

Many a working man of America indirectly owed the living for his family to the Cardinal's faith in the American system of enterprise. In 1929, before the stock-market crash and subsequent Depression, Harvard and the Cardinal had just succeeded in getting out of the theatre business. In the six years past, the Cardinal quietly had already distributed, for Church or charity, $1,276,538; yet, on December 31, 1929, he had $1,082,387 in cash on interest in the banks. This was his own money from the Keith bequest, entirely separate from any funds of the Archdiocese.

In 1933, the year of the Bank Holiday, when Franklin D. Roosevelt became President, when pessimists were at their gloomiest over the future of the country, Cardinal O'Connell took his million dollars and invested it in industrial securities. It was a gesture of his faith in the fundamental economic soundness of the United States.

By 1936, industry had turned the corner, and the Cardinal was seventy-five years old. All through the years, he had held fast to his resolution that he would not profit personally by the Keith bequest, and that he, personally, would see that every penny was distributed to charity. In prudence, he knew that thenceforth he would be living on borrowed time, that death could come like a thief in the night, that it was time to close out the Keith estate.

One Spring afternoon in 1936, he said to his secretary, Father J. F. Minihan:

"Jerry, take your pencil."

Many and many a day or night he must have pondered over the problem, because now, in one afternoon, he dictated, without hesitation, the distribution of more than a million dollars. At the end of the year, when the final accounting of his trusteeship was filed with the court, every i dotted and t crossed, he could write "Balance—None," and sign his name.

Some of the benefactions listed in the accounts from 1923 to 1936, will never be revealed. They were individual charities: boys and girls sent through college who today are doing well in their professions or business; struggling artists helped, when it made all the difference to their career; hospital bills paid for needy sufferers. The Cardinal himself concealed the names of such beneficiaries and their prayers of gratitude must be his reward.

One recurring item of expense through the years illustrates how scrupulous was the Cardinal to treat the bequest individually. Included in the estate was the old summer cottage of the Keiths at Marblehead. The Cardinal never had that property transferred to the Archdiocese, to get the benefit of ecclesiastical tax-exemption.

He paid more than forty thousand dollars in real estate taxes to the town of Marblehead during his lifetime, besides maintaining a caretaker there.

There was nothing elegant about the rambling shingled house at Marblehead, although its ocean view was very fine; but the Cardinal loved its seclusion. Revealing is the remark he is reported to have made to Colonel Edward M. House, the Texas friend of President Woodrow Wilson, who summered at nearby Magnolia and often exchanged visits with O'Connell. House was said to have commented one day that the place hardly seemed handsome enough for the residence of a Cardinal.

"Maybe not," said the prelate, "but I like it. A boy named Willy O'Connell would have thought it a palace."

In his *Recollections of Seventy Years,* the Cardinal wrote "the (Keith) legacy has been used entirely and solely for the benefit and welfare of the Archdiocese of Boston." He was writing in 1933, and his words were true at that time. Later, in the final distribution, he included certain institutions not in the Boston archdiocese; but the records bear out that every cent of the Keith money was used either for relief of the needy, or for the benefit of Catholic institutions.

The Cardinal advanced building of his little Rome in Brighton, for instance, by building the beautiful Keith Memorial Chapel of St. Elizabeth's Hospital ($177,000); and $100,000 more to the hospital itself; St. John's Seminary ($300,000); the episcopal residence and Chancery office at Lake Street ($600,000). In Boston's South End, he built the Cathedral High School ($155,000); and the Cathedral rectory.

Incidentally, it should be noted here that, previously, the Cardinal had provided a gymnasium for the students at St. John's Seminary, Brighton; and one for the Working Boys Home in Newton.

Lowell, his birthplace and the site of one of the Keith theatres, received such benefactions as land for a Boys' Camp ($5,000); land for St. Peter's Church, ($1,000); Keith Academy ($361,000); Keith Hall ($28,000); St. Peter's Orphanage ($25,000); Lowell Charitable Bureau ($2,000).

Education of men for the priesthood was ever an all-important cause to the Cardinal. Besides his third of a million to the Boston Seminary of St. John's, he gave to the North American College in Rome in all $60,000; to Catholic University in Washington, D. C., $50,000; to Boston College $50,000 and thousands for scholarships to Georgetown University, and to Xavier College for Negroes.

Protection of helpless or underprivileged children was close to his heart. The Catholic Charitable Bureau of Boston received $100,000 outright in addition to generous annual donations. The House of the Good Shepherd ($25,000); St. Mary's Infant Asylum ($10,000); the Protectory at Lawrence ($10,000); St. Peter's Orphanage in Lowell ($25,000); the Polish Home of the Little Flower ($5,000); Italian Children's Home ($10,000); St. Vincent's Orphanage in Cambridge ($50,000); Sisters of the Blessed Sacrament, for work among Negroes and Indians ($25,000); St. Vincent de Paul Society of Boston ($25,000). With contributions to Charitable Bureaus in various cities of the Archdiocese, a total of $200,000 was allotted for aid to children, in institutions or families.[9]

The Cardinal thought, too, of aged or ailing priests who had given their whole lives to the service of Christ and might come to lonely old age or illness. He gave $100,000 to the Boston Clergy Fund. He remembered, too, the underprivileged of Nassau where he had spent his latter winters. He gave $1,000 for the poor of Nassau; $500 for education of poor children there; and $1,000 to the Leper Colony of the Bahamas.

The above is only a partial list, describing the major buildings or institutions that benefited from the Keith fund. Direct donations to parishes or Charitable Bureaus in the Boston Archdiocese, for instance, totalled $55,650. Relief of the poor in specific places like Italy, Haiti, Louisiana, the South in general mounted up to some $15,000, given as friends in the clergy—like Cardinal de Lai —made him acquainted with the needs. Flood sufferers in 1935 in the mid-West were remembered with $1,000 to the American Red Cross.

A little insight into the Cardinal's own appraisal of personal heroes he admired may be found in the three names he chose for modest donations to monuments or memorials. Two were converts and literary figures—Father John Tabb and Gilbert Chesterton. The third, Leonard Wood, was admired less for military prowess than for his statesman-like governorship of Catholic natives on their emergence from colonialism, in Cuba and the Philippines.

Our Lord once told His disciples a parable of a certain nobleman, about to go into a far country. The prince gave money to each of his servants and bade them take care of it until his return. The servant who laid in a safe place the money confided to him and did nothing about it, was severely reprimanded. But to him who prudently traded until the five talents yielded ten to give his master on his return, were said those beautiful, familiar words: "Well done, thou good and faithful servant." [10]

William O'Connell's handling of the Keith bequest was in that spirit of Our Lord's teaching. The first estimate, in the accounting to the court in 1923, of the Keith bequest, was set at $601,687. When the books were closed, prudent management had resulted in a total of $2,270,000 cash distributed for benefit of Church and charity.

Nor must this be taken for the whole of the monuments that William Cardinal O'Connell left after him. From other donations given him during his life, he had saved the historic Church of St. Clement in Rome from the undermining waters of the Tiber; he had beautified the parish church in Ireland where his parents were married; he had helped restore the seventh-century abbey of Bobbio, Italy, where died that great Irish saint, Columban.

Surely, he merited, at the gate of Heaven, to hear from the Master he had served all his life,

"Well done, thou good and faithful servant."

CHAPTER TWENTY-ONE

MUSIC AND LETTERS

Io mi son un, che quando amor mi spira, noto ed
a quel modo che ditta dentro, vo significando.

Dante: Purgatorio, Canto xxiv, 52-54

> *(I am one who when Love inspires me, take note and go
> setting it forth after the fashion which he
> dictates with me.)*

Okey, tr.

A MAN IN high office, expected to maintain the dignity of the role assigned him, is under constant strain in public.

All public figures need occasional relaxation from this strain. The world knows that Winston Churchill likes to paint pictures; that Dwight D. Eisenhower enjoys a round of golf. Franklin D. Roosevelt and King George V found solace in their stamp collections.

Cardinal O'Connell relieved tension by long daily walks, and found his recreation in books and music. Evenings he played the piano and sang; sometimes, dropping in for tea at the homes of kin or close friends, he would spontaneously sit down to play their piano. As a boy in Lowell he had lessons and, by the time he was sixteen, was proficient at both piano and organ. While a student at Boston College, he filled in as organist and choir director at St. Joseph's Church, Wakefield, in 1880. Curiously, all of

O'Connell's parish experience would be in a church dedicated to St. Joseph, patron of the Universal Church. First in Wakefield, later at St. Joseph's, Medford, and lastly at St. Joseph's in Boston's West End, the Sunday School work was his favorite pastoral labor. At the Boston church, in working with the children's choir, he noted, "It is surprising and disheartening to find how very few English hymns are fit to sing, and how even fewer have music set to them which is worthy at all of the Church." [1]

The thought stayed in the back of his mind for twenty years, and, once settled as Cardinal, he devoted many evening hours to composing a complete series of hymns for Low Mass with English verses and simple melodies suited for children's voices.

In this he undoubtedly had the assistance of Pio De Lucca, who had accompanied him from Rome, first to Portland, and then to Boston as cathedral organist and music director. The first hymns published were copyrighted in De Lucca's name in 1913 and 1914.[2] The collection, published as The Holy Cross Hymnal and "Affectionately dedicated to The Children of the Archdiocese of Boston," made its appearance about 1915, with copyright in the Cardinal's name. Subsequently, so popular was the collection, that in 1924, a publishing firm took it over and, thirty years later, it is still being put out by the Boston firm of McLaughlin and Reilly Company.

Of the twenty-two hymns of the Cardinal's composition, nine have proved enduringly popular. His Hymn to the Blessed Virgin has been made their own by many women's sodalities. The Hymn to the Holy Name is virtually the official hymn of Holy Name Societies of men throughout the United States. The Prayer for a Perfect Life, re-arranged as a solo, is frequently heard at sacred concerts today.

The composition first published, and probably more often sung since than any other of O'Connell's was his setting for the Latin motet *Juravit Dominus* composed in 1882, when the author was twenty-three years old, studying at the American College. It has been sung there, and in the Boston archdiocese ever since. Young Father O'Connell saw it published, in 1892, when he was a curate at St. Joseph's in Boston, with the inscription "To Rt. Rev. D. J. O'Connell—Sung during the First Mass of Priests at the American College, Rome." [3]

It was a rare Friday afternoon in winter that Cardinal O'Connell and his secretary could not be seen at the Boston Symphony Orchestra, sitting in the front row of the right balcony.

This was also the favored acoustic location of his friend the spectacular Mrs. Jack Gardner, whom he had first met in Rome when she was collecting art objects for her fabulous Fenway Palace, opened in 1903 in Boston. The Cardinal, however, paid the regular twelve-dollar price for his seats. Isabella Gardner was reputed, at the auction for the first season in 1900 in the then new Symphony Hall, to have paid $1120 for seats A 15 and 17, right balcony front row! [4]

The Cardinal's young nieces never remembered his coming to the house on a Sunday afternoon, without sitting at the piano and having them sing with him. He brought from France a special songbook for children and was likely to pay them a nickel apiece to learn the words; with a bonus of a dime for any four-syllable word they could pronounce correctly.

Once, at a public affair, a Universalist minister, chatting with the Cardinal who had praised the Gothic architecture of the minister's new church, chanced to mention what a superb organ the church possessed. The Cardinal's eager interest was so apparent, that the minister generously made an appointment to come with the key on some weekday and let the Cardinal try the organ.

It was a deep, dark secret for some time that the organist whom passers-by heard practising on the organ of the beautiful stone church at Boylston and Ipswich Streets in Boston's Back Bay was, in truth, a Cardinal of the Roman Catholic Church.

Eventually, in 1935, when the depression had hard hit the congregation of the Universalist Church of the Redemption, the Cardinal took it off their hands. It had cost $750,000 when erected in 1926. After remodeling the interior and installing a beautiful altar, the Cardinal dedicated it on December 8, 1935, re-christening it in honor of his titular church of San Clemente in Rome.

After his death, it was made the Eucharistic Shrine of St. Clement's, with the Franciscan Missionaries of Mary maintaining perpetual adoration before the Blessed Sacrament. Today a white-clad nun directs the chant of the Sisters and plays the organ that once was played by the Cardinal of Boston.[5]

Cardinal O'Connell had a well-pitched, though not professionally trained voice, and one of his relaxations was to sing operatic arias, to his own piano accompaniment. The artist Jacob Binder in 1924 was commissioned to paint a portrait of Leo Kolb, of Washington, D. C., who was visiting at the Rawson Road residence. One morning at a sitting, the artist found the Cardinal at home. While Mr. Kolb held the pose and the artist worked at his easel, the Cardinal sat down, running his fingers over the keys, and began to sing the aria, "My Heart at Thy Sweet Voice" from Samson and Delilah.[6]

"Suddenly he looked at me. I had stopped painting, my brush in the air and tears were in my eyes from the emotion pouring through the music," recalled Binder.[7]

The Cardinal chuckled.

"Well, if my singing keeps you from painting, I had better stop," he said, and left the artist and subject alone in the room.

It was William Allen White, the Hoosier philosopher-editor whose Emporia Gazette was nationally known for many years, who told another anecdote. He and Cardinal O'Connell were fellow-passengers on the *Vulcania* in 1933. The Cardinal generally kept to his own suite at sea, but on the morning they were to dock, he came into a deserted salon and found White playing, on the piano, the Pilgrim's Chorus from Tannhauser. The Cardinal sat down and listened, to White's gratification, until the piece was ended.

"Beautiful music, isn't it?" said the Cardinal to White. "This is the way I like to play it."

And he sat down and played it in his own style while White listened.[8]

Hearers differed as to whether the Cardinal's voice was baritone or tenor. He cultivated its pitch by listening to records of great operatic singers and, to the end of his life, it remained "still warm and firm in spite of his eighty years (as) he sings at the end (of solemn high mass at the cathedral) *Sit Nomen Domini Benedictum. . . . Adjutorium nostri in nomine domini. . . . Benedicat vos omnipotens Deus Pater et Filus et Spiritus Sanctus.*" [9] Less than a month before his death, in April, 1944, at the last Sunday at which he pontificated in the cathedral, those present marveled at the bell-like timbre of his voice in that last benediction.

Fiction in literature is a pleasant and often a powerful medium, but sometimes it pre-empts in human minds the more drab and prosaic fact. Five years after the death of William Cardinal O'Connell appeared a novel entitled *The Cardinal,* written by a former Bostonian, Henry Morton Robinson, with its scenes laid in Boston, New England and Rome. The book rapidly became a best-seller.

Like all gifted novelists, the author used, in some cases, true incidents, and historic happenings, although attributed to fictional characters and deftly transposed from actuality. It was, perhaps, inevitable, that Bostonians reading about a locale familiar to them, and still under the vivid recollection of the personality of the man who had been for them so many years THE Cardinal, should have tended to attempt identification of actual personalities with the fictional characters.

One motif, skillfully interwoven in the novel as a thread in the promotion of an obscure young priest to the ultimate rank of Cardinal, was translation from the Italian of a spiritual work by an influential Vatican Secretary of State.

It is well, then, to set the record straight on the translation made and published by Cardinal O'Connell of *The Passion of Our Lord,* by Cardinal de Lai. It should be made clear that in this translation there was no self-seeking, no influence on his career.

The Italian work was published at Rome in 1921, when Cardinal O'Connell had already held for ten years the highest rank to which he might aspire, short of being elected Pope. In that connection, to single out one of the seventy Princes of the Church for the compliment of translating his book, would hardly be a politic way of courting the votes of others in a future conclave.

Cardinal O'Connell himself recorded how he came to translate his friend's spiritual book. One of his well-known habits—a headache to John Riedi and any secretary who had to pack for his journeys—was insistence on a large valise stuffed with books to read. In the hurried preparations for sailing on the *President Wilson* in 1922, when word came of the death of Benedict XV, one of the volumes tossed into the valise (probably with the thought of refreshing the Cardinal's Italian for his stay in Rome) was Cardinal de Lai's book, received some months earlier.

It was not until the return voyage, that Cardinal O'Connell picked up *The Passion of Our Lord* and, Lent having begun, approached it meditatively as spiritual reading. This the book is, of the highest order, with a fresh approach, devoid of sentimentality and yet the more powerful for its stark and historical narrative.

"We had no book just like this in English," wrote the Cardinal a year later. "Then came the decision to translate it." [10]

Thirty years after the translation was first published, men who had been at Chancery in Boston in 1922 and 1923 remembered seeing the Cardinal seated in his study, dictating the translation at sight to a secretary, with frank tears rolling down his cheeks at the most moving passages. Three decades after its first publication, the book was still selling each year to a generation that had not known Cardinal O'Connell.

The work of dictating the translation was done in odd hours, between Archdiocesan affairs, between correspondence with President Harding on important national affairs, between conferences with the American hierarchy of which O'Connell was dean, since the death of Cardinal Gibbons; between consultations with the trustees of Catholic University, of St. John's Seminary, or with lawyers engrossed in settling the Keith estate.

Considering the pressure under which Cardinal O'Connell labored, the translation was a *tour-de-force* and a work that could only have been accomplished by the driving power of a genuine spiritual emotion that gripped him.

Once completed, the Cardinal directed that *The Pilot* put it on sale at the nominal price of one dollar, in order that no Catholic in the Archdiocese should be too poor to buy it. For his personal books, like the collection of his *Letters* in 1915, or *Recollections of Seventy Years* in 1934, the Cardinal was willing that a professional publishing firm should make a profit and pay him royalties. For *The Passion of Our Lord,* he wanted no profit and the credit to go to the original author, Gaetano Cardinal de Lai.

These are the facts. Let the brilliant fictional version remain with the novelists.

The Cardinal also turned his hand to autobiography and memoirs on occasion. Thus in 1915, he allowed a leading Boston publishing firm to bring out a volume of his letters,[11] covering the years as seminarian, parish curate and rector in Rome. Again, for the Jubilee of his ordination, the same firm published his memories of seven decades.[12] In 1926, for the quarter-century mark in his episcopate, the Cardinal had produced a thirty-page essay in a paper pamphlet. Then, too, there are the eleven volumes of Sermons and Addresses of the Cardinal, covering a span of years from the early eighteen-nineties up to 1938.[13]

His last publications included the privately printed slim volume, "A Memorable Voyage," with illustrations, describing the Conclave of 1939; and "A Tribute of Affectionate Memory," published in 1940.

This last was a forty-eight page tribute to his predecessor, Archbishop Williams, and the Cardinal prefaced it with a quotation from the New England poet, William Cullen Bryant (1794-1878), whose *Thanatopsis* he had learned by heart in boyhood. "It was to me like the discovery of a new world in which my imagination revelled with delight." [14] Now, at eighty-one, he chose the lines from "A Walk at Sunset."

> And while the wood-thrush pipes his evening lay,
> Give me one lonely hour to hymn the setting day.

His own reading taste was omnivorous. Boston Public Library's staff was accustomed to send up a basket weekly to the Cardinal's residence, chiefly of works of history, biography or current topics.

Some the Cardinal only skimmed, but from all he gleaned some observation or quotation.

"I look about me now, here in my library," he said, "and I see arrayed, row upon row on the shelves, some of the closest friends I have ever known . . . Plato, Marcus Aurelius and Omar Khayyam with their pages of pagan philosophy, Saint Augustine and Saint Bernard and Saint Thomas, giants of Christian thought . . . my dear old Italian friend, the immortal Florentine, who saw with poetic eye the visions of Hell, Purgatory and Heaven itself. . . . The moment a task is done, I have a book in my hand." [15]

It is in memory of the Cardinal's devotion that the Italian epic of Dante has been scanned to furnish chapter headings of this book. To see Dante's lines thus illustrating various phases of his own life would have pleased Cardinal O'Connell.

The Cardinal, from his seminary days in Rome, had great admiration for the Italian school of painting. During his years as Rector, he made many excursions to various Italian cities to view the works of art. Venice he visited often and an incident in Boston in 1930 brought back to his mind the story of Paolo Cagliari, called Veronese, who was had up before the Holy Office of the Inquisition in Venice in 1573 to justify his artistic license.

Veronese had been employed to re-decorate the refectory of the convent of SS John and Paul (S. Zanipolo in Venetian dialect) burned by German invading troops after using it as a barracks. Frater Andrew Buono commissioned Veronese to paint a mural forty feet by twenty feet of the Last Supper. However, the artist's imagination ran away with his judgment. The central panel showed Christ at table with the twelve Apostles, but to fill the immense canvas, Veronese began adding all kinds of superbly drawn characters from the street scenes of Venice. There are turbaned Turks, fashionable Venetian nobles, quaint Negro dwarfs in livery; beggars, a paunchy Fifteenth Century politician, and even a couple of the hated German soldiers, shown snitching viands and drink in a corner. The last straw, for the affronted monks, apparently, was Veronese's idea of putting a very life-like hunting dog at the feet of Christ, in front of the table.

Veronese had to think fast, when summoned before the dread Holy Office on July 28, 1573 and asked what kind of a Last Supper he thought he had painted.

"It is a picture of the Last Supper," he began, haltingly, and then, with a burst of inspiration, "the last supper of which Jesus Christ partook with his apostles in the house of Simeon, the Pharisee."

"What do those figures armed like Germans with pikes signify?" sternly asked an Inquisitor.

"I need to say a few words to explain," stammered Veronese.

"Say them, then."

"We painters take liberties, the same way poets and lunatics do," apologized Veronese. "I did those two halberdiers, one eating and one drinking . . . because it seemed to me that the owner of the house, being a rich, important person should have such men in his service. . . . I only follow what my masters did. . . . Michaelangelo at Rome in the Pontifical Chapel painted Our Lord and St. Peter and St. John and they are all naked." [16]

This last point saved Veronese's bacon; no one cared to question the taste in art of the Holy Father. They let Veronese change the title of his painting to La Cena in Casa Levi, and today it can be seen, so titled, in the Accademia di Belle Arti in Venice, where William O'Connell, too, saw it fifty years ago.

The Boston version of the Inquisition came about when the Parker Hill Branch of the Boston Public Library was built on Mission Hill. It is one of the Gothic masterpieces of the noted architect Ralph Adams Cram, who had carved above the entrance the seals of the City of Boston and of the Trustees of the Boston Public Library.

Promptly a worthy priest, raising his eyes heavenward, discovered "two naked little boys" carved on the façade, and wrote a letter to the trustees demanding that the indecent carving be removed. The trustees referred the letter to Cardinal O'Connell.

The Cardinal investigated and learned that the seal in question had been designed by the great sculptor Augustus St. Gaudens, in the antique style. The background shows in graceful foliage, the

Tree of Knowledge. In the centre is a pylon holding, like a lectern, an open book and, on either side, stand two male figures holding aloft torches of Learning, all very symbolic, and appropriate for a library, and artistic in design.

For his next afternoon stroll, the Cardinal had Pio drive him to the neighborhood and was fortunate enough to spy the protesting priest reading his breviary in the sunshine. It was a simple matter for the suave Cardinal to invite Father to stroll with him; to discover the new building and to provoke an outburst about the little naked boys. The portly prelate propped his cane and leaned back to see with his own eyes.

"Admirable, Father," he said cheerfully. "How artistic. Does it not remind you of the classic sculpture in the Vatican?"

"But they have no drapes, not even a fig-leaf," objected the old priest.

"Exactly, exactly," returned the Cardinal. "Probably that is why they remind me of the Vatican. So like the undraped figures by Michaelangelo in the Sistine Chapel. Of course you remember, Father. Didn't you make the Holy Year pilgrimage in 1925?"

That settled the question. No more was heard about the unbreeched boys, and the Mayor of Boston at the next vacancy, invited Cardinal O'Connell to become one of five trustees of the Boston Public Library, which post he held from 1932 until his failing sight in 1936 necessitated his resignation. "As I make my fortnightly visits (for trustees' meetings) to the great library," he wrote, "I rarely fail to go into the children's room and look up at the ceiling to behold the racing centuries of Jack Elliott and the fine figure of Maud Howe; and instantly I am back in the great barn-like loft of the Torlonia Palace, watching Jack Elliott painting either the heads or the tails of the dashing equines still racing in their mad course around the ceiling of the children's room. Then I go slowly up the grand staircase and pass the ethereal and restful frescoes of Puvis de Chavannes, and the contrast is, to say the least, striking, although no doubt the works of both artists have undoubted merit." [17]

The Cardinal could remember dropping in for tea on a Sunday

afternoon in Rome of 1898, at the Elliotts' to join there the president of Radcliffe College, Mrs. Louis Agassiz, and the headmaster of Groton School, Reverend Endicott Peabody. Mrs. Agassiz' sister, a convert to the Catholic Church, had been buried, by permission of the Cardinal, in 1918 from the Cenacle Convent he had established in Brighton.[18]

Though she was beautiful, the Cardinal would not have liked Maud Elliott had she been a chatter-box or had she used cosmetics. The Cardinal's ideas on women's dress and decor had never changed from the day when his mother and her friends did not apply powder to their noses and plain black silk was their "best dress."

In newspaper interviews, sermons and speeches to the League of Catholic Women, the Cardinal frequently fulminated against low-necked and short-skirted gowns, and paint and powder. He went so far as to intimate that women wearing lipstick should not be admitted to the altar-rail for Holy Communion.[19] When someone protested that this was pretty sweeping, in view of the common use of lipstick, the Cardinal thought of an unanswerable excuse.

"There is danger of staining the expensive vestments and fine linens of the sanctuary," he answered.

At the reception in Washington honoring the Cardinal's Golden Jubilee, a lady of high society drew a very pointed rebuke. She approached, her figure moulded into a silver lame gown of extreme decolletage, her hair elaborately coiffured and her face a work of art to do credit to a Turner. She caught the Cardinal's eye on her gown, with his best snapping-turtle expression, and gabbled quickly:

"You must pardon me, Your Eminence, for wearing *silver* to your *golden* Jubilee; but we've all been going through a depression, you know."

"I see you have plenty of brass left, anyway," said the Cardinal.

CHAPTER TWENTY-TWO

PROGRESS BETWEEN WARS

Onde convenne legge per fren porre;
convenne rege aver, che discernesse
della vera cittade almen la torre.

Dante: Purgatorio, Canto xvi, 1, 94-97

> *(Wherefore 'twas needful to put law as a curb,*
> *needful to have a ruler who might discern*
> *at least the tower of the true city.)*

Okey, tr.

HISTORY EXEMPLIFIES that the wielder of authority may be tyrannical, or timid. He may dissipate power by excessive personal supervision of details; or he may abdicate his responsibility by delegating it too loosely. The ideal leader is he who inspires devotion to a common ideal, chooses subordinates dedicated to that ideal, and, while requiring stewardship, yet gives rein to initiative.

The test of William O'Connell's leadership is found in the great growth of the faith, of Catholic institutions, of prudent administration of the Church's affairs over the thirty-seven years of his rule as Archbishop of Boston.

From three-quarters of a million souls in 1907, the Catholic population of the Archdiocese increased to a million and a quarter, approximately, at his death. This despite two World Wars and the stringent restriction of immigration which, in Archbishop Williams' time, had been so heavy from Catholic countries of Europe. Parishes, divided from old ones or newly created, increased from 194 to 322; the number of priests almost tripled, from six hundred to more than fifteen hundred; with admissions to the diocesan seminary similarly tripled. More than twenty new religious congregations established communities in the Archdiocese under the Cardinal's patronage; diocesan elementary schools were doubled and high schools tripled, taught by some three thousand dedicated religious Sisters or Brothers.[1]

Converts to the Catholic faith, from all walks of society, became so numerous that the Cardinal instituted the custom of adult Confirmation at the cathedral, with as many as seventeen hundred in a year being included.

In his first three decades in office, the Cardinal carried to virtual completion, with establishment of the Archdiocesan building and oratory dedicated to St. Thomas More, at 49 Franklin Street in downtown Boston, the re-organization of archdiocesan affairs and charities, housed in appropriate structures and locations.

"I have worked hard for sixty years. It never hurt me," he said tersely.[2]

A few among the men whose talent and great spirit the Cardinal first perceived, later crowned with recognition by Rome, may be mentioned. John B. Peterson, selected as first rector of St. John's Seminary under O'Connell, ended as Bishop of Manchester, N. H. A youth from Whitman, whom the then Archbishop O'Connell in 1911 sent as a seminarian to the North American College in Rome, became his own Auxiliary in 1932, and, in 1946, after the Cardinal's death, is known to the nation as Francis Cardinal Spellman, Archbishop of New York. Richard J. Cushing, educated at St. John's Seminary, ordained in 1921, archdiocesan director of the Propagation of the Faith for many years, on June 29, 1939 was consecrated by the Cardinal as his Auxiliary Bishop and, on the Cardinal's death was named Archbishop of Boston. The Cardinal did not live to see five other priests of his Archdiocese consecrated as Bishops by 1950. They were the late Bishop Louis

Kelleher, and the late Bishop Thomas F. Markham; Most Reverend Edward Ryan, Bishop of Burlington; Most Reverend Eric F. MacKenzie, D.D., Auxiliary Bishop of Boston; and Most Reverend John Wright, D.D., Auxiliary Bishop of Boston, 1947-1950; Bishop of the new Diocese of Worcester from 1950. Also, in September, 1954, another native of the Archdiocese was consecrated Auxiliary Bishop, Most Reverend Jeremiah F. Minihan, D.D.

In the wide field of the missions, O'Connell had taken a zealous interest. In 1908 he was the keynote speaker at the first Catholic Missionary Congress in Chicago and in 1913 welcomed its second by invitation in Boston. Clerics from all over the United States, Canada, Mexico, Puerto Rico and the Philippines took part in the mission rallies held in seventy-five churches of the Archdiocese of Boston on the Sunday when the Cardinal preached in the Cathedral of the Holy Cross.

"No narrow horizon hems in our outlook," he said. "The Negro and the Indian at our own doors; the Catholic families in out-of-the-way communities, struggling against odds to keep the light of faith burning; the Filipino to whom we owe a generous and watchful interest; the multitudinous Orient, the isles of the sea, the burning heart of Africa, the ice-ribbed circle of the North—there is no field where the children of men sit in darkness and spiritual hunger that is foreign to the deliberations and purposes of this Congress of men of God." [3]

He reported that the Archdiocese of Boston in the past year had contributed $123,000 to the Society for the Propagation of the Faith (then, as from its foundation in 1822, at Lyons, France) and paid tribute to the $11,000,000 it had sent to America in the early days.

"With justifiable pride, I may say, too," he remarked, "that the new Seminary for Foreign Missions which is to train youth for 'fields afar' is largely a development of the mission spirit that has grown up in Boston with the spread of interest in the work of the propagation of the faith." [4]

In 1913, today's widely known Maryknoll was indeed new and the names of its pioneers, Fathers James Anthony Walsh and

Thomas Frederick Price too familiar to his audience to need mention. O'Connell himself, from his first coming to Boston, had been sympathetic to the hopes of the young Boston priest-editor of *The Field Afar*. Apparently, only the financial and administrative burden of re-organizing St. John's Seminary with archdiocesan clergy, enjoined on O'Connell in 1909 by Pius X, had prevented the foundation of Maryknoll in the Boston Archdiocese. This is indicated in a letter from James Anthony Walsh to Father Price. The latter, be it remembered, had been a classmate of William O'Connell at St. Charles' College in the 1870's. The Cardinal, in his memoirs, devoted several pages to a vivid account of Price's experience in shipwreck on a voyage from his home in North Carolina to enter St. Charles'. The youth had escaped drowning by the providential drifting by of a plank, linked in his mind with a vision of the Blessed Virgin. "I wish I could properly describe Price's own narrative of this miraculous intervention," wrote the Cardinal. "I stood as if rooted to the spot, gazing with awe at one to whom Heaven itself had given such a wonderful sign of predilection and protection . . . in after years, when he came to me, as Archbishop of Boston, for counsel and aid in founding with Father James Anthony Walsh, the Society of American Missions *(sic)*, I recognized in him the saintliness of his youth." [5] The archives of Maryknoll bear out O'Connell's original desire to underwrite foundation of the new missionary society, and its frustration. Six months before permission of the hierarchy had been obtained and definite plans begun at the meeting of the archbishops in Washington, April 27, 1911, James Anthony Walsh was writing to Father Price:

"Shortly after Archbishop O'Connell became Coadjutor, I had occasion to tell him the condition of our work; and when I added that I looked forward to a Foreign Mission Seminary as the logical outcome of this work, he commended the idea suddenly and warmly and implied that I had hit on his own plan. On this occasion, Cardinal O'Connell stated that if he were in full power, he would at once convert the house of philosophy into a Foreign Mission Seminary and place me in charge. . . .

"Since His Grace has come into power, he has not alluded to the conversation in question. Twice, however, he has suggested that I look forward to a visit to the Far East so as to make personal observations on the needs and opportunities.

"I brought up the subject of the Seminary again, once, to His Grace in the Summer of 1909 and while he admitted that such an institution might come soon, he did not appear at the time especially interested. It would not have surprised me at any time, however, in the past year, if His Grace had told me to start a Foreign Mission Seminary. He has a wide view of the Catholic Church and if other important matters were not pressing him and his attention happened to be centered on this need, I believe that he would act with his customary vigor." [6]

It is obvious, from Father Walsh's letter that he understood the pressing indebtedness of archdiocesan institutions inherited by O'Connell when he succeeded to the See in 1907. It might be inferred, from the reference to "the Summer of 1909" that O'Connell may have told him, confidentially, on his return from Rome, of the new plans for St. John's Seminary, made public in 1911. These plans, enjoined by Pius X and urged by Cardinal Satolli in June of 1909, would have made O'Connell's original idea of using the house of philosophy as cradle of the new Mission Society not feasible.

However, the Cardinal remained a warm sympathizer with the plan; contributed financially to it; and granted an *exeat* to one of his ablest priests, Father Walsh, to let him become, with Father Price, co-founder of the first community in the United States of priests dedicated to the Foreign Missions.

Early in April, 1910, a paragraph in the back pages of *The Field Afar* asked for someone to translate, as a labor of love, a book on the missions in Italian, *Operarii Autem Pauci*. Only two offers were received; one from a schoolteacher in San Francisco. The offer accepted was that of a young priest, graduate of the North American College in Rome, stationed at St. Paul's in Cambridge. When the translation was completed and forwarded for Imprimatur, the

Cardinal chuckled and sent word for young Father Joseph F. McGlinchey to call at Chancery.

"I am appointing you to succeed Father Walsh as Director of Propagation of the Faith," said the Cardinal to the amazed priest, only four years ordained.

Zeal and the sincere desire to serve was what the Cardinal was looking for, and he knew devices for finding it out. Father Mc-Glinchey would direct Propagation of the Faith for seventeen years, until the Cardinal promoted him to be pastor of St. Mary's Church in Lynn, replacing him with another zealous young priest, Father Richard J. Cushing.

Although his own talents were in the administrative field, and his life from 1895 spent behind a desk, dealing with paperwork, the Cardinal had a deep sense of the commission of Christ: "Go ye into all the world, preaching and baptizing." In the first year as Archbishop, he had told the Catholic Missionary Congress of November, 1908 in Chicago: "The providential hour of opportunity has struck. . . . All indications point to our vocation as a great missionary nation." [7]

He recognized that great areas in the United States needed the preaching of the gospel of Christ, too. In inviting the Church Extension Society, founded by the future Francis C. Kelley, Bishop of Oklahoma, to hold its second missionary congress in Boston in 1913, Cardinal O'Connell was in accordance with the Holy Father.

Cardinal O'Connell was one of the first backers of the original director of the Church Extension Society, Father Francis Clement Kelley, at a time when many of the American Hierarchy, particularly Archbishops John Ireland and John J. Keane were dubious about the work.

"It is no tardy act of justice to say here that Cardinal O'Connell broke the Eastern ice for us," wrote Bishop Francis Clement Kelley of Oklahoma in 1939.[8] "I shall never forget the opening session of that Congress when, before a packed auditorium, the Cardinal half-turned to Archbishop (James E.) Quigley and said with slow and meaning emphasis on every word 'Chicago and Boston understand each other.' The two Archbishops met for the first time at that Congress. It was as if the Cardinal said 'The East understands the West.' "

It was, also, a sign of a new outlook in the American Church. The days when the viewpoint of Cardinal Gibbons, John Ireland, John Keane, Denis O'Connell had dominated were past. The elder generation was approaching its sunset and the new one, trained in Rome to a universal, world-wide sweep of thought, coming up.

Hanna in San Francisco and O'Connell in Boston could bridge the continent with a campaign for Christ on a Ford truck. O'Connell would back both James Anthony Walsh for Foreign Missions and Francis Clement Kelley for Home Missions. There was nothing parochial about O'Connell's vision.

For a man whose critics liked to accuse him of being a conservative, Cardinal O'Connell made some rather striking innovations in his day. Certainly never before had a Prince of the Church spoken on Boston Common, in the shadow of Bulfinch's gold-domed State House, and under the white steeple of Brimstone Corner, on the very soil where once the Puritans had whipped Quaker women, near the site of the old Town Jail where Cotton Mather decided a poor Irish woman was in league with the Devil because she knew her *Pater Noster* in Latin!

Yet William Cardinal O'Connell, on Sunday, August eighteenth, 1918, stood there to welcome back the Caravan of Christ he had blessed on July first, 1917, beside Holy Cross Cathedral, and sent on its mission across the continent to his old fellow-seminarian in Rome, Archbishop Edward J. Hanna of San Francisco.

It was the first time in the United States, perhaps in the world, that the new machine, the automobile, had been blessed as a means of bringing the gospel to the man in the street.

The idea originated with two zealous converts who found their way to Christ's Church through endeavors in Socialism to improve a sorry world. Mrs. Martha Moore Avery came of old Yankee stock; David Goldstein was Jewish. They met in the Socialist Party of Massachusetts; they encountered and battled Communism in its ranks; and they both found in the Catholic Church the ideal of social justice and the salvation of the individual.

Burning with zeal, they desired to adapt the soap-box techniques of the Socialists to campaigning for Christ. They broached their plan to Cardinal O'Connell at Granby Street.

"It's striking," said the Cardinal, frowning a moment. "But it's thoroughly American. I don't know but that it is all right." [9]

The auto-van, painted yellow-and-white in the Papal colors, was built on a Ford chassis, and opened to provide a pulpit, under a crucifix, with an American flag at one side. Mrs. Moore Avery and Goldstein spoke at open-air meetings in all the Massachusetts towns and cities. They, and their helpers, formed the Catholic Truth Guild, its motto, suggested by Cardinal O'Connell: "For Faith and Fatherland."

Thousands heard the clear presentation of Christian doctrine; asked questions, took home the pamphlets with which the van was stocked. Some called the auto-van "Rome's Chariot" but the Catholics styled it "the Cardinal's car."

Goldstein and Arthur S. Corbett manned the auto-van on the trans-continental campaign, four months in California and four months on the route back to Boston, with thirteen thousand miles logged. The enthusiastic Knights of Columbus in California bought a new chassis with eight-cylinder engine as their contribution for the return journey. Perhaps the crowd at the home-coming reception on Boston Common was disappointed that the Cardinal did not wear his flowing red robes and biretta. Nevertheless his was a tall and impressive figure in clerical black, with touch of red at the throat, as he mounted the travelling pulpit to say:

"What a wonderful journey you have made, the first of its kind, perhaps, in the history of the world. . . . You have scattered a sacred seed all along that glorious path, of the love of religion and the love of America. . . . The track you have traced from the old settlement of the sons of St. Francis to Boston will be a sacred bond which binds us all stronger to our holy Church and our beloved country." [10]

In the saintly Pope Pius X, many men of his day found inspiration. It is not surprising, then, to find that Cardinal O'Connell in his addresses and pastoral letters anticipated the subjects of

encyclicals issued by the learned librarian Achille Ratti after his
election as Pius XI. It would be 1922 before Pius XI commended
to the clergy and the faithful the practice of Retreats and the
Spiritual Exercises of St. Ignatius Loyola. O'Connell, a dozen years
earlier had invited the Passionist Fathers and the Religious of the
Cenacle to the archdiocese and aided them in building Retreat
houses in Boston.

Following the lead of Pius X, O'Connell, as Archbishop, delivered to his flock a pastoral letter on Modernism, the heresy
which he defined as the spirit of rationalism in religion. In so far
as the movement affected Catholics, it was chiefly felt in Europe;
but O'Connell perceived the insidious error in a hard and doubting
spirit by which Christ would be shorn of His Divinity and authoritative teaching deemed restraint of liberty of thought. Prophetically,
in 1907 O'Connell warned that any danger to the Faith is of
world-wide influence. He lived to see the globe encompassed by
two World Wars. He recognized the coming of the sway of science
and technology and did not despise the true progress of which our
modern age may legitimately boast, but he pointed out:

"There is a superstitious Reason as well as a superstitious Faith.
. . . Both sin by excess, but neither is the true fruit of that reasonable Faith which is the highest faculty of man's intellect.

"Thousands, who would resent the thought of submitting to the
teachings of the Church, of Jesus Christ, are ready to follow
blindly a leader whose watchword is science. The charlatan of
yesterday becomes the oracle of today if he base his vain pretensions on something that appeals to intellectual pride.

"The non-Catholic universities of this country are pervaded by
a philosophy akin to that which is at the root of the Modernist
errors. Scientific and historic literature are impregnated with it
. . . show a manifest eagerness to glorify any movement set afoot
by erratic scholars which aims to weaken in the popular mind
the strength of historic and traditional Christianity." [11]

So said O'Connell, the watchman. He would not have been
surprised, forty years later, to see an awakened nation holding

Federal inquiries in Boston into the Communist allegiance of university and high school teachers. He suspected the subversive attack on the minds of youth when it was only a worm in the bud. But that was because he thought with the mind of the Church, had been trained in the lore of her centuries-old experience. The Shepherds of the Church, Leo XIII and Pius X saw these things, wrote them in their encyclicals. O'Connell's courage to say them openly for all to hear, simply for all to understand, constantly to warn his fellow-citizens—that courage was his own.

"The atmosphere of the age is impregnated with unbelief," he warned. "The very prosperity of the age is producing moral weakness. . . . Keep your minds free from error by acts of faith in God. . . . Keep your hearts free from sin . . . by the purity of unspotted lives, the honesty of unsoiled hands." [12]

Catholic education was another objective for which both the Boston Cardinal and the eleventh Pope Pius drew inspiration from Pius X. One of the first Apostolic Letters of Pius XI, *Quandoquidem* [13] exhorted bishops to take charge of their diocesan seminaries. O'Connell, after direct consultation with Pius X at Rome, had done so in 1911 in his own See.

O'Connell from the beginning had encouraged and aided his alma mater, Boston College. Under his patronage Emmanuel College, the first local Catholic college for women would be opened in Boston by the Sisters of Notre Dame; the Religious of the Sacred Heart would found the College of the Sacred Heart in Newton and the Sisters of St. Joseph would open Regis College with its magnificent campus in Weston. Parochial schools and high schools were multiplied also.

The Cardinal had long been putting into practice the principles uttered by Pius XI in the constitution *Deus Scientiarum Dominus,*[14] reorganizing Catholic universities.

"We are living through a very critical era. . . . For some centuries now there has been developing outside the Church, a corrosive, critical, skeptical spirit . . . which . . . began by repudiating revealed Religion. . . . More recently it has attacked Morality, denouncing all our inherited moral notions as a code of outworn taboos, ridiculing the very notion of sin. . . . Having tried to strip man of his true grandeur potentially as a child of God. . . . Modern Thought in our own day . . . tries to rob even the natural man of all right to respect. Man is reduced . . . to an animal or a machine, a slave of necessity . . . a puppet driven hither and thither. . . .

"To my mind, one of its (the university's) greatest duties today is to oppose a bulwark against the disintegrating and destructive tendencies running riot in the intellectual world and in individual and social life." [15]

The Cardinal so strongly felt the function and need of the Catholic University that, in addition to serving as a trustee through the years, at his death he left it a bequest of fifty thousand dollars from the funds at his disposal.

On the same occasion of his Golden Jubilee in the priesthood, addressing the Bishops of America, assembled to honor him at Washington, he reiterated:

"We can never be too grateful to God for the privilege of laboring for him in a country which . . . has never denied Him . . . and where, thank God, the Catholic priest and the Catholic bishop are honored and respected by the whole people. . . . Americans, whatever their creed . . . acknowledge the power for good exerted in and out of season by the Catholic priests and Bishops, who, abstaining from any meddling interference in the political world, being . . . outside and above all parties, love their country with an absolutely unselfish love. . . . I am proud beyond words of being one with you in labor, devotion and love. . . . United by faith to the See of Peter in all things spiritual, we are united in devotion to the cause of Christ and the welfare of America and the peace of the world." [16]

If Pius XI will be always remembered and cited for his great encyclical *Quadragesimo Anno,* on the social and industrial problems of the period between World Wars I and II, Americans should recall Cardinal O'Connell's Pastoral Letter of 1921, when Achille Ratti was still Archbishop of Milan. It was written in response to the frequent questions and discussions of Protestant clergymen of

Boston, to set forth the Catholic position on ideals in industrial relations.[17]

"The existence of deep-seated discontent and far-reaching resentment in the industrial world of today is not to be questioned," wrote the Cardinal.

"Wage-earners are restless; the wealthy are apprehensive; petty strikes are of daily occurrence; great strikes threaten national disaster; class consciousness is on the increase; class hatred is being fomented by unscrupulous agitators. . . . Misguided men, oftentimes ignorant of the true issues involved, have lent themselves to the propaganda of radicalism." [18]

Having drawn a picture so true in its outlines that it might stand in 1951 as truly as in 1921, the Cardinal went to the heart of the matter.

"Underneath the turmoil, lies a wrong philosophy of life, a misunderstanding of the destiny of man and his relations to his Creator. The question of human and divine rights involved in the industrial issues of today is a moral question. . . . To find a remedy for the evils of the industrial world, to reconcile conflicting interests, to make practical application of the religious ideals of Christianity in every-day life, to restore peace on earth is a work that should appeal to every lover of his faith and his flag. . . .

"The Church is by right and principle the unflinching defender of the people's rights. She alone has taught the rich their duty to the poor, the divine authority of law, the personal responsibility of every man. Today, she condemns the cruel arrogance of wealth and power; tomorrow, with voice no less authoritative, she condemns mob law and mob violence. . . . She is no truckler to majorities. She can lose and wait. Time and the all-prevailing justice of God are her vindication. . . .

"She has defended, and will ever defend, rights inalienable to men, such as the right to live, to be educated, to enjoy liberty, to labor, to rest with recreation, to worship God. . . . These rights carry with them corresponding obligations and duties. . . . There is no place in the modern world or society for the idle. . . . However, we must not look on labor . . . as a commodity to be bought or sold. Man is not an irresponsible machine. He has intellect and free will—an immortal soul.

"Labor is the university in which all men are trained. We learn obedience, self-sacrifice, patience, fortitude and oftentimes humility, when we compare our work with that of our fellow-men. . . . Suitable wages are necessary, that man may have food, clothing, shelter, and recreation. Demands on endurance must be reasonable, working conditions should be healthful and pleasant.

"The workman thus treated should be honest, subordinate, devoted to the interests of his employer and considerate of his associates. . . . Employers should see that of their profits a fair amount is set aside for the wage of their workingmen. Employers should be faithful to the just agreements which they have made . . . have regard for the dignity of the workingman, his right to health, safety and recreation (with) ample time for the due performance of civil, domestic, and religious duties.

"The aloofness of the employer from the worker, the concentration of wealth in the hands of a few, the oppression of the worker are abuses . . . still altogether too common. . . . The right of men to organize is a natural, inalienable right. When capital is obdurate in its evil ways, there is only one refuge left to the oppressed, and that refuge is Organization. . . . Nor can the state, which is founded to maintain and guard the interests of the individual and the family, invade these rights. This is one of the points in which Catholicity differs sharply from Socialism which unduly exalts the rights of the state and gives it supreme jurisdiction over the natural rights of the individual and the family." [19]

The entire Pastoral is well worth reading. The excerpt last cited above has especial significance, because its viewpoint was responsible for embroiling Cardinal O'Connell in a bitter political dispute on national lines three years later.

This was the famous Child Labor Amendment to the Constitution, agitated for many years and finally passed by Congress, subject to ratification by the states, in 1924. Proponents of the effort to protect children from unmerciful exploitation had twice unsuccessfully sought to end it by the powers of Congress. A Supreme

Court decision of 1918 ruled that a law forbidding interstate transportation of goods manufactured by child labor was unconstitutional. Again, in 1922, with the Cardinal's old friend, William
Howard Taft, newly sitting as Chief Justice, the Supreme Court
found unconstitutional a Congressional Act seeking to impose a
tax of ten percent of annual profits on employers of child labor.
Taft, in his opinion, made the same point that was in the mind of
the Cardinal: "The good sought in unconstitutional legislation is
an insidious feature, because it leads citizens and legislators of
good purpose to promote it without thought of the serious breach
it will make in the ark of our covenant." [20]

There was no dispute about the evils of child labor in the old
days of sweatshops, of boys and girls in textile factories, as in
O'Connell's youth in Lowell; in mines or tobacco manufactories.
Social workers like Jane Addams or Florence Kelly, clergymen of
all denominations, men and women of good will everywhere,
wanted children protected from exploitation by ruthless employers.

It was truly painful to men like William Howard Taft and William Henry O'Connell to be regarded as an enemy to little children
or a proponent of sweated labor for youth, because they opposed
legislation on grounds of principle.

The Cardinal, when the humanitarians had forced a Constitutional Amendment through Congress, had an even stronger reason
for opposing ratification in his growing awareness of the infiltration
of Communistic ideology and action in this country.

He branded the Child Labor Amendment boldly as "this soviet
legislation" [21] and urged his Archdiocesan clergy to inform their
parishioners on the issue, with the object of defeating ratification
at the Massachusetts polls in the November election of 1924.

Looking back, from the vantage of the Nineteen-Fifties, it is
clear that the Cardinal was on the winning side of the argument.
Only twenty-eight states ever ratified the Amendment in the next
thirty years, eight short of the number necessary for adoption. At
the same time, the agitation had had its beneficial effect so that by
1952 forty-seven of the forty-eight states had adopted local restric-
tions on child labor.

In 1924, however, the fight was hot and personalities unbridled. Cardinal O'Connell saw clearly the principle involved in Federal control over the individual, usurping parental rights to child education and control. He soon found himself involved in controversy with many of the American hierarchy, leading clergy and laymen or laywomen.

The Cardinal's wrath was aroused when the national body of Catholic laywomen, of which his Boston League of Catholic Women was a member, passed a resolution which seemed—or could be construed—to endorse ratification of the 1924 Child Labor Amendment. His wrath boiled over when astute propagandists of ratification, on the eve of the Massachusetts election, took out of context statements by certain Catholic personages, connected with the National Catholic Welfare Council and with the faculty of Catholic University. The press and electorate of the Boston Archdiocese was flooded with releases and fliers proclaiming that leaders of the Catholic Church favored ratification.

Since Massachusetts voters, by a heavy majority, voted against ratification at the polls, in spite of the propaganda, the Cardinal would have saved himself many headaches, had he let his temper cool off and forget his provocations. It had become too personal with him for that, however. Boston ladies of the League of Catholic Women, who went to St. Louis to a convention, requesting that the national group repudiate the alleged endorsement, injudiciously reported back that feelings had run so high that one delegate on the floor publicly referred to the Boston Cardinal in derogatory terms.

The Cardinal took the affair up with his brother Bishops, and found nearly all of them holding views opposite to his. "Boston is having a brainstorm," wrote one prelate to another at the time. "He is one against a hundred."

The estimate may not have been accurate; but the issue was joined. The Cardinal took the position that the N.C.W.C. had no authority to appear to commit the hierarchy of the Catholic Church publicly on such issues, when each bishop had sole spiritual and moral jurisdiction in his own diocese.

In the end, the matter was referred to Rome, and Rome, as usual, viewed it without heat or prejudice. The argument was solved by dissolving the National Catholic Welfare Council and erecting in its place the present National Catholic Welfare Conference in which the setup has precluded such situations.

An entirely different question but one involving the same principle of administration by lay or ecclesiastical authority in which O'Connell participated was that concerning collections for the missions, by the Society for the Propagation of the Faith.

"When I became Archbishop," he wrote, "the management, control and distribution of these vast sums of money were still in the hands of this lay Board in France at Lyons. I was convinced that the whole condition was abnormal, and while the motives were, no doubt, excellent and the success of the organization obvious, still, the preponderant influence of the whole work was that of a few laymen of France who were now the head of a great religious work. . . . In 1909 I had occasion to visit the Holy Father and, during my stay in Rome, I called on the Cardinal-prefect of Propaganda, Cardinal Van Rossum, a Hollander, and I had a long and very frank conversation with him on the subject. . . . Fortunately for all concerned . . . the administrator of the work in Lyons, once the truth of the situation had been presented by Rome, rose nobly to the situation, accepting in the most Catholic spirit, the decision of the Roman authorities . . . to take over this and similar societies . . . in order to remove even the slightest suspicion of anything savoring of nationalistic purpose. . . . The work of reorganization was soon begun by the Roman authorities . . . and today is in perfect working order, thanks to the magnanimity of the Lyons Board." [22]

CHAPTER TWENTY-THREE

MORALS OR POLITICS

. . . saper d'alcuno e buono; degli altri
fia laudabile tacersi.
                    Dante: Inferno, Canto xv, 103-104

*(it is good to know of some and of the rest
it will be laudable to keep silence.)*
                                    Carlyle, tr.

IN THE nearly forty years that William O'Connell ruled the Archdiocese of Boston, plenty of legends sprang up. Some of them appeared in print, with more or less inaccuracy. A national magazine reported that the Cardinal was spoken of with bated breath in the halls of the Massachusetts legislature as "Number One." Bostonians knew well enough that the familiar sobriquet for His Eminence was "Number Eighty," from the license plate of his automobile.

Some of the allegations became so fantastic that the Cardinal, on his sixty-ninth birthday, interpolated a denial of rumor into the dedication of the chapel of the Immaculate Conception. This is over the crypt where he planned to be buried. The occasion was only a month after the presidential election of 1928, when Massachusetts voted for Alfred Emmanuel Smith, but the nation elected Herbert Hoover.

"After the election someone had the audacity to pretend that

223

I contributed money towards the campaign," fulminated the Cardinal, at the chapel dedication. "I have never contributed a cent in my whole life to any campaign or any individual running for office, or to any party. As an American citizen, I vote according to my conscience and it is nobody's business for whom I vote or why I vote." [1]

Many of the Cardinal's flock were prominent in the politics of the Democratic Party, for instance, Mayors John F. Fitzgerald, James Michael Curley, Frederick W. Mansfield, Maurice Tobin of Boston. The first Catholic to be elected Governor of Massachusetts was David I. Walsh, later, for twenty-six years, United States Senator. Curley, Tobin, and Charles F. Hurley were all Massachusetts governors in the Cardinal's lifetime. Tobin went on to be Secretary of Labor in the Truman Cabinet.

In no campaign and for no candidate did the Cardinal issue or permit an endorsement from him. He stood aloof from internecine contests among Catholic candidates. He left to law-officers and the courts castigation of Catholics indicted for offenses.

Frederick Mansfield was a candidate for mayor of Boston in 1929 unsuccessfully; again, with victory, in 1933.

"In all the years I was a candidate, and the years I was in office at City Hall," said Mansfield after the Cardinal's death, "I never heard from the Cardinal, nor did any of the monsignor's gossipers credited with doing his errands, come to see me. After I retired from politics, as Henry V. Cunningham had died the Cardinal did send a monsignor—to ask if my office would care to handle the legal matters for the Archdiocese."

The average citizen—or even the average Catholic—has no idea of the legal questions that arise in the daily business of a large diocese. There are questions involving wills and bequests to the Archbishop, or parish churches or charitable institutions; matters of insurance; transfers of real estate; trusts for perpetual care in cemeteries. Even Cardinals and Archbishops have to make wills, like the humblest layman. Such matters, involving expert legal knowledge and representation in courts, were handled for the Cardinal first by Cunningham and later by Mansfield.

The Cardinal maintained friendly relations with many of the
non-Catholic clergy, whom he sometimes met almost daily when
he took his walk down Commonwealth Avenue. Dr. Paul Revere
Frothingham of the Arlington Street Unitarian Church was a
neighbor, and Bishop William Lawrence of the Protestant Episcopal Diocese of Massachusetts another. The Cardinal, perhaps
because of his father's death from cancer of the throat, and certainly because of the almost daily necessity of making public addresses or sermons, always took pains to walk with the wind at
his back. One raw, easterly afternoon, walking west on the avenue,
he met Bishop Lawrence who said briskly: "Your Eminence is
walking the wrong way, with the wind on your back and the sun
dazzling your eyes."

"The sun is always in my eyes when I gaze on the Episcopal
Bishop of Massachusetts," returned the Cardinal suavely.

Men of high office in the nation turned to Cardinal O'Connell
for counsel. When it was a question of nominating a Justice of the
Supreme Court of the United States, President Warren G. Harding
held the appointment of Pierce Butler in abeyance for two weeks
until he had a favorable report from the Cardinal.[2] Both Calvin
Coolidge and Franklin D. Roosevelt, by proxy, while in office as
President, came to convocations of Catholic University in Washington, at the Cardinal's invitation.

Franklin D. Roosevelt, on the Cardinal's Golden Jubilee, termed
him "a great churchman and a great American citizen." [3] At the
Mass for his Golden Jubilee, June 8, 1934, a Metropolitan Opera
tenor sang *Panis Angelicus* in the Cathedral of the Holy Cross,
while thousands heard tributes to him spoken in Gaelic, French,
Italian, Polish, German, Arabic, Lithuanian, Portuguese, Syro-
Maronite, Syro-Melchite, and English. It was a dramatic instance
of the diverse origins of the American Catholics to whom he had
ministered in Boston over the years.

Republican or Democrat, the Cardinal had no favorites in partisan politics. His preaching and his practice were always for honest
government and good citizenship at every level. Just after World
War I, scandal overtook some high-placed members of the Knights

of Columbus who were removed from office for malfeasance. The Cardinal manifested his sentiments by staying away for five years from the annual Patriots' Day banquet of the K. of C., while the unhappy business was before the courts. When he again accepted an invitation to the annual affair, he spoke of it bluntly.

"I have been absent now for several years from this annual banquet. No one has regretted it more than I. But your Order is not exempt from conditions that face other societies. There are critical times when we must exercise great patience until the crisis is past. Happily the crisis is past. I need not be more explicit. Now I can come here and feel that my presence is a real approbation of your present attitude. . . . I remember the foundation of this organization and I know well the spirit which animated its founders . . . was certainly religious and patriotic. It is clearly your present duty to keep it so. . . .

"Are you quite sure that the public attitude of some conspicuous individuals, who have gained prominence by your supposed or alleged support at the polls . . . is not reasonably the cause of the suspicion that this organization is manipulated by clever men for purely political purposes? . . . Beware of it, if you expect our approval." [4]

That was straight talk, but the same advice and admonition the Cardinal had given over and over, from the pre-war days of the Catholic Union or the American Federation of Catholic Societies, to the Holy Name Societies he encouraged in every parish. It was not a Catholic bloc that he wanted to see in America, but every Catholic voting according to conscience. His reiteration of this theme gave scope, in 1937, for a political maneuver of which the Cardinal had no knowledge until it had been accomplished. It was the first year that clean-cut, handsome young Maurice Tobin [5] was candidate for Mayor of Boston. The campaign was heated. On the morning of Election Day, on every subway stand and street corner, the front page of the Boston Post flaunted a banner in black type across the top of the front page:

"Voters of Boston: Cardinal O'Connell, in speaking to the Catholic Alumni Association, said: 'The walls are raised against honest men in civic life.' You can down those walls by voting for an honest, clean, competent young man MAURICE TOBIN today, etc." [6]

The *Boston Post* was not strictly accurate in quoting the Cardinal who actually had said, four days earlier: "There are many educated, fine men, but walls are built around honest men. Honest men are excluded. There are those who hold high positions who are false to their principles. We know them well. But the public finally learns the truth. . . . That is what has happened in many European countries. The final triumph of education is to save the world from this chaos." [7]

A few years later the story had been so distorted that national circulation was given to a version such as: "Anyone who votes for a person they know to be dishonest or otherwise unfit for office commits a sin—Cardinal O'Connell." [8]

That was not what the Cardinal said. It happened to suit politically-minded people to take his words out of context and use them in a form easily misunderstood to promote political objectives. By reference to his original words, it is plain that he was speaking in generalities, and specifically applying his principles to the scene in Europe. It was the age-old game of rumor-rumor, who's got a rumor? The public is quick to repeat a catchword, but slow to check the actual source.

The Cardinal frequently made public pronouncements in connection with proposed legislation which he felt would affect morals. Prohibition was an instance. He held the Catholic viewpoint that abstinence or temperance are virtues; but that compulsory prohibition is an infringement of individual liberty. When the controversial issue of aid to education was fought over in the Massachusetts Constitutional Convention of 1917, Cardinal O'Connell took the stump [9] in opposition to the amendment proposed by Martin Lomasney which would have prohibited public funds for "any church or religious society or any college or other institution which is not a public institution established by law." Lomasney was hitting at non-Catholic bodies, such as Harvard or Massachusetts Institute of Technology which had been generously endowed by the state legislature from time to time. Eighty-five out of ninety Catholic delegates, including ex-Governor David I. Walsh, had voted for the amendment and were embarrassed when the Cardinal publicly called it "an insult to Catholics." Massachusetts citizens, however, ratified it at the polls by a two-to-one majority.[10] In the 1930's, the Cardinal roundly and publicly condemned the radio priest, Rev. Charles Coughlin of Royal Oak, Michigan, who had acquired a fervent following in the Boston archdiocese. The Cardinal forbade his clergy to take part in partisan politics, saying, "No individual priest has the right to speak for the whole Church. He has absolutely no right to commit the Church to any particular philosophy of economics. His mission is to preach the word of God and not arouse animosities and feelings of partisanship." [11]

Father Coughlin retorted that "the Cardinal has no jurisdiction over me . . . for forty years Cardinal O'Connell has been more notorious for his silence on social justice than for any contribution he may have made in practice or doctrine toward the decentralization of wealth." [12]

That same year a statement by the Cardinal on a bill establishing a State lottery in Massachusetts, by vigorous excoriation of the lottery project, printed in all the newspapers the next morning, made headlines all over the country. It produced a change of heart in enough legislators to bring about reconsideration, and, in the end, defeat of the bill.

After the death of Cardinal Gibbons in 1921, William O'Connell was dean of the American hierarchy until his death, almost a quarter of a century later. Cardinal Farley had died in 1918. Denis J. Dougherty of Philadelphia was created Cardinal in 1921; William Mundelein of Chicago and Patrick J. Hayes of New York in 1924.

Cardinal O'Connell stood consistently on his principle that the Church should not mingle in politics, even though in his days came the greatest fervor of Catholic sentiment, when Alfred Emmanuel Smith was the Democratic Party's candidate for President in 1928. On moral issues, however, the Cardinal conceived it a duty to speak boldly, even though it put him in the van against liberal views of the times. It must have been satisfying to him when the Massachu-

setts electorate confirmed his opposition to the Child Labor amendment, and so-called "birth control" legislation; as well as the state
lottery. He respected the laws, refusing to use his office to intervene. He withstood considerable pressure to petition for clemency
in the Sacco-Vanzetti case which stirred Boston profoundly from
1921, when the two Italian-born draft-dodgers and radicals were
convicted of murder, until their execution in 1927. The wife of
Governor Alvan T. Fuller was a Catholic, and the Governor, under
Massachusetts law, had power to pardon the condemned men or
commute the death-sentence to life-imprisonment. Sympathizers
who had raised large sums of money for the protracted defense of
the pair, brought to America a sister of Bartolomeo Vanzetti to
make an emotional appeal as a Catholic to Cardinal O'Connell. It
must have been a distressing interview for the Cardinal. He received the unhappy woman kindly, but made plain to her that he
would not intervene in the process of the law of the land. President
Calvin Coolidge had taken the same stand. Governor Fuller, because of the intensity of feeling, appointed a distinguished committee to review the case in its entirety and advise whether there
had been any miscarriage of justice warranting clemency. The
members were President A. Lawrence Lowell of Harvard, President Samuel W. Stratton of Massachusetts Institute of Technology
and the old friend and neighbor of O'Connell, Judge Robert Grant.
The committee's report found that both Sacco and Vanzetti had
been proved guilty beyond a reasonable doubt of the murders of
Frederick A. Parmenter and Alessandro Berardelli in a pay roll
robbery. They were executed August 23, 1927.

Of course, those who held different views from the Cardinal,
termed him conservative, or even reactionary, but he held to his
course, reiterating the moral theme that as Catholics grew in numbers and entered into office-holding, each individual should be an
exemplar of good morals.

"This land has been given over by God's Providence to the
rule of all the people, and every citizen must, in accepting its
benefits, accept also the responsibility of guarding its welfare and
helping on its prosperity," he said, "and since the impending ills

of the body corporate are not physical, but moral in their nature, the Church whose field is the moral world, must confront them now as she has done in all the ages since the days when Peter and Linus, Cletus and Clement, faced them in the Roman Empire and by the power of the Cross defeated them in their very stronghold." [13]

In his sixties, the Cardinal rarely accepted engagements, keeping his evenings clear for reading, writing of the innumerable sermons, addresses and pastoral letters required by his office, and planning.

The success of his administration was largely due to the thought he devoted to planning ahead; and the ability he had to delegate responsibility for carrying out the plans. Two priests, each heading an Archdiocesan bureau that grew to handle more than a million dollars in charitable outlay in the course of a year, testified that in twenty years, the Cardinal had never visited their office to check over the work. He scrutinized the regular reports he required from all departments and, if satisfied, left the man alone.

Under the Cardinal's leadership, Boston was the first American diocese ready to hold a synod revising local legislation in conformity with the new Canon Law. It met on April 7, 1919.[14] One of its fruits was the remarkable record of the Boston archdiocese during the depression when not only did the new and old parishes and charitable institutions weather the financial tempest, but were able to expend hundreds of thousands of dollars in charitable relief.

It made few headlines in his day, but probably the greatest contribution of Cardinal O'Connell on a national scale was his insistence that Catholicism was a spiritual, moral and religious force, to be ever dissociated from politics. Day in, day out, for fifty years he preached and practised it—to his flock in Boston, in meetings of the New England bishops and of the American hierarchy.

"In the tremendous growth of Catholicism . . . is a religious organization for the present and future of America on which she can rely, as the very cornerstone of law and order, the prop and support of government, a bulwark against the corrupting forces of anarchy and decay, of irreligion and of infidelity. No government owns her (the Catholic Church); but all governments need her . . .

she holds the rich to a moral reckoning in a world which has gone mad; she stands by the poor. She loves even the blackest sinner and sends to his knees the false-hearted pharisee. . . . Beyond our lives we (Catholics) love our faith; and with these lives we stand ready to defend the land which gives us liberty. The Catholic Church and all her children love America for the liberty she has promised. Let America learn to love the Catholic Church!" [15]

Twice this rigorous resolution of principle must have been sorely tested, since William O'Connell was a son of Irish-born parents with all the Celt's indignation at the century-old sufferings of Ireland and warm-blooded sympathy for kinsfolk across the sea. Each time, although some of his own failed to understand, he stood firm on principle.

The first test arose at war's end in 1918, when the Paris Peace Conference and Woodrow Wilson's Fourteen Points raised hopes— soon dashed—that self-determination would be applied for Ireland's freedom.

The Cardinal's speech in Madison Square Garden, on December tenth, 1918, has been called, by those who heard it, the most magnificent oratory of his lifetime. Already, on November fifth, a week before the Armistice, he had spoken to the war-time English Ecclesiastical Mission visiting this country, urging Ireland's independence:

"May not an O'Connell one day go back a pilgrim to Lough Derg, the shrine of his ancestors, and there, on the soil hallowed by the footsteps of St. Patrick, kneel, and thank God that at last Erin, long-suffering, unhappy but ever faithful Erin, is herself once more, self-governed, self-ruled, self-sustained? God grant it soon." [16]

At Madison Square Garden, after recounting Ireland's wrongs, with stinging irony, he thundered:

"Is it the Bolsheviki only who now are to be acknowledged as free? Is it because, being Catholic, the Irish people repudiate Bolshevism, that they are now to be repudiated and their just claim forgotten and neglected? . . . Was the great war a conflict for true freedom under right of all alike, or was it a grim hoax played upon the ingenuous by the shrewd manipulators of clever phrases?" [17]

The history of the next thirty years supplied the answer to his questions; but the trials of the next six months brought division among the Irish themselves in which O'Connell felt he should play no partisan role. In March of 1919, he was warning the Ancient Order of Hibernians in his cathedral:

"Let us go on doing our duty simply and well and, by so doing, teach the great lesson. . . . The one thing that can keep this country in order and under the law . . . is a clean conscience before God, full obedience to His holy law. . . . Let me say to you that in all patience we should work out our salvation, with the firm determination to have the right but with the patience of Christ who worked out all things well." [18]

Consistent with his principles, when the League of Nations controversy blazed hotly, in 1919 and 1920, Cardinal O'Connell said nothing, for or against. It was under debate in the United States Senate; and there he left it to the determination of the people's elected representatives, under the Constitution.

A test of his natural sentiments came in 1928 during the campaign when emotions ran so high over the candidacy of Irish Catholic Alfred Emmanuel Smith. As a man, a human being, every fibre of his heart yearned for Smith's success. As a Prince of the Church, he knew it his duty to stand aloof from secular, temporal politics.

He had his chance to state his stand, indirectly, the next year when the Te Deum was sung in the Cathedral of the Holy Cross for the signing of the Lateran Treaties which ended the captivity of the Holy See and established Vatican City as an independent, neutral seat for the head of the Catholic Church.

O'Connell had been only eleven years old when Victor Emmanuel II's troops occupied Rome and sequestrated the patrimony of Peter. He had spent ten years altogether in Rome, viewing at first hand the trials of the Popes who followed Pius IX as prisoners of the Vatican. Now he had lived to see the day when patience was rewarded; justice achieved without bloodshed.

It was with deepest joy that, after the Te Deum, he gave a powerful historical address to the thronged congregation.

"If this Church is to be universal—to minister to the faithful of all lands, of all times, of all races and of all nations—the head of that Universal Church must obviously and naturally be under the domination of no one nation or no one race; neither should he be the subject of emperors, kings or potentates. . . .

"The Pope might be Italian by birth, or French or German or English or any other nationality, but once placed in . . . the headship of the Catholic Church, the Church Universal, he is the successor of Peter . . . subject in spiritual authority to no civil power . . .

"In a word, the Catholic Church can never be a national church in any sense . . . (but) this conflict is no new thing; it has gone on from the very beginning of the public ministry of Christ Himself and, no doubt, will continue to go on . . . it can all be summed up in . . . the defense on one side of unity and universality for spiritual truth, and, on the other side, the local, civil, material power attempting to wring from the spiritual that which the spiritual can never yield, namely giving to Caesar that which belongs to God. . . .

"To the prayer for the Pope and for Italy, we add another, very dear and close to our hearts. God bless America whose history thus far has been that of respect for religion and profound reverence for the things that are highest and best in spiritual life." [19]

It was a joyous pilgrimage which the Cardinal led that Spring from Boston to Rome. Although in his seventieth year, his strength was still equal to a twelve-mile walk.[20] He had reached a milestone in the erection of the one hundredth new parish since he headed the Archdiocese in 1907. He was dean of the American hierarchy and "recognized as one of the ablest leaders of the Roman Catholic Church." [21]

He recalled with pleasure afterward "the great Mass on Sunday in the Church of Santa Susannah . . . one of the glowing and memorable incidents . . . the three visits to the Basilicas . . . the audience with the Holy Father . . . the address of the Pope . . . the cordial, whole-hearted reception given to me in two private audiences . . . I took great pleasure in caring for the pilgrimage. I really gave myself to it in Rome in a way which I never did before."

It seemed, in those years of the brief interlude between two World Wars, as though the sunshine of peace were returning to a troubled world. With pleasure the Cardinal looked forward to revisiting the fair country of his parents' birth where De Valera and the Irish Republicans had come to power through the elections of February, 1932.

In June of 1932, Cardinal O'Connell led to the Thirty-first Eucharistic Congress, held in Dublin, the largest individual pilgrimage, numbering over fifteen hundred, from the Boston Archdiocese. On the voyage over on the Cunarder *Samaria,* forty Masses were celebrated each morning; the rosary was recited in common every afternoon, and lectures on Ireland and her history in the evenings re-animated love of the old country in each heart.

"Here in Ireland, where our forefathers lived and suffered for the Faith," said the Cardinal in his broadcast to America, June twenty-seventh, "our pilgrims have made a renewal of that loyalty and fidelity to the Faith of Christ, given to His Holy Church and which the children of Erin have kept, knowing it to be God's gift and therefore their most precious possession in life."

At the close of the Congress, with his nephews and nieces and a few close friends, the Cardinal kept a rendezvous with an Irish cousin, Dr. Philip O'Connell, principal of the Clonmel Technical School in County Tipperary, whose genealogical researches had revealed the family history. It was a personal pilgrimage for the Cardinal, his first opportunity to visit Ireland since the few days fifty years before, en route to seminary life in Rome.

At Lurgan parish church in County Cavan, he could see the stained glass window over the high altar which he had presented in memory of his mother and father, and kneel at the sanctuary step where they had knelt for their marriage almost a century before.

The party stopped by lovely Glendalough in County Wicklow to visit the shrine of St. Kevin, toured County Meath to the Hill of

Tara, ancient capital of Ireland; across the Boyne to the town of Kells.

It was only five miles more into County Cavan, ancestral district of both the O'Connell and Farrelly families. As a trustee of Catholic University in Washington, D. C., Cardinal O'Connell took pains to visit, at Edenburt, the birthplace of Dr. Philip J. Garrigan, 1840-1919, vice-rector of Catholic University who had borne the burden of its early days of organization while the rector, Monsignor John J. Keane was touring America and Rome for support. Dr. Garrigan (who was Bishop of Sioux City when he died in 1919), had been brought to America as a child. His family emigrated at the same time as John and Brigid O'Connell, settling in Lowell, and it was he who had visited O'Connell, a seminarian at the American College, bringing him the gift of the four volumes of St. Thomas Aquinas' *Summa.*

At Fartagh, the Cardinal gazed with indignation at the ruins of the O'Connell homestead from which his kinsfolk had been evicted half a century before; and, at Enagh, he pointed out the house where he, in 1881, had spent a couple of days with his maternal uncle, John Farrelly. The people of Virginia, the modern center of the district, turned out in a reception that was a grand reunion of O'Connells and Farrellys.

In his response to the welcome, the Cardinal recalled boyhood memories of his mother's stories of the beautiful countryside, and his own pleasure in again seeing the Hill of Bruise, towering six hundred feet above the plain, and the wooded shores of Loch Ramoy and the pleasant valley of the River Blackwater. His chief pleasure, he said, was in seeing the neat homes and prosperous conditions of Ireland's new day, in contrast to the sad conditions that had driven his parents to emigrate in 1849.

"I am ashamed," he told a companion, "of the wave of hatred that swept over me against the conditions that drove them out."

The Cardinal toured Ireland from Dublin to Galway, to rejoin the *Samaria,* stopping to visit Maynooth College on his way; and saying his last Mass in Ireland at the Dominican Church in Galway.

It had been a very heart-warming and happy journey, the last carefree holiday the Cardinal might enjoy, for he was coming back to the mounting problems of the great depression, the bitterness of the November elections when Franklin Delano Roosevelt defeated Herbert Hoover. The Bank Holiday loomed ahead, when the Cardinal would have to appeal to his people:

"There is an army of men asking food for their little ones, of elderly men and women shut out from employment by the depression, of persons crying from their hospital beds, of youth who must keep their ruddy cheeks and self-respect. It is estimated that there are eleven million unemployed in the United States today . . . thirty to thirty-five million, assuming their dependents, suffering directly from unemployment—one-fourth of our population.

"Our obligation is clear as the noonday sun . . . public relief has reached its limits. Private agencies now have a duty to shoulder . . . I appeal in the name of our dear Lord. . . . Open your purse and give generously." [22]

CHAPTER TWENTY-FOUR

OUR LADY OF PERPETUAL HELP

Donna, sei tanto grande e tanto vali
che qual vuol grazia ed a te non ricorre
Sua disïanza vuol volar senz' ali.

Dante: Paradiso, Canto xxxiii, 13-15

(Lady, thou art so great and hast such worth that
if there be (any) who would have grace yet betaketh
himself not to thee, his longing seeketh to fly
without wings.)

Wicksteed, tr.

THE THOUGHTS, the prayers, the dreams of every individual are intensely personal, for the greater part passing in silence, unknown to humans around them.

The interior spiritual life of a person is rarely exposed to the public; yet intimates sometimes obtain a glimpse through casual acts or reactions. The servants of Cardinal Merry del Val, O'Connell's beloved and inspirational friend, for instance, knew that the noble-born son of a wealthy family slept until his death on an iron cot, with laced pallet instead of springs or mattress. Whether living in the Vatican apartments as Secretary of State, or the Palazzo Marta as archpriest of St. Peter's Basilica, Merry del Val retained the ascetic bed he had purchased as a seminarian. It was typical of his quest for humility. Each morning, after his daily Mass, Merry

237

del Val recited a Litany of petitions for humility of his own composition. It received wide circulation after his death, when the cause for his beatification was introduced in 1953.

William O'Connell had humility enough, at least, to discern in their lifetime, the holiness and saintly qualities of Merry del Val and of Pius X. In his own life, he was reticent; the only personal prayer to be found in his writings is very short:

> Dear Lord, take my years of worthless toil and make them flower. Take, too, the trials, the grief, aye, and the tears that have fallen through long gray hours when unwavering faith was wrestling with the shadows. The past is past forever. Pardon, Lord, for all its errors, mistakes and its defects.[1]

One of O'Connell's most ardent pastorals was that for Lent of 1911 on the Blessed Sacrament.[2] He constantly urged upon his flock daily reception of Holy Communion and, by permission of Benedict XV, formed in 1920 a League of Daily Mass for the Archdiocese of Boston.[3] In this, naturally, he was making no innovation but carrying on the Church's traditional teaching.

O'Connell made a pilgrimage to the Holy Land in January of 1924, "as result of a desire which was developed strongly by his work in translating into English the story of the Passion by Cardinal de Lai." [4]

He was the first American Cardinal ever to visit Jerusalem. The journey could have been a succession of receptions and honors. It could have been a popular pilgrimage with hundreds of lay-persons and clergy under his leadership, participating, as at Rome or Dublin on other occasions.

Instead, the Cardinal chose to go quite simply, accompanied only by two Boston priests, sailing on the *Empress of Scotland,* with three hundred other passengers. He turned the voyage into a spiritual retreat, by secluding himself, and not going ashore at the various ports for excursions.

"My purpose was purely a spiritual one. . . . Before I started, I received messages from various people of high position offering me hospitality and kindnesses, but I waived them all, because I knew that would distract me from the sole purpose of my voyage. . . . I was an humble pilgrim and my mission was purely personal and devotional. . . . I was consequently left free . . . (for) the complete realization of my dream, which was purely and simply a spiritual pilgrimage to the holy places." [5]

In reading of the exterior life and deeds of William O'Connell, it should not be forgotten that for sixty years, in common with every man ordained to the priesthood of the Holy Catholic Church, he had the obligation of reading his Office, which consumes an average of an hour of prayers, psalms and meditations daily. Also, daily, he began his day at six o'clock, by celebrating Mass in his private chapel, which with preparation and thanksgiving after, meant another forty minutes devoted to worship of God. Daily, too, he said at least one rosary, fifteen minutes of meditation on the events in the lives of Our Lord and His Blessed Mother with the refrain of invocation: Holy Mary, Mother of God, pray for us sinners now and at the hour of our death.

Frequently, also, the duties of his station in life necessitated pontificating at the cathedral or at solemn high Mass in one of the churches of the archdiocese.

Of his private prayer, his interior life, it is more difficult to find a record.

Despite his imperfections of disposition, his impetuous character, the errors of his human judgment, he was, quite simply, a man of prayer, devoted to God and ever seeking to go to Jesus through Mary.

When the most bitter sorrow of his life overwhelmed him, he could be seen, time and time again, going on foot, inconspicuously like the humblest of his flock, to the Mission Church on the hill in Roxbury, to kneel at the shrine of Our Lady of Perpetual Help.[6]

This bitter sorrow, a blow striking both his heart and his pride, was the defection from the priesthood of a nephew, James P. E. O'Connell. The uncle had had the handsome, brilliant youth as a seminarian under him in Rome in 1900. He had made the nephew's education and theological training his own financial responsibility; as Archbishop had personally administered to him the Holy Orders. As Cardinal, he could not resist raising him to the post of Chancellor of the Archdiocese, despite his youth and lack of experience. Thus to the sorrow felt over the defection of any priest, was added the sting of regret for his own blindness in judging character. His conscience, too, felt the tragedy of their parting scene, embittered with vain remonstrance and angry reproaches.

The two never met again, the nephew out-living the Cardinal by a few years, after a respectable business career far from Boston, and dying in communion with the Catholic Church. The scar in the heart of the Cardinal never healed; the need for prayer and personal penance never left him.

To his credit, the Cardinal met the tragedy manfully. Those most intimately in his service knew no outburst of self-pity or of anger. He took to kneeling for hours in his private chapel, or through sleepless nights at the priedieu in his bedroom; but he forced himself to stony composure in public.

Perhaps the nearest the Cardinal came to referring to his trouble was in a sermon at the cathedral on his sixty-eighth birthday when he said: "I do not mean that I claim to have had more than my share of difficulties which come to a man who is in a very important place, but I only say that I have had enough to make me feel surer than ever that the great thing in life is, first of all, the sense of God's presence, and that everything will have its day and wrong will be righted finally." [7]

In those lonely, troubled years the Cardinal turned to Mary, the Mother of Sorrows, for help in his interior spiritual life. From the patterns of her virtues, he sought to conform his own nature more acceptably to God. [8]

CHAPTER TWENTY-FIVE

CARDINALS AT HARVARD

Non e il mondan romore altro che un fiato
di vento.

Dante: Purgatorio, Canto xi, 100

(Earthly fame is naught but a breath of wind.)
Okey, tr.

WILLIAM O'CONNELL became Archbishop of Boston and the city's first resident Cardinal in the last decade of the old "Brahmin" culture. As Van Wyck Brooks would say, "Boston prayed over the Florentine library and Mrs. Jack Gardner's Venetian palace, and it even made Florence and Venice Bostonian somehow because of its regard for Italian culture. The cult of Dante had woven itself into the fabric of Boston life." [1] Harvard College, across the Charles River, was both nucleus and symbol of the mental climate that had bloomed from the Transcendentalism of the Nineteenth Century.

Before 1915, a liberal arts education was chiefly restricted to the wealthy who could afford foreign travel. For the middle or laboring classes cultural facilities were so few that Andrew Carnegie would spend sixty-four million dollars to build seventeen hundred free public libraries dotted over the map.[2] A child born in 1900 would have grown to manhood before he could hear the first radio broadcasting program (1920); or read the first popular news weekly (1923) or sit in a theatre to hear the first sound-track movies (1927).

The accidental circumstances of his life and education had prepared William O'Connell to fit into the select circle of Boston Brahmins on his arrival in 1906, and his years in Rome had made him acquainted with many of them. Larz Anderson's rich relatives, the Bellamy Storers, who were devout Catholics with their daughter married to Count Pierre de Chambrun, aided Boston intellectuals to discover that a Catholic archbishop could be cultured, too. Maria Longworth Storer collected Church prelates with avidity, and pursued O'Connell from her Boston home at 56 The Fenway. When Archbishop O'Connell, on the evening of February tenth, 1910, in the Cathedral of the Holy Cross, delivered an address to the St. Vincent de Paul Society on Joan of Arc, in the front pew sat Mr. and Mrs. Bellamy Storer and Mrs. Jack Gardner.

The unique Mrs. Gardner, who had spent three million dollars for her art collection in Fenway Court and refused Duveen's offer of fifteen million for it,[3] frankly wept like a school girl through O'Connell's eloquent homily on the little French shepherdess who saved France at the head of an army and died in flames at the stake. O'Connell, on May twentieth, 1909, had been in St. Peter's in Rome for the beatification of Joan of Arc.

Mrs. Gardner would often imperiously invite him to the dinners or notable evening musicales at Fenway Court, but O'Connell was under no illusions as to her attitude. He told a friend, who had expressed the hope that Mrs. Jack might be on her way into the Catholic Church, "She has no such aspiration. She only likes me around for my decorative value as a cardinal."

Through Mrs. Gardner, originated one of the enduring friendships of the Cardinal's life, with her three nephews, Harold Jefferson, Julian L., and Archibald Cary Coolidge.[4] With the Coolidges, O'Connell had a link with Harvard more amicable than he had with Harvard's presidents, Charles W. Eliot and A. Lawrence Lowell. Eliot and O'Connell held opposite views on most current topics but the Coolidges were congenial. The Cardinal could write: "In God's own time there will be a clearer understanding of the great spirit of unity for which our Blessed Lord prayed. Meanwhile I thank God that there are souls like you who are of the Spirit of Christ and His Church." [5]

In 1908, as Archbishop, O'Connell had given a $10,000 clubhouse for Catholic students at Harvard, installing as its zealous chaplain a future rector of St. John's Seminary, Reverend Charles A. Finn. Mr. Lowell, inducted as president of Harvard in 1909, presumably was not pleased when the site for the new St. Paul's Church in Cambridge was changed, under the Cardinal, from Massachusetts Avenue to the old McKay estate at Mount Auburn and Bow Streets, near the gate of Harvard Yard. [6]

"There is very grave danger not far distant from this sacred edifice," the Cardinal had said as he laid the cornerstone in 1916. "It is the growing tendency to separate science from faith and spiritual from material forces. Prominent educators are striving to undermine the foundation of all truth, the source of all knowledge, all life—Christian faith. . . . Knowledge is good and of exceeding value; but faith is essential and should go hand in hand with science throughout life." [7]

President Lowell and O'Connell inevitably approached the concept of a university from opposite viewpoints. Lowell recalled the founding of Harvard in 1636 by a money grant from the General Court of the Massachusetts Bay Colony and its naming, in 1639, for the Congregational minister, Rev. John Harvard of Charlestown, who left half his estate and all two hundred and eighty books of his theological library to the new college. The original intent was to educate orthodox Puritan clergy and aboriginal Indians. The rise of Unitarianism had liberalized the objectives; attendance at chapel had ceased to be compulsory in 1886. Darwinism and new materialistic philosophies and sciences modernized Harvard.

There was another matter on which the views of Lowell and O'Connell diverged. During the years before the entry into World War I of the United States, a wave of admiration for Belgium's sacrifice had grown into a cult of hero-worship for Cardinal Mercier, who remained at his post throughout the German Occupation. O'Connell had first met the Belgian in 1914, after the conclave which elected Benedict XV. The coronation was held hastily to allow the cardinals to return to their own countries, where already war was raging. "There were Cardinals sitting side by side, belonging to the very nations that at the moment were suffering the dire ravages of war. . . . There was an exterior dignity and charity such as only the Catholic Church can offer, a perfect brotherhood in the faith," he recalled.[8]

O'Connell, like every other cardinal, had taken the same oath that Mercier did on his elevation—to defend the Faith even to the shedding of blood. The current cult of Mercier seemed to him more political than religious: "He did his duty, and the singular thing is that the world at once proclaimed him a hero, especially the English-speaking world—that is to say, the Protestant world. . . . I cannot help wondering why Cardinal Mercier was admired as a hero throughout the Protestant world for obeying a principle which, under other circumstances, has not been accorded the same applause." [9]

In 1919 the honest differences of viewpoint between President Lowell of Harvard and Cardinal O'Connell of Boston led, behind the scenes, to an amusing comedy of manners.

After the November, 1918, Armistice of World War I, both President Wilson and Cardinal Gibbons had journeyed to Belgium to urge Desire Cardinal Mercier to visit America. A State visit to the United States by King Albert and Queen Elizabeth was also arranged; but the Cardinal's tour was to be separate from that of the Royal party.

On May seventh, 1919, Cardinal O'Connell, writing to Mercier at Malines, Belgium, enclosed an official invitation from Mayor Andrew F. Peters to be the guest of the City of Boston, and to stay as the Cardinal's guest at his residence, on Rawson Road, Brookline.[10] On August eleventh, the Cardinal informed Peters that Cardinal Mercier had accepted both invitations and would arrive in Boston on October fourth.

Some very pretty social skirmishing ensued, to determine whether Mercier was to be received as a Belgian patriot or a Roman Catholic cardinal. Mayor Peters proposed to hold a civic reception in the Abbey Room of the Boston Public Library. This would have insured a small audience, with tickets limited to the Boston Brahmins. Cardinal O'Connell side-stepped it neatly by stipulating the affair should be in historic Faneuil Hall, traditionally open to all citizens of Boston, "at the noon hour for the convenience of business men."

Next arose the question of Harvard University which proffered an honorary degree to Cardinal Mercier to be awarded during his visit. Now William O'Connell had been living five miles from Harvard for the past thirteen years without hearing a whisper of a degree for Boston's first Cardinal. The Harvard invitation made no mention of him, even though it would be from his house, as his guest, that the Belgian Cardinal would start for Cambridge.

Cardinal O'Connell drew up a neat program which accounted for every hour of the weekend that Mercier would be in Boston; despatched it to Mercier, who was arriving shortly in New York to go on a tour. O'Connell then disappeared into the blue, as far as Harvard or Mercier could discover. Actually he left Boston September tenth and went "on retreat" for the rest of the month, delegating Monsignor Michael J. Splaine to deal with all correspondence.

Splaine had a busy three weeks. Invitation lists had to be drawn up and seating arrangements perfected for a luncheon at the Rawson Road residence on Saturday noon; a dinner to be given Saturday night by James J. Phelan at his home on Chiswick Road, Brookline; a Pontifical Mass at the Cathedral of the Holy Cross on Sunday morning, with Their Majesties, the King and Queen of Belgium attending; a reception Sunday afternoon at the League of Catholic Women; a State dinner Sunday night tendered by Governor Calvin Coolidge; a visit to Boston College Monday morning; the Mayor's reception at Faneuil Hall Monday noon; a luncheon at St. John's Seminary and reception by the clergy afterwards.

On receipt of the program, Mercier's secretary queried whether the visit to Boston College might not be transferred to Saturday, to allow a visit to Harvard on Monday. He was informed that Boston College, being non-residential, the Belgian Cardinal would find few, if any, students there on a Saturday. This led to a worried appeal from Mercier himself, addressed to the Cardinal:

"There is one thing which puzzles me a little. I venture to open my mind about it with all the brotherly feelings I foster for Your Eminence.

"Long ago the Havard (sic) Universite Authorities sent me an invitation which I accepted, just as I have done with the other principal American universities, such as Yale, Columbia, Princeton. After having taken the advice of my eminent and wise brother, Cardinal Gibbons, I came to the conclusion that I could not, without offending most respectable american (sic) feelings, omit a visit to the great national institution in question.

"I add, and Your Eminence will agree with me, that visiting the Universities, the most considerable one could not be excluded; as much the more that Havard (sic) was the American Institution to come to the assistance of our Louvain University; and its President belongs to the General Committee for the reconstruction of the same.

"Allow me to suggest that a visit at Havard (sic) might be settled, if a little change could be made in the programme you have been so kind as to submit.

"I remain, my dear Lord Cardinal, your devoted Brother in Christ

(signed) D. J. MERCIER
Archbishop of Malines." [11]

The exchange that followed between Cardinal Mercier, his would-be hosts at "Havard" and Monsignor Splaine who was holding the fort at the Granby Street Chancery office, must be imagined, since no records can be found, except a formal note signed by Cardinal O'Connell:

"I wish to say that I do not know of anything which should interfere with a visit to Harvard University if you wish to make one; and that the reason the visit was not included in my program was because I did not know when you wished to make the visit." [12]

The President of Harvard in 1919 was the distinguished Abbott

Lawrence Lowell, born December 13, 1856 in Boston, for whose family both the cities of Lawrence and Lowell, birthplace of Cardinal O'Connell, are named. President Lowell was also a cousin of Right Reverend William Lawrence, Protestant Episcopal Bishop of Massachusetts, who was currently raising by his persuasive efforts a ten-million-dollar endowment fund for Harvard. The President of Harvard sent no letter to the Cardinal of Boston, but, at the eleventh hour, on the twenty-ninth of September, the following communication was addressed to Cardinal O'Connell:

"Harvard University will entertain His Eminence Cardinal Mercier on Monday afternoon, October the sixth, and the President and Fellows request the honor of your presence and cordially invite you to join the academic procession which will form at half-past three o'clock in the College Yard at the Johnston Gate and then proceed to Sanders Theatre.

JOHN WARREN
University Marshall."

To His Eminence
WILLIAM CARDINAL O'CONNELL [13]

It was, perhaps, an insult, to have been studiously ignored through the month when Harvard was arranging the affair for Cardinal Mercier, and now, grudgingly, at the last moment, to be invited. However, Cardinal O'Connell would not cherish a personal grudge. His attitude, ever since his creation as first Cardinal-Archbishop of Boston, had been that no one was obliged to like him as a man; but no one was entitled to disregard the dignity of his office as a Prince of the Church.

All the cross-currents of feelings were well concealed and the visit of Cardinal Mercier to Boston was a great success. Cardinal O'Connell met him at the station as he arrived from Springfield by train and representatives of the governor and mayor were on hand to extend greetings. Enthusiastic crowds lined the streets as the two prelates drove through Boston to the adjoining town of Brookline where O'Connell still maintained his residence on Rawson Road.

Under the changed program, Cardinal O'Connell had had to notify intended guests of the cancellation of the luncheon planned at his residence for Saturday noon. Cardinal Mercier who was nearing his sixty-eighth birthday and had been enduring a strenuous program of travel and receptions, was happy to be able to relax and rest and chat a little with his brother-prelate.

The scene Sunday morning was unparalleled in the history of the Cathedral of the Holy Cross—with the Catholic King, Queen and Crown Prince of Belgium on thrones within the sanctuary, opposite the thrones for the two Cardinals, and the Old World ceremony of incensing monarchs, as well as prelates, carried out during the Mass.

The program went through without a hitch, ending with the convocation at Harvard on Monday afternoon when Cardinal Mercier and Cardinal O'Connell marched in the academic procession and the Belgian Cardinal received an honorary degree along with Their Majesties of Belgium.

Honors from many institutions were showered upon the Cardinal as he approached his Golden Jubilee, the fiftieth anniversary of his ordination, in 1934. Boston College, at Commencement, June 10, 1931, had already bestowed on him her highest acclaim as patron of Arts and Letters. (Salutatorian that day was John J. Wright of Massachusetts, future secretary to the Cardinal, Auxiliary Bishop of Boston and first Bishop of Worcester.)

The Catholic University of America in Washington held a convocation on November 14, 1934, awarding him an honorary degree of Doctor of Laws. The anniversary date, June 8, 1934, was marked by presentation to him from the priests of the archdiocese of a magnificent golden chalice. After the Cardinal's death, Archbishop Cushing devoted this chalice to use at the Eucharistic Shrine in the church the Cardinal had bought and re-named St. Clement's for his own titular church in Rome.

The French Ambassador journeyed to Boston on August 12, 1935 to decorate the Cardinal with the highest gift of France, the

Grand Cross of the Legion of Honor. Italy's King sent him the Cross of the Crown of Italy.

Harvard Stadium was the scene of a reception and music festival in his honor by the Mayor and citizens of Cambridge. But from Harvard University came no formal recognition.

In 1933, A. Lawrence Lowell became President-emeritus of Harvard. The new President, James Bryant Conant, was a young and earnest scientist, whose life in the laboratory had been so secluded, that a reception was arranged at Fenway Court to allow Boston society to know him. Mrs. Jack Gardner had been dead nearly ten years, bequeathing her Venetian palace and its art collection as a permanent museum for the people of Boston. In her memory, the Cardinal decided to accept the invitation to the reception in her old home for young Dr. Conant. It illustrates well the esteem for the Cardinal in the non-Catholic community after thirty years in their midst.

"The Cardinal stole the show," all Boston was saying next day.

Wearing his imposing Roman purple, with his handsomest jeweled cross and ring, the Cardinal entered the cortile, bright with flowers, lights and fountain; majestically ascended the colonnaded stairs, admired the room with walls covered with ancient Spanish embossed leather, and paused in the great Louis Seize salon to admire Rubens' Rape of Europa. As everyone knows, the huge painting shows an immense bull, plunging through the waves, with the beautiful maiden on his back.

There, beneath the painting, for the next hour, the Cardinal had to stand, gorgeous in his robes, greeting the throng that had, spontaneously, formed in line to shake his hand. Even the retired Episcopal Bishop of Massachusetts, William Lawrence, stood in line. Meanwhile the man in whose honor the reception was being held, waited at the other end of the palace in the Rembrandt room.

It is pleasant to record that when the Cardinal finally freed himself from the unscheduled reception line, and started to find the new President of Harvard, he met Dr. Conant hastening down the long tiled corridor to find the Cardinal. The handshake they exchanged that evening was the start of a happy experience for the Cardinal.

Shortly after his seventy-seventh birthday, the Cardinal recognized the necessity for a crucial decision. Characteristically, he discussed it with none, until his mind was made up—none, that is, save his constant counsellor, Our Lady of Perpetual Help.

For some three years, now, his eyesight had been dimming with the slow growth of a cataract on his one good eye. Diabetes, for many years proudly concealed, had afflicted him, forcing him to a Spartan diet that left him most days hungry, since he would not be slave to the new device of injections of insulin. The sight of the left eye long ago had been destroyed.

Two years ago, he had consulted privately a brilliant young surgeon of the Massachusetts Eye and Ear Infirmary, Dr. Edwin B. Dunphy who had told him that an operation was the only hope. But no surgeon in the world would promise that such an operation would be successful.

Still, O'Connell was not yet ready to lay down the reins. His mind, ripened by experience, was still keen; his body vigorous. He resolved to let the operation wait. The surgeon accepted his decision without argument. No one would wish to be known as the man who had blinded a cardinal!

For many months, the Cardinal took his regular walks, pontificated at the Cathedral, addressed meetings, received callers, all in a world of greyness. He managed it superbly. There was always Jerry Minihan's strong arm to guide him as he walked. Well-trained Chancery officials dealt with correspondence and made competent digests of matters for his decisions.

Then, suddenly, the words of a caller presented necessity for action. The caller was James Bryant Conant, President of Harvard, chemist internationally renowned.[14] His errand was to enquire courteously if Cardinal O'Connell would accept an honorary degree at Harvard's Commencement of 1937.

Like the blue flash of lightning across a grey sky in the winter thunderstorms characteristic of Boston's bizarre climate, thirty years of life flashed through the Cardinal's mind in a moment, and, though the implications were clear to him, his decision was unhesitating. Imperturbable as ever, in audience, he bowed and graciously accepted the proposed honor.

"Jerry," he said, later that day, "make an appointment for tomorrow with Dr. Dunphy."

And, to Dr. Dunphy at the surgeon's office, he said firmly that he had decided to undergo the operation on his eye.

"Let it be done the first week in April, please," he said.

Any other time but April, the surgeon returned. He would be on his annual vacation in Bermuda then. The steamer tickets were bought, hotel reservations made, arrangements completed for care of his patients. Surgeons, arbiters of life or death so often, harried and driven by the needs of hundreds of patients or teaching obligations, often become as authoritative, as inflexible as a cardinal. William O'Connell, for all his seventy-seven years, had not the obstinacy of senility. He recognized that this time he could not command, he must sue.

He took the doctor into his confidence. He must avoid the pneumonia season and build up bodily strength by his annual stay in Nassau's sunshine. Equally, he must be recovered from the operation by June.

"My dear doctor," he said, in his attractive, compelling voice, "can you imagine the joy in Philistia if a cardinal of the Church went staggering and stumbling to receive a degree from Harvard?"

The simple selflessness, the entire dedication to the dignity of the Church, carried conviction to the non-Catholic surgeon. The Bermuda vacation was postponed. The Cardinal's plans were carried out to the letter. There was to be no publicity whatever, he decreed. The operation must be done in complete privacy in his own bedroom. He gave the surgeon carte blanche for whatever arrangements would be necessary. So it was done. A miniature operating room theatre was installed temporarily at Lake Street. One of the new crank-up-or-down hospital beds just coming into use replaced the old brass bedstead.

The surgeon assembled his team of assisting surgeons, head operating room nurse; special nurses around the clock, male orderly;

all engaged for the April date, and none of them knowing who would be their patient. The operation was to be at two o'clock in the afternoon. That morning the team assembled at the doctor's office and drove out in a body to the rendezvous.

Dr. Dunphy never had a more cooperative patient than the Cardinal. He remembered how, the night before the operation, when he called for a final check-up, the Cardinal had said to him:

"Doctor, have I ever mentioned religion to you, ever asked your religious belief or practise?"

"No, Your Eminence," said the Doctor, expecting an ante-mortem sentimental sermon on Catholicism.

"I do not intend to do so now," said the Cardinal, turning his almost sightless eyes toward him. "I have only one request. To-night, will you say a prayer asking God to guide your hand tomorrow according to His All-knowing purpose?"

The young surgeon dared not, at that suspenseful moment, confess that for three months he had been praying constantly, so conscious was he of the great responsibility on him.

The operation was performed under a local anesthetic and the Cardinal lay as though carved in granite. For the four days after, when not the slightest movement was permitted, he continued to lie motionless. Many patients complain bitterly of the back strain and pain following this immobilization.

"Does your back hurt?" enquired the doctor.

"Nonsense, Doctor; you didn't operate on my back. Never mind my back. Tell me, how is my eye coming?" was the answer.

In ten days, the Cardinal, with Moro for company and Jerry's arm to lean on, was walking as usual in his garden with only the new black glasses to betray that anything had happened. The secret had been faithfully kept. No hint of it appeared in the newspapers. The operation was completely successful, restoring sight in the one good eye for the remaining seven years of his life.

It was not for himself that Cardinal O'Connell took the calculated risk of total blindness, had the operation failed. The Harvard degree was a symbol to him of victory in a cause to which he had dedicated his life, to bring the Roman Catholic Church in Boston out of the catacombs. As a young curate in the old West End slums, fresh from Rome, it had humiliated him for his Faith, to hear anti-Irish prejudice linked with bigotry against his Church. In those ten years he had evolved his own patient, persevering, lifelong custom of adding to his night-prayers the invocation: Saint Patrick, pray for us. Saint Bridget, pray for us. This was his secret protest at the old Boston custom of referring to Irish men as "paddies" and women as "biddies."

Consciously, doggedly, through all the years, he had tried to form himself, to conduct himself as an exemplar to Yankeedom that a Catholic could also be a gentleman, a scholar; a good citizen and loyal patriot; on a par with men of any other ancestry or belief.

In 1919 he had steeled himself to meet and endure the tacit disdain of an honorary degree awarded, not to him of Boston, but to his guest and brother-Cardinal of Belgium. He understood very well the Anglophile spirit that could overlook the Catholicism of Mercier to honor the patriot-ally of Britain's stand in the dark days of 1915-16. He understood, but it made the slight to himself no less bitter.

Never had the Cardinal wavered from his Catholic concept of a university. He loved the tall tower of the new St. Paul's Church, of red brick like the Harvard Freshmen houses by the river and the ancient dormitories in the Yard. Its architecture he praised for its reminiscence of Della Porta's church of St. Joseph, built for the Roman Carpenters' Guild in 1538 over the historic Mamertine Prison where Peter and Paul were incarcerated. When it was completed, in dedicating it, he reminded his people again:

"When, centuries ago, some of the great schools of Europe forgot their duty to their Mother . . . they missed the real thing. They have not all the truth, unfortunately. They have missed the way because they cut off the light. . . . It is well that here, face to face with this justly famous school . . . should stand the living proof that this is not all of life, that wealth and learning and position and influence are but ephemeral." [15]

Now, at long last, after thirty weary years, lonely years, the moment was at hand when America's proudest and greatest uni-

versity would witness to the world that a man could be born of
Irish immigrants, could be a Catholic and a priest, and also could
be ranked a citizen of distinction in the land.

William Cardinal O'Connell was willing to take the calculated
risk of total blindness, were the operation unsuccessful, rather than
impair the dignity of his cardinal's purple by stumbling on the platform when the degree was conferred. His courage was rewarded.
His prayers were heard. In the copy of "Recollections of Seventy
Years" which he sent, after the operation to the surgeon, he wrote,
with clear vision and firm hand, "In recognition of a great service."
He meant a service to the Church, not to himself.

One human touch crept in. He had, early in his first acquaintance
with the eye-surgeon, asked if the depression was affecting many
patients. The surgeon said yes, that while he, himself could intermit
fees in case of need, the hospital bills in certain cases were a great
hardship. The Cardinal wrote out a check in four figures.

"I give you this as a trust fund, on condition," he said, "that
you never reveal to your patients the source of the aid."

Now, after his own operation and the experience of near-blind-
ness preceding it, the Cardinal made a change in his will. St. Raphael's Guild for the Blind was left an equal share in his residuary
estate with the Charitable Bureau and the Seminary and the St.
Vincent de Paul Society.

CHAPTER TWENTY-SIX

ELECTION OF A POPE

Con l'ali snelle e con le piume del gran disio . . .
Dante: Purgatorio, Canto iv, 1, 28-29

(With swift wings and with the plumes of great desire . . .)
Okey, tr.

O N JUNE twenty-fourth, 1937, at the Harvard Commencement, the Boston Cardinal received the honorary degree of Doctor of Laws. Others honored at the same time included the New England poet, Robert Frost; the chairman of Harvard's Tercentenary observance in 1936, Jerome D. Greene; the chairman of the National Commission for Fine Arts, Charles Moore; the President of Cornell University, Dr. Edmund E. Day; and the Boston bibliophile and publisher, Charles H. Taylor.

"William Henry Cardinal O'Connell: For three decades, Archbishop of Boston, a son of this Commonwealth, honored as a faithful shepherd of a multitude of devoted citizens," ran the translation of the Latin citation for the degree. Its meticulous language implied delicately that the honor was not awarded to a Prince of the Catholic Church, but to a good American citizen who had been born Willy O'Connell, of Lowell in the Commonwealth of Massachusetts. Three days later, the Cardinal presided at the first Mass ever celebrated in Harvard Stadium, a memorial service for the war dead.

On his seventy-eighth birthday that year, dedicating the new Cathedral rectory in the South End, he could look back with satisfaction on virtual completion of the dream of rebuilding the material framework of the Archdiocese. The Keith millions had been all distributed for charity and accounting made. The fire which in 1936 virtually destroyed Philosophy House at St. John's Seminary had enabled him to reconstruct the old building handsomely; the gymnasium had been dedicated and the new St. Clement's Hall would be opened in 1940 as a seminary. The various Diocesan bureaus had been brought together in a convenient downtown location at 49 Franklin Street, and St. Thomas More's oratory dedicated on the ground floor as its Eucharistic heart of inspiration.

The country had emerged from the great depression and, thanks to prudent stewardship, the Archdiocese of Boston had come through uncrippled and strong enough to complete the building program while dispensing notable charity to the afflicted.

His health was equal to the physical burden of ceremonies or administrative affairs that might well weary a man half his age. The Cardinal discovered that much of the credit was due to the tact and devotion of the man who had been his secretary now for some years, Father Jeremiah F. Minihan. Father Minihan learned early that opposition only made the Cardinal more obstinate; that with increasing age, he tended to make his first judgment a No from which he disliked to retreat. The young secretary diplomatically began sorting the mail so that only routine or pleasant news was in the first batch on the Cardinal's table in the morning.

Later in the day, while accompanying him on the invariably long walks, the secretary would broach the subject of some problem, and let the Cardinal mull over it and discuss it as they strolled. Finally, one day, the Cardinal looked at him quizzically.

"Young man, how is it that there never are any thorns in the first morning mail? Well, well, *solvitur ambulando*. Don't think that I don't know what you are doing. But I appreciate it, I appreciate it," he said.

He came to enjoy the companionship, the thoughtful service of the younger man. Little private signals were worked out. There was one, often employed at the approach of a well-meaning bore, which meant Father Minihan was to summon Pio Zappa to bring the car around. "Your Eminence, the car waits. You remember that appointment?"

Another originated in a reminiscence of the Cardinal's boyhood days in Lowell. He recalled that in a neighboring house lived a small girl whose mother was forever calling her in piercing tones that could be heard half a mile. When the Cardinal was feeling good-natured and lighthearted, and wanted Father Minihan, over the seminary grounds or through the marble halls of Lake Street, would echo that clarion call, in a sort of tribal chant:

"Ka-a-atie—An-n-niee-e!"

Even though Cardinal O'Connell, storming into the apartment of the newly elected Pius XI a scant hour after the 1922 Conclave was concluded, had won the change from ten to eighteen days at the death of a Pope for calling the Conclave, the two fruitless dashes, in 1914 and 1922 rankled deep. In 1938, when Pius XI had a serious illness, Cardinal O'Connell told his household officers that he had made up his mind that he would not go to Rome a third time. However, the case did not arise that year, as the Pope recovered.

The Cardinal left New York on the *Lady Rodney* in mid-January, 1939, for his winter vacation at Nassau, with a reservation to return to Boston March seventeenth.

At six o'clock on the morning of February tenth, the telephone at The Hermitage awakened Father Minihan who ran down stairs to learn from Bishop Bernard, the Apostolic Vicar of the Bahamas, that Pius XI had died a few hours earlier.[1]

The Cardinal, too, had been aroused by the urgent ringing of the telephone and was waiting to hear the news.

"Lord have mercy on him," he said. "Well, let us go say our Masses for the repose of his soul."

At breakfast he was very quiet. All morning it was obvious that he was beset by a temptation of declining to make the journey.

There were good excuses that might have been made. He was well past his seventy-ninth birthday. February is pneumonia season in Boston or Rome; all his life he had been vulnerable to bronchial diseases. From the days of his bishopric in Portland, for forty years, physicians had urged on him the advisability of taking winter vacations to avoid exposure to infections. A trans-Atlantic voyage in winter would be a stormy one.

Then, too, buried in his memory were the frustrating experiences of the vain dashes across the sea in 1914, 1922. Even extension of the time for sealing the conclave to fifteen days would hardly be margin enough, and it was impossible to know if the Camerlengo would choose to exercise the discretion allowed to prolong it to eighteen days. They had elected a Pope without him twice already; would his presence or absence matter a third time? So he debated with himself.

Minihan, unobtrusively, had slipped out to the village to explore the possibilities. A steamer was lying off Nassau, due to sail at midnight. Another would leave New York February fifteenth.

"Let us go to the chapel," said the Cardinal, after lunch.

He knelt a long time at his prie-dieu; turned finally with tears in his eyes.

"I will go," he said. "Call Boston to pack my robes."

The next few hours were a bustle of packing, of telephoning, of making lists of requisites. The Cardinal made the five o'clock tender to the big ship lying out in the harbor. Father Minihan finished the final packing and arrangements to catch the seven o'clock tender. He was fearful of the reception he might get from the Cardinal; but the Cardinal had thought of that. As the tender approached the ship, the old prelate, leaning over the rail, called out the joking familiar summons, knowing that Minihan would not think him frivolous:

"Ka-a-atie An-n-nie-e!" It was his way of appreciating the call to duty.

His brother-Cardinals of the Western hemisphere were ahead of him. Cardinal Villeneuve of Quebec happened to be in Rome already. Cardinals Dougherty of Philadelphia and Mundelein of Chicago were able to catch the Italian liner *Rex* in New York on February eleventh. From South America, Cardinals Copello of Buenos Aires and Leone of Rio de Janeiro had boarded the *Nep-*

tunia and were en route. The *Saturnia,* sailing from New York February fifteenth, was committed to a leisurely tourist cruise, but the *Neptunia* was able to speed her voyage; Italian line officials arranged that Cardinal O'Connell's party should transfer at Gibraltar or Algiers to the *Neptunia.*

Late that day at Algiers, hundreds of passengers on both ships lined the rails to watch the Cardinal and his party descend the gangway to a small boat and cross to board the *Neptunia,* waiting with steam up for the last dash to Naples. The South American Cardinals welcomed their confrere.

The Italian government, when the *Neptunia* docked on the first day of March, at eight o'clock in the morning, at Naples had a special train waiting to whisk the three prelates to Rome. The South Americans took the train, covering the distance in two hours.

O'Connell, with the memory of his bitter disappointment on his last train ride to Rome in 1922 strong upon him, insisted on starting at once by motor. To guard against a possible motor breakdown, the party was divided among three automobiles. The Cardinal rode in the first one with his secretary, Monsignor Minihan. No mishap occurred and the six-hour journey brought them to the Grand Hotel in Rome a few minutes after two o'clock.

The Cardinal paused only for a light luncheon and change from travelling clothes to the purple robes of mourning worn by cardinals while the See of Peter is vacant. Then he proceeded, with Monsignor Minihan who was to be his conclavist, to the Vatican. It was less than an hour before the doors were to be locked. Five thousand miles he had journeyed, by sea and land. He reached the door with only minutes to spare, last of the sixty-two Cardinals to arrive.

The historic moment of his life—the event toward which he had bent his hopes and twice seen his efforts frustrated, in 1914 and in 1922—had now struck. The great bell of St. Peter's, tolling overhead as they crossed the wide colonnaded piazza, reverberated joyously in the heart of the aged Cardinal from Boston. The sun, breaking through a sudden shower, encircled the Vatican with a rainbow in happy omen.[2]

While Cardinal O'Connell's ship was speeding across the Atlantic, the solemn Pontifical Requiem Masses were sung day by day, in St. Peter's where the dead Pope lay in state in the Chapel of the Blessed Sacrament. The funeral and burial took place on the evening of February fourteenth.

Pius XI, three years earlier, had shown his affection for Cardinal Eugenio Pacelli by naming him Camerlengo, responsible for details of administration, on the death of a Pope. Preparations were begun for the Conclave to elect a new Pope. Monsignor Arborio Mella di S. Elia was named governor and Prince Ludovico Chigi Albani della Rovere, marshal of the conclave. The Little Sisters of the Holy Family began readying their kitchen to cater to sixty-two Cardinals, en route from the far corners of the earth.

From the earliest days, election of Peter's successors has followed what we of today term the democratic process. When human emotions and abuses threatened the integrity of elections, the Lateran Council, back in 1059, restricted actual election to Cardinals and, as early as 1179, we find written decrees that a two-thirds majority was necessary for election. From 1274, it had been a regulation that the cardinals be isolated from the world during their deliberations. Thus arose the expression, the conclave, from the Latin phrase *cum clavi,* locked up with a key.

The Australian ballot system, of which modern democracies are so proud, originated only in 1867. The cardinals in conclave for centuries have exercised a secret ballot. It was achieved by giving each a large sheet of paper. At the top, a cardinal wrote his name, turned down the paper to cover it, and sealed it with wax. At the bottom, he wrote a motto in Latin, known only to himself, folded it and sealed it with wax. In the middle space, clearly visible, the cardinal wrote the name of his choice for Pope. No canon requires that the choice be made from the College of Cardinals; but naturally, among the seventy selected to the honor of a red hat for pre-eminence in work for the church, it is more likely that a qualified candidate will be found.

In 1939 an ancient custom still was in force, providing that, on a candidate receiving a two-thirds majority, the waxen seals be broken and the ballots scrutinized to make certain the successful candidate had not voted for himself.[3]

Cardinal O'Connell and the two South American cardinals, Capello of Buenos Aires and Leone of Rio de Janeiro, did not reach Rome in time to attend the Mass of the Holy Ghost in the Pauline Chapel on the morning of March first; but they were in time to gather with the other cardinals in the Pauline Chapel that afternoon to march in procession to the Sistine Chapel while the choir intoned *Veni Creator*. There all renewed their oaths and, with the officers of the conclave, took vow of secrecy as to the proceedings. As they left the Sistine Chapel, the Noble Guards waited, to escort each to his cell, while the Camerlengo and governor and marshal oversaw the search of the Vatican palace for possible intruders, the severance of telephone communication and the locking of the door to the outer world, by Camerlengo Pacelli on the inside, and Prince Chigi on the outside.

Few men attain the cardinalate in modern days in comparative youth. William O'Connell had been fifty-two years old when the red hat came to him in 1911. Now he was nearly eighty years of age, but he thanked God for the *vigor in arduis* of his motto that had upborne him through the tension of the stormy sea-voyage and left his tread still firm, his mind and faculties clear. One of his confreres, Cardinal Baudrillart, had brought a wheel-chair into the conclave for getting about over the long marble corridors of the thousand-room Vatican building. The doors of the conclave were locked at 7:17 P.M. on Wednesday night, March first. Cardinal O'Connell could take his light supper, read his breviary and say his rosary, and compose himself for grateful rest in his cell. At nine o'clock Thursday morning, the Cardinals gathered in the Sistine Chapel for Mass; the sacristan recited the *Veni Creator;* the tellers were chosen by drawing names from a velvet pouch; and the voting began. In front of Cardinal O'Connell's canopied chair, as with the other cardinals, stood a small table with paper, pen, sealing wax, taper and matches.

At the top of a sheet, the Cardinal wrote his own name, folded the sheet down and sealed with wax softened over the lighted taper.

Then he thought of a secret motto by which to identify his ballot and wrote it in Latin—*e pluribus unum,* maybe. In such tense moments, the most banal phrases swim to the top of the mind. Folding the paper from the bottom to conceal the motto, he sealed that, too, with wax. Then he paused for a silent invocation of the Holy Ghost.

Perhaps his mind went back to 1914, or 1922, when if the ship had been speedier, he might have cast his ballot for his beloved friend, Merry del Val, or that other good friend, Cardinal de Lai. Now the times were different. Both his friends were dead. This was no time to elect to Peter's chair some old man whose time drew near. Ethiopia, Spain, China—bombs, bullets, bloodshed in the past three years—presaged more and greater conflicts.

Cardinal O'Connell wrote a name in the center of his ballot.[4] In his turn, as senior of the Cardinal-Priests, he walked to the altar in his trailing purple robes of mourning, knelt a moment, and tilted his ballot from a paten into the large chalice.

Back in their chairs, the cardinals waited, while delegated officials brought in the ballots of two cardinals sick in their cells; Tommaso Boggiani and Francesco Marchetti-Salveggiani.

Then the tellers began reading aloud the written names. No cardinal had received the forty-two votes necessary for a two-thirds majority.

Once more the prayerful, deliberate process of balloting was repeated and again no candidate had the majority.

It was noon. The master of ceremonies and the sacristan were called in for the solemn process of burning the ballots in the stove set up at the back of the Sistine Chapel, with a long pipe carried out through the end window. Wet shavings were mingled with the paper and waxen seals to make black smoke that would tell a waiting world no Pope was yet elected. The Cardinals returned to their cells and thence to the dining chamber.

After dinner, some rested in their cells, others walked in the fresh spring air in St. Damasus Square, reading their Office or saying a rosary.

A few of the cardinals began packing up their bags in their cells, because, from the first ballot, it had been apparent to all that the slender, dark-haired Camerlengo, Pacelli, Pope Pius XI's "trans-Atlantic Secretary of State"—was the leading candidate. His name had stood out in the first ballot; had nearly reached the necessary two-thirds in the second.

At four o'clock that afternoon, the sonorous bell in St. Damasus Square tolled for the third round of balloting and again the cardinals gathered in the Sistine Chapel. They wrote their names, their mottoes; sealed them; inscribed their choice for the next Pope, and deposited the slips in the great chalice.

Despite the vow of secrecy, and the reticence preserved by responsible cardinals, a whisper went around Rome that the third ballot had given sixty-one out of sixty-two votes for Eugenio Pacelli. The only vote against him was presumably his own.

To William O'Connell, by right of being senior Cardinal-Priest, with the senior Cardinal-Deacon Caccia Dominioni and the Dean of Cardinals, Pignatelli di Belmonte, went the honor in the name of the Sacred College, of approaching the chair in which sat Pacelli to ask officially:

"Do you accept your lawful election as Bishop of Rome?"

With Pacelli's broken-voiced "Si!", the acclamations broke forth. The canopies above sixty-one chairs were furled. The cardinals gathered around the one canopied seat where sat the new Pope, the two-hundred and sixty-first.

Eugenio Pacelli was the ninth Cardinal to become Pope whose Title had been the ancient church of SS. John and Paul. In 1946, when the former Auxiliary Bishop of Boston, Francis Cardinal Spellman was elevated, Pius XII made him Titular of his own former church, under the charge of the Passionist Fathers since 1773.

Since taking the name of Pius XII, the Holy Father is often spoken of as *Pastor Angelicus,* a phrase assigned to his reign in the ancient, but unofficial "Prophecy of Malachi." For the benefit of the curious, it may be said that the phrase foretold for the successor of Pius XII is *Pastor et Nauta.*

None of this future speculation intervened at that solemn moment. The Dean of Cardinals, reverting to the fact that when Christ chose Peter to be chief shepherd of His flock, He changed his name from Simon to Peter [5] asked:

"What name will you bear?"

"I will be called Pius, because of my grateful memory of Pius XI."

There was a brief pause while Pius XII was dressed, in the sacristy, in a white cassock and rochet with red stole and mantle and returned to sit before the altar.

One by one, Cardinal O'Connell among them, the older men knelt to kiss the foot and the hand of the new Pope, while officials jubilantly burned the ballots; and white smoke, swirling over the Vatican, told all Rome of an election. Half an hour later, at six o'clock, when Cardinal Dominioni stepped out onto the balcony above the entrance to St. Peter's, fifty thousand people were gathered around the obelisk filling the immense square. As Dominioni's voice, carried abroad by loud-speakers, announced that Eugenio Pacelli was the new Pope, roars of rejoicing drowned his words, and impulsively the great crowd began singing a Te Deum.

It was the first time in recorded history that a conclave had lasted only one night and day. It was also the sixty-third birthday of Eugenio Pacelli, the new Pope.

William Cardinal O'Connell stood in the *Sala della Benedizione,* above the entrance to St. Peter's watching the sea of faces, hearing the shouts and songs of rejoicing.

He was eighty years old. Five Popes had already reigned in his lifetime, Pius IX, Leo XIII, Pius X, Benedict XV, and Pius XI. He had known four of them, but never before had it befallen to him to exercise the solemn, the awe-inspiring responsibility of helping to choose a Vicar of Christ.

Now, below, quick sharp commands brought the troops lining the square to attention. Along the corridor from the interior came the processional cross, the sedan-chair. A hush fell as the great mass of people went on their knees at sight of the white-clad figure of the new Pope, standing in the floodlights at the front of the balcony. Slowly, solemnly, he raised his arms and imparted the historic Papal blessing—*Urbi et Orbi*—to the city and the whole world, the faithful kneeling before him, and the world beyond the shadows where the sun of a tomorrow was already rising on the other side of the globe. The bells of St. Peter's rang out, as the Pope withdrew; the voices of the seminarians filled the air, as the Cardinals followed the Pope back to the Sistine Chapel and knelt once more before him to promise loyalty and obedience.

The first official audience to the cardinals and Vatican officials and diplomats was held the next morning, March third; and for the third time the Cardinals made obesiance and kissed the hand and foot of Pius XII, seated before the altar in the Sistine Chapel, in white cope and mitre now as Bishop of Rome and Successor to Peter.

The coronation was held on March eleventh in the outer loggia of St. Peter's, sixty feet above the square, so that thousands might view it. After the fall of Rome in 1870, Leo XIII in 1878 had been crowned in the Sistine Chapel, as had Benedict XV, while Pius X, in 1903 and Pius XI in 1922, had had the ceremony within St. Peter's. Cardinal O'Connell thus witnessed the historic coronation in the view of the people that is traced back to the eighth century.

First, however, came the Papal Mass, inside St. Peter's. The procession, led by Swiss guards in their medieval uniforms, descended the Scala Regia to the vestibule of St. Peter's. The Cardinals walked at the end, immediately in front of the gilded sedia gestatoria with nodding ostrich plumes in which sat the Pope, blessing the cheering multitude crammed into the vast basilica. There was a halt at the Chapel of the Blessed Sacrament, for adoration of the Eucharist, then the procession went on to the altar of St. Gregory the Great, where the Pope vested, and proceeded to the main altar and the new Pope celebrated the Mass. At the altar of St. Gregory, William O'Connell, in keeping with his office as a Cardinal-Priest, vested in a chasuble before taking his place in the apse, with his train-bearers sitting at his feet.

By noon, O'Connell had to don cope and mitre to take his place beside the gilded throne with red velvet canopy for the coronation itself, when Pius XII was invested with the triple crown denoting his office as *Pater principium et regum; Rector orbis in terra; et Vicarius Salvatoris nostri.*[6] Following the Pope's blessing to the multitude, the procession returned to the Hall of the Paramenti where O'Connell and the other Cardinals gathered about the Holy Father once more expressed their congratulations. To them said Pius XII: "We entreat you, members of our Senate of the Church, at this solemn moment when the majesty and the burden of the papal diadem has been placed upon our head, indeed, we beseech you, our most intimate Counselors, in the words of St. John Chrysostom: 'You who know our work thoroughly, assist us with your prayers, your zeal, your devotion and cheerfulness, that we may be your glory and you may be ours.' "

The days intervening between the conclave and the coronation were truly happy ones for Cardinal O'Connell. His suite was thronged with callers. Ambassador to Britain Joseph P. Kennedy and his wife, the former Rose Fitzgerald of Boston, came. Kennedy was official United States representative at the coronation. American Ambassador William Phillips, accredited to the King of Italy, called. The Irish Ambassador to the Vatican, William J. B. Macaulay had an American wife, the former Mrs. Nicholas Brady, Papal Duchess whose one-time home at Manhasset, Long Island, had, in 1936, given hospitality to the new Pope when he visited America as Cardinal Pacelli in 1936.[7] Another Boston caller at the Grand Hotel was Amory Matthews, Catholic convert whose father Nathan Matthews was once Mayor of Rome, host to Theodore Roosevelt in 1910. Amory Matthews was a Papal Chamberlain.

"Alfonso XIII of Spain,[8] whose suite was next to mine, paid me a visit and we had a delightful conversation," recalled the Cardinal. "Prince and Princess Barberini, Don Lelio Orsini and others came, recalling memories of the old days when I was rector of the North American College in Rome. Few of my old acquaintances among the Cardinals are alive but it was pleasant to see Prince Belmonte. Cardinal Belmonte and I are the only surviving Cardinals created by Pius X of holy memory." [9]

The Cardinal also found vigor to revisit places of beloved memory in Rome. He walked on the Pincian hill and in the Borghese

Villa gardens once more. He paid his official *ad limina* calls as Archbishop of Boston, to sign the register at the basilicas of St. Peter's, St. Mary Major, St. John Lateran and St. Paul's-without-the-Walls. He knelt again at the shrine of Our Lady of Perpetual Help on the Esquiline hill. It was Lent; the Stational Church for Monday of the second week in Lent was his own Titular Church of San Clemente; the Cardinal was able to visit it on that solemn day, the sixth of March in that year. He joined with students of the North American College in reciting the rosary in the church with Prior O'Daly of the Irish Dominicans.

Two days later, he was welcomed back at Via dell' Umilta within the walls of the old college where, first as seminarian and later as rector, a full ten of the eighty years of his life had been passed. He spoke briefly but with inspiration to the students in their black cassocks, but when they began singing the familiar old Latin hymns, he broke down with memories, retreating alone to the beautiful college church of St. Mary of Humility. There were tears still in his eyes as he emerged and he shook his head at the seminarians who crowded about him in the cortile, anxious to take snapshots.

"No, no, boys," he said gruffly, reluctant to be photographed while manifesting such emotion.

He had several private audiences with Pius XII during his stay. Afterwards he spoke with admiration of this fifth Successor to St. Peter whom he had known in his long lifetime.

"I have known the Holy Father since his boyhood and have long been an intimate friend of his family. . . . When he visited Boston three years ago he was my guest. . . . He has had a unique training for the great duties which lie immediately ahead of him. . . . As Camerlengo he showed me every courtesy; he deferred the Conclave out of consideration for me. He is a man of vast understanding and experience. . . . He is above all a man of great piety. He is a saint." [10]

The Cardinal sailed for home from Naples on the *Vulcania*, arriving in New York March thirtieth and taking the Eastern Steamship's *St. John* for the overnight completion of his notable

two-months' journey. Next morning "at ten o'clock I was again
at my desk, taking up the many affairs of the Diocese. . . . On
Sunday, April second, I presided at High Mass at the Cathedral
and . . . extended to the congregation the paternal blessing which
the Holy Father had commissioned me to bring to clergy, religious
and laity," wrote the Cardinal in the last of his published books.[11]

Three indelible memory-pictures those with the Cardinal in
Rome in 1939 carried away.

One was, on his return to the Grand Hotel from the conclave,
on the Wednesday evening, smiling at them in the lobby, entering
the lift to ascend to his room with never a word after the emo-
tionally exhausting experience. In the privacy of the small elevator,
he made a fist of his right hand, turned it to show the sapphire
flash of his Cardinal's ring, shook it in a gesture of victory! Without a word, he drove home to their minds the long, long effort,
from 1914, again in 1922, to fulfillment at last in 1939 of the inner-
most meaning of a cardinal's purple—the responsibility, under the
Holy Ghost, to choose a successor to Peter's Chair.

It was the ring Leo XIII had given him. At long last, a trust was
discharged. From henceforth the Holy See would have the voices
of all a narrowing world represented in electing Christ's Vicar to
head His visible Church. Australia, the Orient, North and South
America, Africa—now it was manifest that the Church was universal, and all her sons, of every race or color or continent, would
share in her highest counsels. By jet-plane, by steamer or sub-
marine, by train or on foot, the Cardinals of the Sacred College
would gather in conclave. That, wordlessly, was what the gesture
of the flashing ring on the hand of the eighty-year-old cardinal
meant.

The second memory was of the end of the audience with Pius
XII, the first granted after his election, even before his coronation.
The words of congratulation had been spoken, the amenities exchanged, the others had made their three bows and withdrawn to
the door of the audience-chamber.

Two figures were henceforth etched in memory. One was that of
the tall, black-haired man, all in white, the new Pope Pius XII,

extending his two hands to the stout, silver-haired figure in flowing scarlet. Slowly, painfully, the scarlet figure was sinking to his knees.

"Non, carissimo cardinale, non inginoc hiarsi!" [12]

"Si, si, Santo Padre."

So, for an instant they contended, the white Vicar of Christ who remembered O'Connell at the hundredth birthday of his own grandfather; and the scarlet-clad veteran of half a century in the service of Christ's Church.

The imperious, disciplined will of William Cardinal O'Connell won. His aged joints and muscles obeyed his will and, despite the restraining hands of him who, but yesterday, had been Eugenio Pacelli, William O'Connell knelt on both knees to the Pope he had helped to elect.

The third memory was stamped a few days later, as the Boston party sailed for home. There had been honors paid; there had been the magnificent ceremonies; there were ecclesiastics and officials accompanying them to Naples, to the raising of the gangplank.

The steamer drew away from the pier. The Cardinal stood in the stern watching that last view of Italy and the plume of Vesuvius' smoke against the sky. He raised his right hand.

"Vale Roma!" he said softly.

He knew he would not see Rome again.

CHAPTER TWENTY-SEVEN

LAST DAYS

In terra e terra il mio corpo, e saragli tanto con
gli altri che il numero nostro con l'eterno
proposito s'agguagli.

Dante: Paradiso, Canto xxv, 124-26

> *(Earth in the earth my body is, and there shall it be*
> *with the rest until our number equalleth the Eternal*
> *purpose.)*

Wicksteed, tr.

THE WORLD knows today, after the difficult years from 1939,
that Pius XII is a man of noble character, of heart burning
with charity, of intellect resolute and brilliant to meet the problems
of wars, woes and vicissitudes.

William O'Connell, who helped elect him, lived long enough to
know, too, that Pius XII had a tender respect for old age. As Papal
Secretary of State, as a visitor to Boston and America in 1936,
Eugenio Pacelli was in position to be thoroughly aware of ecclesi-
astical conditions. In 1906, Rome had not hesitated to name a
Bishop-Coadjutor for Archbishop John Williams.

Now, in 1939, Rome, with its long vision, selected the man fitted
to rule the See of Boston one day; but spared the aging Cardinal
the pang of receiving a Coadjutor.

His heart was already smitten because, on June fourth, 1939, suddenly, of a Sunday afternoon, the Cardinal's brother Edward had died. Edward, barely a year older, had been William's closest family tie through the years. He had brought him to Boston as superintendent of Holy Cross cemetery, to have him near. He had watched Edward's children grow up, dropping in often at the house on the hill beyond his own residence. When young Joe went to break the news of his father's death, the Cardinal said no word. He only fell on his knees and prayed. Then he arose, went with Joe to the Waban Hill house and led the family in the rosary.

The Cardinal had pontificated at many a funeral of laymen or priest in the cathedral, but for his own brother, he said the Requiem Mass simply in the family parish church of St. Ignatius, even though, then, it was only the auditorium of Boston College; and he went, eighty years old though he was, to Holyhood cemetery to say the committal prayers, and knelt to do so. Now he only of the eleven children of John and Brigid O'Connell, was left.

Three weeks later, in Holy Cross cathedral, the aged Cardinal went through the long ceremony of consecrating the new Auxiliary Bishop Rome had given him, Richard J. Cushing. Bishop Francis Spellman had been promoted to be Archbishop of New York. The Cardinal assigned Spellman's church of the Sacred Heart in Newton to the new Bishop who, for so long and notably, had directed the Bureau of the Propagation of the Faith in Boston. It was a relief, a comfort, to have a strong young Auxiliary who could travel about the archdiocese for Confirmations.

The war that broke out in December, 1941, when Japan, the country he had visited and admired, attacked America at Pearl Harbor, tried his spirit sorely. His world was peopled now with violent men—Hitler in the Germany he had loved; Mussolini in his beloved Italy; Tojo in Japan. It was a sad way to remember the world he had lived in.

He carried on, indomitably. His voice still rang out more clearly, his Latin words more distinct, at cathedral services than those of the younger generation. He had a new secretary in 1943 because he had made the sacrifice of naming Monsignor Minihan as Chancellor to carry on the diocesan daily duties he knew were beyond him. The secretary was Father John J. Wright, recently back from studies in Rome, able to chat with him in the liquid Italian that still was fabric of his mind, quick to rise to his lips.

One of the secretary's duties, to spare the Cardinal's one good eye, was to read aloud to him. It was educational, but not always diverting, since the Cardinal chose the books to be read. It is a mark of youth to prefer the latest books, the most topical articles. Age tends more and more to retrace memories of a vanished day in works of biography, history and memoirs. Age realizes, instinctively, the force of the epitaph on the tomb in St. Peter's of Adrian VI; "To judge a man, even of the highest virtue, it is necessary to know the time in which he lived." [1]

O'Connell, in the spring of 1944, like all America, like all the free and democratic world, was beset with thoughts of war. The first faint promise of victory was dawning in that spring. Rommel's Nazi legions had been driven from Africa by American troops. Mussolini's star had set and Italy, under new alignment, had thrown off the Fascist yoke to join British and American forces in ousting the Nazis. Stalin, victorious in Russia against Hitler, was pressing for a second front in subjugated France. The press had carried news of American bombs rained on St. Laurence-without-the-Walls in Rome with Pius XII hurrying to aid the stricken people; but indignation of the Christian world had brought assurance that there would be no more bombs over Rome.

Rome—where since 1940, the North American College had been desolate, vacated under the necessities of war.

The Cardinal was unusually silent during his customary afternoon drive. Pio Zappa rolled the car along at exactly twenty-one miles an hour by the river with the sun lighting up the red brick masses and gold, red, blue and green cupolas of the Harvard houses on the opposite shore. The young secretary unconsciously began humming a tune.

"What are you humming?" said the Cardinal suddenly.

"Cavalleria Rusticana," said Father Wright, guessing wildly.

"No," corrected the Cardinal. "It was *Connais tu le pays?* from *Mignon*. That was the first opera I ever heard—from a twenty-sou seat in the gallery in Paris, the autumn of 1881, on my way to Rome."

Rome! Again he was silent until the car stopped under the porte-cochere at the Lake Street residence. Usually, on alighting from the car, he walked for an hour before going in. That day, as Pio held the door, the Cardinal reached out a hand for support.

"My legs feel like wooden sticks," he said, in Italian.

"Better the legs wooden than the head," returned the man who had been driving the Cardinal, with horses or motorcar, for more than forty years, in Rome or Portland or Boston.

"We had best go in," said the Cardinal. "We won't walk today; you can read to me instead, Father."

But when Father John Wright picked up the book they had been reading and opened to the page with the bookmark, the Cardinal halted him.

"I don't want to hear any more about Peter Cooper," he said firmly. "Read me something about Rome. Read me Wiseman's Last Four Popes."

The book, Father Wright said, was down at the Chancery office. Well, go fetch it, bade the Cardinal; he would wait. The young secretary went across the field and returned with the faded red volume from the *Works of Cardinal Wiseman.*[2]

"Begin where he tells about the re-opening of the *Venerabile,*" directed the Cardinal. The secretary found the page and read:

"On the eighteenth of December, 1818, the writer of this volume arrived in Rome, in company with five other youths, sent to colonize the English College in that city after it had been desolate and uninhabited. . . ."

"That will do, Father," interrupted the Cardinal unexpectedly. "You remember the College on Via dell' Umiltá. You were there. The American College is closed now, but this war will end, too. A new rector will go back and some young men, too. I hope it is on a Sunday that they re-open it. I hope they will have Benediction and that they will sing the Litany of Loreto.

"You need not read any more. Run along. Jerry will be here soon. I would like to sit here and think."

At five o'clock when Monsignor Minihan came in, he was still sitting in the chair. There was the usual light supper, and desultory reading and conversation. The Cardinal retired a little earlier than usual after reciting his night prayers with Monsignor Minihan. During the night he suffered a cerebral hemorrhage. He lingered for six days, conscious, clasping firmly in his hands the crucifix that had been his as a seminarian in Rome; blessing with the crucifix the nephews and nieces, the priests of his household, Bishop Cushing who led them in recitation of the rosary. But they never heard again the strong, melodious voice.

His last words had been of Rome. Somehow it seemed as though he had never left Rome. He had carried Rome in his thoughts and aims and prayers for sixty years. Rome was the heart's center for a Catholic. Rome! Never again in this world would he see Rome; but never, in this world, did he forget Rome.

Terminal pneumonia set in. The Cardinal's heart ceased beating fifteen minutes before six o'clock on Saturday evening, April twenty-second, 1944. It was the feast-day of two Popes martyred in Rome, SS. Soter and Caius, sixteen centuries earlier.

The obsequies lasted five days with thousands standing in April showers outside the crowded cathedral where the first Cardinal-Archbishop of Boston lay in state, the great amethyst ring Leo XIII had given him on his finger, the red *galero* at the foot of the bier. On the morning of April 28 he was buried at a Mass sung by the Apostolic Delegate and Archbishop Cicognano in the presence of the only living American Cardinal, Archbishop Dougherty of Philadelphia.

Characteristically, he had the last word. At St. Peter's Church in Lowell, they had built a crypt, hoping that there, some day, would lie the Cardinal who once had been baptized in old St. Peter's, Willy O'Connell of Gorham Street. In the Cathedral of the Holy Cross on Washington Street, Boston, there was a crypt where already lay two Archbishops, his predecessors in the See.

"I wish to do this myself . . . no committees," the Cardinal had written in 1912 to Prior Nolan at San Clemente. That was the way he did things to the end. His Last Will and Testament directed that he be buried in the Chapel of the Blessed Virgin that he had built on the grounds of St. John's Seminary.

True to his nature, he had the final word. He was ready to meet the God to whom he had vowed his life in early manhood. He had done the best he knew through the sixty-odd years; as seminarian,[3] as priest, as rector in Rome; as bishop, archbishop. In his prime, he had come to the purple and in his old age he had seen achieved his objective—that, in future, any cardinal of the global Church might join in election of the Supreme Pontiff of the Church of Christ.

He was ready to say the *Nunc Dimittis*. Lord, let thy servant depart in peace.

ACKNOWLEDGMENTS

FIRST AND foremost, my gratitude is due to His Excellency, Most Reverend Richard J. Cushing, D.D., Archbishop of Boston, who originally suggested the writing of this work so that information might be gathered from the many persons now living who knew His Eminence, the late Cardinal O'Connell, and afforded all possible encouragement and help during the work's progress.

It would be invidious to single out individuals, and impossible for lack of space to list all who have generously given of their time to aid me with personal reminiscences. With most of the individuals, it was a labor of love in memory of their friend and Shepherd, for which thanks of mine would be superfluous.

A debt of gratitude for aid in research in records and archives, however, will at once serve to acknowledge painstaking cooperation and to indicate sources explored for data.

With humblest appreciation, the writer will ever remember the gracious reception accorded her at the Vatican by the Holy Father, Pope Pius XII, now gloriously reigning; and the gracious act of the Pontiff in granting special permission for information to be made available from the Vatican archives for this work.

In that connection, appreciation is also expressed to His Eminence, Nicola Cardinal Canali, President of the Pontifical Commission for the Government of the State of Vatican City; to His Excellency, Most Reverend Giovanni Battista Montini, Pro-Secretary of State to His Holiness, Pope Pius XII; to His Excellency, Archbishop Albareda, O.S.B., Prefect of the Vatican Library; to Right Reverend Joseph McGeough, Secretariat of State, Vatican City; and to Count Pietro Enrico Galeazzi, Governor of Vatican City.

Scholars in Rome whose courteous and illuminating aid were of the greatest assistance include:

North American College: Most Reverend Martin J. O'Connor, D.D., Rector; Very Reverend Robert J. Sennott, Vice-rector; Reverend George Schlichte, Vice-rector.

The Jesuit House, Borgo San Spiritu, 5; Rev. Vincent J. McCormick, S.J.; Rev. E. K. Burrus, S.J.; Rev. Thomas M. Lannon, S.J.

San Clemente Collegio, Via Labicana, 5; Very Reverend Leo C. Lennon, O.P., Prior; Rev. Raphael S. Hannigan, O.P.; Rev. Romuald Dodd, O.P.; Rev. Austin L. Flannery, O.P.

Church of St. Alphonsus, Via Merulana: Rev. Eric Wuenschel, C. SS. R.

Supreme Sacred Congregation of the Holy Office, Vatican City: Right Reverend Hugh O'Flaherty.

Shrine of St. Columbanus, Bobbio, Italy: Most Reverend Bernardo Bertoglio, Bishop of Bobbio; and Reverend Don Pietro Malacalza, pastor, San Columbano.

Ireland: Dr. Philip O'Connell of Clonmel, historian and genealogist.

Portland, Maine; Diocesan Archives: Most Reverend Daniel J. Feeney, D.D., Bishop-Coadjutor of Portland; Rev. Edward A. Gallagher, Archivist. Rt. Rev. Philip Desjardins, St. Hyacinthe's Church, Westbrook, Maine.

Boston, Massachusetts, Archdiocesan Archives; Right Reverend Walter J. Furlong, Chancellor; Miss Anna Kelly.

Massachusetts Historical Society, Boston; Mr. Stewart Mitchell, Director; Mr. Stephen Riley, Librarian.

Boston Athenaeum; Mr. Walter Muir Whitehill, Director.

Boston Public Library: Dr. Milton Lord, Director.

Harvard University: Mr. Philip McNiff, Director, Lamont Library.

Boston College Bapst Library: Rev. Terence L. Connolly, S.J., Librarian; and Mr. John O'Loughlin and Mr. Thomas V. Reiners, assistants.

Holy Cross College, Dinand Library: Rev. William L. Lucey, S.J., Librarian.

Creagh Memorial Library, St. John's Seminary, Brighton: Rev. John Broderick, Director.

THE PILOT, Boston: Very Rev. Francis J. Lally, editor.

Catholic University, Washington, D. C.: Most Rev. Bryan Mc-Entegart, D.D., Rector; Rev. Dr. Henry J. Browne, Archivist; Rt. Rev. Maurice J. Sheehy, and Rev. Dr. John Tracy Ellis.

National Catholic Welfare Conference, Washington, D. C.: Rt. Rev. Howard Carroll, Director.

Library of Congress, Washington, D. C.: David C. Mearns, Chief Manuscript Division and his assistants, Dr. D. B. Powell, and Katharine Brand.

United States Department of State, Washington, D. C.: Dr. Carl Lokke, Chief, National Archives.

St. Charles College, Catonsville, Md.: Very Rev. George S. Gleason, S.S., President.

St. Bernard's Seminary, Rochester, N. Y.: Rev. Robert F. Mc-Namara.

Sophia University, Tokyo, Japan: Very Rev. Theodore Geppert, S.J., Rector; Rev. Bruno Bitter, S.J.; and Rev. William H. Healy, S.J.

St. Matthew's Cathedral, Washington, D. C.: Miss M. E. Quill, secretary.

Mission Church (Our Lady of Perpetual Help), Boston: Very Rev. John J. Hosey, C. SS. R., Rector; and Rev. Joseph F. Scannell, C. SS. R.

Catholic Foreign Missionary Society, Maryknoll, N. Y.: Most Rev. Raymond M. Lane, M.M., and Rev. Robert Sheridan, M.M.

The Paulist Fathers: Rev. Joseph McSorley, C.S.P., and Rev. James E. Joyce, C.S.P.

Among Church dignitaries in America who kindly favored the writer with encouragement and information for the project, special gratitude is due to Most Reverend Amleto G. Cicognani, Apostolic Delegate to the United States; His Eminence, Francis Cardinal

Spellman, Archbishop of New York, and Most Reverend John Wright, Bishop of Worcester, and Most Reverend Jeremiah F. Minihan, Auxiliary Bishop of Boston.

Boston clergy whose intimate years of service with His late Eminence, Cardinal O'Connell, afforded reminiscences generously made available, include the Vicar-General of the Archdiocese; Right Reverend Augustine F. Hickey of St. Paul's Church, Cambridge; former Rectors of St. John's Seminary, Right Reverend Charles F. Finn, Holy Name Church, West Roxbury; and Right Reverend Edward G. Murray, Sacred Heart Church, Roslindale; former Chancellors of the Archdiocese, Right Reverend Richard J. Haberlin of St. Peter's Church, Dorchester; and Right Reverend Jeremiah F. Minihan of St. Catherine's Church, Norwood; the former Director of the Propagation of the Faith, Right Reverend Joseph F. McGlinchey of St. Mary's Church, Lynn; the former director of the Catholic Charitable Bureau, Right Reverend Michael J. Scanlan, St. Rose's Church, Chelsea; and Right Reverend Robert H. Lord, Diocesan historian, St. Paul's Church, Wellesley.

To these, and to all the other men and women who have shared reminiscences with the writer, and particularly to Mr. Joseph E. O'Connell, nephew; Mrs. Mary O'Connell Ryan, niece; and to Mrs. Josephine Kirk, niece, and her husband, Judge Paul Kirk, deepest thanks are accorded. Their cooperation was invaluable.

DOROTHY G. WAYMAN

APPENDIX

THE LAST WILL and Testament of William Henry O'Connell, Cardinal-Archbishop of Boston, after provision for his faithful servants, left his personal estate of about One Hundred Thousand Dollars, to Church and charity. It was signed on the seventeenth day of November, 1943, six months before his death; and was admitted to probate in Suffolk Probate Court, Boston, on June twenty-sixth, 1944. It reads as follows:

In the name of the Holy Trinity, Amen.

I, William Henry O'Connell, Cardinal of St. Clement's, Archbishop of Boston, humbly ask pardon of God for my failings and weaknesses and beg His Divine Mercy on my soul. I humbly ask the forgiveness of all whom I may have injured or offended, as I freely forgive all who have ever offended or injured me. I beg the prayers of priests and people for the repose of my soul. I give thanks to Almighty God for the many graces and favors that He has given me throughout my life; particularly for the inestimable grace of living and dying as a faithful son of the Holy, Roman, Catholic and Apostolic Faith.

With a deep sense of gratitude to Almighty God for His goodness and generosity, I desire that whatever I own be given to charity. I direct that my funeral obsequies be as simple as possible; that I be buried in the Chapel of the Blessed Virgin on the grounds of St. John's Seminary, Brighton, Massachusetts.

I give, devise and bequeath to my successor as Roman Catholic Archbishop of Boston, a corporation sole, all the property, real, personal and mixed, including all my book-plates and copyrights which I hold as Archbishop of Boston, a corporation sole.

I suggest that the Jackson Estate which was left to the American Cardinals as Trustees and which I administer in succession to Cardinal Gibbons as Dean of the American Hierarchy, be administered by the Cardinal who succeeds me as Dean of the American Cardinals in accordance with the established practice of the Trustees.

After the payment of my just debts and funeral expenses, and the amounts which may be assessed and payable as inheritance or excise taxes, I give, devise and bequeath as follows:

First; to the Society for the Propagation of the Faith, Boston branch, 49 Franklin Street, $2,000 for Masses for the repose of my soul.

Second: to Christian Riedi and Pio Zappa, who for thirty years or more have given such devoted and true service to me, the sum of $10,000 each.

Third: To Mary Hynes Riedi and Delia Hynes, who have been in my domestic service for more than a quarter of a century, the sum of $5,000 each.

Fourth: To the Particular Council of the Society of St. Vincent de Paul of the Archdiocese of Boston, $5,000 to be used for relief of the poor and needy of the Cathedral of the Holy Cross parish, Boston.

Fifth: To the pastor of St. Peter's parish, Lowell, Massachusetts, my native parish, $5,000 to be used for the relief of the poor of St. Peter's parish, Lowell.

Sixth: All the rest and residue of my property, real, personal and mixed, and wherever situated, I leave to be divided in equal shares to (a) St. John's Seminary, Brighton; (b) the Society for the Propagation of the Faith, Boston branch; (c) the Catholic Charitable Bureau, 49 Franklin Street, Boston; and (d) the Catholic Guild for the Blind, 49 Franklin Street.

Seventh: I appoint my nephew, Joseph E. O'Connell, Newton; and Right Reverend Jeremiah F. Minihan, present Chancellor of the Archdiocese, to be co-executors under this will and I request that they be exempt from furnishing any surety or sureties on their official bond.

Eighth: (Here follows the routine legal clause empowering the
executors to settle the estate.)

In witness whereof, I, William Henry O'Connell have hereunto
set my hand and seal this 17th day of November, 1943

Witnesses: EDWARD G. MURRAY
GEORGE M. DOWD
JOHN J. WRIGHT.

BIBLIOGRAPHY

THIS BOOK does not pretend to be a record of every act of William Henry O'Connell in his ecclesiastical offices as priest, bishop, Cardinal. It is, rather, a study of the character, in the setting of his own times, of a man born in humble circumstances who rose to be Dean of the American Hierarchy.

A complete Bibliography would be of scant interest to the lay-reader and superfluous for scholars. Here follows, therefore, a list of the principal works that aided in reconstructing the early years of the Cardinal's life, many of which are quoted in the text. They fall into natural subdivisions.

The Cardinal's Own Published Writings

Sermons and Addresses. Vols. i-iv. Copyright, 1915. Pilot Publishing Company, Boston.

————. Vols. v-xi. Copyright, 1938. Pilot Publishing Company, Boston.

Letters of Cardinal O'Connell. Vol. i. Copyright, 1915. The Riverside Press.

Reminiscences of Twenty-five Years. Copyright, 1926. The Pilot Publishing Company, Boston.

Recollections of Seventy Years. 1934. Houghton Mifflin Company.

Golden Jubilee. Copyright, 1935. Riverside Press.

A Memorable Voyage. Copyright, 1939. Privately printed.

A Tribute of Affectionate Memory to Most Rev. John J. Williams, Archbishop of Boston. Dated August 30, 1940.

The Passion of Our Lord. (Translated from the Italian.) Copyright, 1923. Pilot Publishing Company.

Archdiocese of Boston

History of the Archdiocese of Boston. Three volumes. By Robert
H. Lord, John E. Sexton and Edward T. Harrington. 1945.
The Pilot Publishing Company.

A Brief History of the Archdiocese of Boston. By Rev. Michael J.
Scanlan. 1908. Nicholas M. Williams Co.

A Brief Historical Review of the Archdiocese of Boston, 1907-
1923. 1925. Pilot Publishing Company.

Cardinal O'Connell; A Biographical Sketch. By Rev. John E. Sexton. 1926. Pilot Publishing Company.

Lowell, Massachusetts

Lowell As It Was And Is. By Rev. Henry A. Miles. 1845. Powers
and Bagley, Lowell.

History of Lowell. By Charles Cowley. 1868. Lee & Shepard, Boston.

Report Upon the Schooling and Hours of Labor of Children Employed in the Manufacturing and Mechanical Establishments
of Massachusetts. By George E. McNeill, 1875. Wright & Pot-
ter, State Printers, Boston.

History of Middlesex County.

American Notes. By Charles Dickens.

Charles Dickens. Two volumes. By Edgar Johnson. 1952. Simon
& Schuster.

The Lowells and Their Seven Worlds. By Ferris Greenslet. 1946.
Houghton Mifflin Co.

Diary of a Tour in America. By Rev. M. B. Buckley of Cork, Ireland. 1889. Sealy, Brigers and Walker, Dublin.

St. Charles College

St. Charles College 1848-1948. Historical sketch by Rev. John J.
Tierney, S.S.

Boston College

A History of Boston College. By Rev. David R. Dunigan, S.J.
1947. Bruce Publishing Company.

Rome in the Old Days

Baedeker's Central Italy. 1909. Karl Baedeker, Leipzig.

A Backward Glance. By Edith Wharton. 1936. D. Appleton-Century.

Roman Spring. By Mrs. Winthrop Chanler. 1934. Little, Brown.

Autumn in the Valley. By Mrs. Winthrop Chanler. 1936. Little, Brown.

Italian Yesterdays. Mrs. Hugh Fraser. 1913. Dodd, Mead.

The Sunny Side of Diplomatic Life. By Lillie De Hegermann-Lindencrone. 1914. Harper & Bros.

Roma Beata. By Maud Howe Elliott. 1907. Little, Brown.

John Elliott, The Story of an Artist. By Maud Howe Elliott. 1930. Houghton Mifflin.

Roman Mosaics. By Hugh MacMillan. 1892. MacMillan & Co.

Rambles in Rome. By S. Russell Forbes. 1899. Rome, 8th edition.

Pilgrim Walks in Rome. By Peter J. Chandlery, S.J. 1903. The Messenger Press.

Roman Fountain. By Hugh Walpole. Doubleday Doran. 1940.

When in Rome. By Streeter and Weisbecker. 1950. Rome.

O Roma Felix. By Msgr. Hugh O'Flaherty and Bishop John Smit. Verdesi, Rome.

Roma Domenica; Note Storiche. By P. Alberto Zucchi, O.P. Vol. 1. Firenze, 1938.

History of The American College at Rome. By Rev. Henry L. Brann. 1910. Benziger Brothers.

The Holy Year of Jubilee. By Herbert Thurston, S.J. 1949. Newman Press.

Recollections of the Last Four Popes and of Rome in Their Times. By Cardinal (Nicholas) Wiseman. 1858. P. O'Shea, New York.

Walks in Rome. By Augustus J. C. Hare. 1887. Smith, Elder Co., London.

(Other books on Rome might be listed; but there is no end to them.)

Boston in the 1890's

Golden Yesterdays. By Margaret Deland. 1941. Harper Brothers.
Americans in Process: North and West Ends of Boston. By Robert A. Woods. 1903. Houghton Mifflin.
Memories of a Happy Life. Bishop William Lawrence. 1926. Houghton Mifflin.
Boston and the Boston Legend. By Lucius Beebe. 1936. D. Appleton-Century.
Symphony Hall, Boston. By H. Earle Johnson. 1950. Little, Brown.
Boston—Historic Towns Series. By Henry Cabot Lodge, 1891. Longmans Green.
Fourscore: An Autobiography. By Judge Robert Grant. 1934. Houghton Mifflin.
Boston Landmarks. By M. A. De Wolfe Howe and Samuel Chamberlain. Hastings House, New York. 1947.

Boston after 1906

Walks and Talks About Boston. 1916. Ball Publishing Co.
The Early Days of Maryknoll. By Bishop Raymond A. Lane. 1951. David McKay Co.
Campaigning for Christ. By David Goldstein and Martha Moore Avery. 1924. Pilot Publishing Co.
Twenty-Five Years in Massachusetts Politics. By Michael E. Hennessey. 1917.
Life in America. Two volumes. 1951. Houghton Mifflin.
Since 1900. By Oscar T. Barck, Jr., and Nelson M. Blake. 1949. The MacMillan Co.
The Big Change. By Frederick Lewis Allen. 1952. Harper Bros.
Sharps and Flats in Five Decades. By Rev. William J. Finn, C.S.P. 1947. Harper Bros.
In Memoriam: Bellamy Storer. By Maria Longworth Storer. Privately printed. 1923.
Isabella Stewart Gardner and Fenway Court. By Morris Carter. Houghton Mifflin, Boston. 1925.

Personalities of the Cardinal's Times

Numerous books about the Popes of his life-time: Pius IX, Leo XIII, Pius X, Benedict XV, Pius XI and the present Holy Father, Pius XII.

Theodore Roosevelt and His Time. By J. B. Bishop. Two volumes. 1920. Charles Scribner's Sons.

The Life and Times of William Howard Taft. By Henry F. Pringle. 1939. Farrar & Rinehart.

The Bishop Jots It Down. By Bishop Francis C. Kelley. 1939. Harper Bros.

The Autobiography of William Allen White. 1946. The MacMillan Co.

Boston Mahatma; The Public Career of Martin Lomasney. 1941. By Leslie G. Ainley. Bruce Humphries, Inc.

The Purple Shamrock. By Joseph F. Dinneen. 1949. W. W. Norton Co.

David I. Walsh: Citizen-Patriot. By Dorothy G. Wayman. 1952. Bruce Publishing Co.

The Life of Archbishop John Ireland. By Msgr. James H. Moynihan. 1953. Harper & Bros.

Americanism: A Phantom Heresy. By Abbe Felix Klein. 1951. Aquin Bookshop.

Recollections of Three Reigns. By Sir Frederick Ponsonby. 1952. E. P. Dutton & Co., Inc.

Father Hecker and His Friends. By Rev. Joseph McSorley, C.S.P. 1953. Herder Book Co.

The Life of James Cardinal Gibbons. By Rev. John Tracy Ellis. Two vols. 1952. Bruce Publishing Co.

Edward Kavanagh. By William L. Lucey, S.J. 1946. Marshall Jones.

Cardinal Merry del Val. By Msgr. Vigilio Dalpiaz. 1937. Burns, Cates & Washburn, London.

Rafael Merry del Val. By F. A. Forbes. 1932. Longmans Green & Co.

Twenty-four American Cardinals. 1947. By Brendan A. Finn. Bruce Humphries.

Popes and Cardinals in Modern Rome. By Carlo Prati. 1927. The Dial Press.

Our American Cardinals. By James J. Walsh. 1926. D. Appleton & Co.

Henry Adams and His Friends. Ed. Harold Dean Cater. 1947. Houghton Mifflin.

Duveen. By S. N. Behrman. 1952. Random House.

New England: Indian Summer. By Van Wyck Brooks. 1940. E. P. Dutton Co.

The Life of Cardinal Mercier. By John A. Gade. 1934. Charles Scribner's Sons.

A Reporter at the Papal Court. By Thomas B. Morgan. 1937. Longmans Green.

On Shrines

San Clemente in Rome. By Louis Nolan, O.P. 1914. Rome.

San Clemente, Pope and Martyr and His Basilica in Rome. Joseph Mullooly, O.P. 1873. Rome.

Italy and Ireland in the Middle Ages. By Vincenzo Berardis. 1944. Dublin.

The Life of St. Columban. By Jonas. Rev. James Wilson, tr.

On Japan

Speaking Diplomatically. By Lloyd Griscom. 1940.

Larz Anderson; Letters and Journals of a Diplomat. By Isabel Anderson. 1940. Fleming Revell Co.

World Mission. Summer. 1953. Vol. 4, No. 2. Tokyo's Catholic University. By Norbert J. Tracy, S. J.

Mittheilungen aus dem Deutschen Provinzen. Vol. xi. 1927-29. By Joseph Dahlmann, S.J.

Revue d'Histoire des Missions. Vol. 12. 1935. L' Universite Catholique de Tokyo—Ses Origines.

The Woodstock Letters. Vol. 61. 1932. In Memory of Father Joseph Dahlmann, S.J. By John Laures, S.J.

World Mission. Winter, 1952.

The Church in New Japan. By Most Rev. Maxmilian de Fursten-
burg. Apostolic Internuncio in Japan.

Miscellaneous

The Wisdom of Catholicism. Ed. by Anton C. Pegis. 1949. Random House.

Histoire Generale de l'Eglise. L'Abbe J-E Darras. 1859. Paris.

Dante's Divine Comedy. Temple Classics edition. 1900. J. M. Dent
& Sons, London.

Fiction

The Cardinal. A Novel by Henry Morton Robinson. Simon and
Schuster, New York. 1950.

The Lady & The Painter. The story of the fabulous Mrs. Jack
Gardner and John Singer Sargent. By Countess Eleanor Palffy.
Coward-McCann, New York. 1951. Pages 212-218 give a
fictional picture of Cardinal O'Connell.

FOOTNOTES
Legend of Abbreviations

AABO.   Archives of the Archdiocese of Boston.

ACUA.   Archives of the Catholic University of America.

ADP.   Archives of the Diocese of Portland.

AOP.   Archives of the Dominican Order, Rome.

ASJ.   Archives of the Society of Jesus, Rome.

AV.   Archives of the Vatican.

HAB.   Lord-Sexton-Harrington: *The History of the Archdiocese of Boston.* Boston, 1944.

Letters.   Cardinal O'Connell: *Letters of Cardinal O'Connell,* Boston, 1915, I.

Recollections.   Cardinal O'Connell: *Recollections of Seventy Years.* Boston, 1934.

Reminiscences.   Cardinal O'Connell: *Reminiscences of Twenty-five Years.* Boston, 1926.

Sermons.   Cardinal O'Connell: *Sermons and Addresses.* I-VII, Boston, 1922; VIII, Boston, 1927; IX, Boston, 1930; X, Boston, 1931; XI, Boston, 1938.

Notes for Preface—In Memoriam

1. *Letters,* I, p. x.
2. *Sermons,* VIII, 120.

Notes for Chapter One

1. HAB., iii, 47. Pope Pius IX erected the Sees of Philadelphia, Boston, Milwaukee and Santa Fe in a brief dated February 12, 1875.

2. Julia, Nov. 1, 1838; John, June 24, 1841; Brigid, Feb. 3, 1843; Luke, Jan. 6, 1845; Mary, Feb. 8, 1847; Matthew, Jan. 7, 1849.

3. A debt of gratitude is owed to Dr. Philip O'Connell, principal of Clonmel Technical School in County Tipperary and author of the

History of the Diocese of Kilmore, 1937; *Schools and Scholars of Breiffne,* 1942. Both works are dedicated to the author's cousin, Cardinal O'Connell. Dr. O'Connell's researches in County Cavan genealogy are exhaustive and were made available to the biographer with generous cordiality.

4. Published in the *Irish Ecclesiastical Record,* June, July, 1949.

5. The old register of baptisms for St. Peter's Church, Lowell, is at the Chancery Office, Archdiocese of Boston.

NOTES FOR CHAPTER TWO

1. Greenslet: *The Lowells and Their Seven Worlds.* Boston, 1946, p. 126.

2. Cowley: *History of Lowell.* Boston, 1868, p. 156.

3. *Ibid.,* p. 200.

4. Miles: *Lowell As It Was and Is.* Lowell, 1845.

5. Boston *American,* Oct. 27, 1928.

6. Cob, a short-legged, stout horse.

7. *Recollections,* p. 6.

NOTES FOR CHAPTER THREE

1. Boston *Post,* March 1, 1925.

2. *Recollections,* pp. 37-39.

3. The certificate is in the possession of Judge Paul G. Kirk and Mrs. Kirk.

4. The priest, probably, was not "an uncle." The only priest kin to the family known to have been out of Ireland was Rev. Peter O'Connell of Fartagh who entered the Grand Seminary at Montreal in 1846. He died in Montreal, Jan. 17, 1854, five years before William O'Connell was born.

5. *Recollections,* p. 47.

6. Boston *Post,* Dec. 6, 1924. "He loved music and played the piano and organ equally well in high school days. He was a splendid singer."

7. *Letters,* p. 11.

8. *Ibid.,* I. 29.

9. *Recollections,* p. 52.

10. *Letters,* p. 25.

11. *Ibid.,* p. 30.

12. *Ibid.,* p. 30.

13. Dunigan: *A History of Boston College,* Milwaukee, 1947, p. 128. A Debating Society was organised in 1868 under Father Fulton, S.J.

NOTES FOR CHAPTER FOUR

1. The author is indebted to Monsignor Hugh O'Flaherty, official of the Supreme Sacred Congregation of the Holy Office, Vatican City, for aid in research to clarify the history of S. Maria dell' Umilta.

2. In 1946, when Bishop Martin J. O'Connor of Scranton, Pennsylvania, became Rector, he undertook the task of repairing damage occasioned during the war when the college was temporarily closed. The work, carried out under the direction of Count Enrico Galeazzi of the Permanent Commission for the Care of Historic and Artistic Monuments of the Holy See, faithfully preserves the original character of the old buildings, despite judicious modernization of living facilities. Even the garden of the inner cloister was restored with shrubbery, fountain and flower beds according to the seventeenth century plan. In 1953, with the opening, on October fourteenth, of a new building for seminarians on the hill across the Tiber at Vatican City, the North American College devoted the historic property at Via dell' Umilta, 30, as a residence for American priests pursuing graduate studies in Rome.

3. William H. B. Deasy, from the Boston Archdiocese, arrived in Rome earlier than O'Connell and Ford in the Fall of 1881. After his ordination, Dec. 20, 1884, he remained in Rome as Vice-Rector under Monsignor Denis O'Connell.

4. Brann: *History of the American College, Rome.* New York, 1910. p. 202. The buttons of the students' cassocks were red, as late as 1895, though later changed to a blue color.

5. *Recollections,* p. 105.

6. Brann: *History of the American College, Rome,* p. 500.

7. *Letters,* pp. 79-80.

8. *Ibid.,* p. 61.

9. *Ibid.,* p. 88.

10. *Ibid.,* p. 89.

NOTES FOR CHAPTER FIVE

1. Hegermann-Lindencrone: *The Sunny Side of Diplomatic Life,* p. 134.

2. Eugenio Pacelli, later Pope Pius XII, born in 1876, said his First Mass on April 3, 1899, at this altar in the basilica of Santa Maria Maggiore in Rome.

3. Dante: *Purgatorio,* Canto x, 73-76, "There was storied the high glory of the Roman prince whose worth moved Gregory to his great victory; of Trajan, the emperor, I speak."

4. *Letters,* pp. 91-92.

5. Monsignor Jeremiah F. Minihan recalls the Cardinal, at the age of eighty, having the car turned back to fetch the triptych which had not been packed for a one-night absence. "I have said my night-prayers

before that picture ever since I was ordained and I don't propose to change now, even for one night," said the Cardinal.

6. *Letters*, p. 94.
7. *Recollections*, p. 357.
8. *Letters*, p. 102.

NOTES FOR CHAPTER SIX

1. *Sermons*, X, 194-200.
2. *Letters*, p. 108.
3. Rev. Denis F. Sullivan, ordained at Troy, N. Y., Dec. 20, 1879; assistant at Immaculate Conception Church, Malden, 1881-94; pastor, Sacred Heart Church, Lynn from 1894 till his death, July 22, 1905.
4. Woods: *Americans in Process*, Boston, 1902. A pioneer in the field of Social work in Boston, Robert A. Woods made an intensive survey of the immigrant population in the North and West Ends of Boston at the period when young Father O'Connell was a curate at St. Joseph's Church, West End.
5. Greenslet: *The Lowells and Their Seven Worlds*. Boston, 1946, p. 132.
6. Lodge: *Boston*. Boston, 1891, p. 204.

NOTES FOR CHAPTER SEVEN

1. Woods: *Americans in Process*. Boston, 1902, p. 174.
2. *Letters*, p. 126.
3. *Ibid.*
4. Ainley: *Boston Mahatma*. Boston, 1949, p. 244.

NOTES FOR CHAPTER EIGHT

1. Vide Elliott: *John Elliott: The Story of an Artist*. Boston, 1930.
2. HAB., iii, 99.
3. *Letters*, p. 89.
4. HAB., iii, 188.
5. *Recollections*, p. 286.
6. ACUA., *Cooper Papers*. Dated May 22, 1901.
7. *Ibid.*
8. Rt. Rev. William Byrne, O'Connell's former pastor at St. Joseph's, Boston, in 1902 became pastor of St. Cecelia's. The church had so many memories for O'Connell, that, as Archbishop of Boston, he reserved the parish to himself, from Msgr. Byrne's death in 1912 until just before his own death. Rt. Rev. Francis L. Phelan was named pastor in 1943.
9. *Letters*, pp. 169-170.
10. *Ibid.*, p. 171.

11. Cater: *Henry Adams and His Friends.* Boston, 1947, p. 291.

12. ADP. Dated Sept. 11, 1893.

13. *Letters,* pp. 171-173. O'Connell also met Satolli again, at the Catholic Summer School, July 7, 1895, when the Apostolic Delegate presided with Archbishop Michael J. Corrigan of New York.

14. *Ibid.,* pp. 158-160.

15. ADP. Dated from Rome, Oct. 7, 1895.

16. *Letters,* p. 177.

17. *Sermons,* II, 117.

NOTES FOR CHAPTER NINE

1. Ellis: *The Life of James Cardinal Gibbons.* Milwaukee, 1952. i, 151.

2. *Letters,* p. 90.

3. Copyright, Louis H. Ross & Co., Boston, 1892.

4. *Reminiscences,* p. 22.

5. HAB., iii, 179.

6. *Reminiscences,* p. 21.

7. Satolli's red hat dated from Nov. 29, 1895.

8. HAB., iii, 160 *et seq.* Chapter Six, "The Stormy Period," gives many details of these difficulties in Boston in the years when O'Connell was a curate there.

NOTES FOR CHAPTER TEN

1. *Letters,* pp. 187-88.

2. *Ibid.,* p. 191.

3. Brann: *History of the American College, Rome.* New York, 1910. The complete English text, pp. 350-380. "The Influence of Rome," by Msgr. William O'Connell, Archbishop of Boston . . . read at the Jubilee Accademia of the American College, June 12, 1909. The original Italian text is found in *Sermons,* iii, 412 *et seq.*

4. Anderson: *Larz Anderson: The Journals of a Diplomat.* Boston, 1940, p. 153.

5. Maria Longworth Storer to William Howard Taft. Dated Aug. 16, 1903 from Colorado Springs.

6. Klein: *Americanism: A Phantom Heresy.* Atchison, 1950, p. 77.

7. *Ibid.,* p. 112-113. Dated at Rome, May 18, 1898.

8. Dated Jan. 22, 1899.

9. *Letters,* p. 196.

10. *Ibid.,* pp. 215-16.

11. *Ibid.,* p. 243. Dated March 18, 1898.

12. Pilgrims will recall Giulio Romano's huge painting of this Battle of the Milvian Bridge in the Vatican Museum.

13. *Letters,* p. 194.

14. Halecki: *Eugenio Pacelli: Pope of Peace.* New York, 1951, p. 17.

15. Hegermann-Lindencrone. *The Sunny Side of Diplomatic Life.* New York, 1914, p. 151. She was the former Lily Greenough of an old family of Cambridge, Massachuetts, herself an accomplished musician. She spent many years in Rome with her Danish diplomat-husband.

16. *Letters,* pp. 235-6.

17. *Ibid.,* p. 218.

NOTES FOR CHAPTER ELEVEN

1. *Letters,* p. 196.
2. *Ibid.,* pp. 195-96.
3. The Boston *Herald,* Nov. 16, 1924.
4. Thurston: *Holy Year of Jubilee.* Westminster, Md., 1949, p. 2.
5. *Letters,* p. 240.
6. Brann: *History of the American College, Rome,* p. 248.
7. Psalm XV; 6.
8. ACUA., *Cooper Papers.* Dated May 22, 1901.
9. Burton: *The Great Mantle.* New York, 1950, p. 142. When Giuseppe Sarto was elected as Pius X, as Merry del Val was assisting him to change his red robes for white, the new Pope dropped his red biretta on the head of the younger man, as sign that he would shortly create him a cardinal.
10. *Reminiscences,* p. 2; and *Recollections,* p. 213.

NOTES FOR CHAPTER TWELVE

1. *Daily Eastern Argus,* July 2, 1901.
2. *Ibid.*
3. *Ibid.,* July 5, 1901.
4. Portland *Daily Press,* July 5, 1901.
5. *Ibid.*
6. *Sermons,* X, 115-116.
7. Bishop Healy died on Aug. 5, 1900.
8. *Recollections,* p. 227.
9. McKinley's death came on Sept. 14, 1901.
10. ADP. Letter of O'Connell from Rome, Jan. 30, 1899: "My dearest Julia. . . . Remember, my salary is $1,000 a year and last year I did not touch a penny of it for myself. . . . Dear Sister, with all my crankiness, I never have but one feeling for you and that is of love and sincere affection."
11. *Ibid.,* from Rome, Nov. 29, 1899: "A week from tomorrow is my birthday and I know Aunty Fay will remember me. Forty years ago she held me in her arms at the baptismal font. I am afraid she could not do it now."

12. Brigid O'Connell Hatch, born Feb. 3, 1843; died at Brookline, Oct. 1, 1918.

13. *Letters,* p. 229.

14. Lucey: *Edward Kavanagh.* Boston, 1946, p. 82.

15. Buckley: *Diary of a Tour in America.* Dublin, 1889, p. 135.

16. *Ibid.,* p. 138.

17. HAB., ii, 430.

18. *Recollections,* pp. 216-17.

19. *Ibid.,* pp. 217-20.

20. The date was July 28, 1903. The text is in *Sermons,* ii, 290.

21. *Sermons,* ii, 281. *Ad Clerum.* May 31, 1903.

22. *Ibid.,* 325. Authority of the Church. Ash Wednesday, 1904.

23. *Ibid.,* 324.

Notes for Chapter Thirteen

1. AABO. Holograph memorandum, undated.

2. Ellis: *The Life of James Cardinal Gibbons.* Milwaukee, 1952. 11, 119n.

3. Pringle: *Life and Times of William Howard Taft.* New York, 1939. i, 228.

4. Storer: *In Memoriam: Bellamy Storer.* Boston, 1923, p. 42. Dated March, 1899.

5. *The Letters of Theodore Roosevelt.* Cambridge, 1953. ii, 1299. Dated May 18, 1900.

6. AV. William O'Connell to Rampolla, dated April 20, 1903.

7. Storer: *In Memoriam: Bellamy Storer.* Boston, 1923, p. 80.

8. ADP. Satolli to O'Connell, Oct. 5, 1904.

9. AABO. A copy, dated April, 1904 exists which specifies that the letter was written and signed by all before William O'Connell was made aware of its contents.

10. Moynihan: *The Life of Archbishop John Ireland.* New York, 1953, pp. 165-66. See also Farrell: *Archbishop Ireland and Manifest Destiny.* Catholic Historical Review, XXXIII, October, 1947, 269-301.

11. ADP. Holograph, dated 22 IV '98.

12. *Ibid.* Dated July 20, 1892.

13. *Ibid.* Copy of a typed letter dated Feb. 23, 1904.

14. ACUA. *Papers of Denis O'Connell* have the same correspondence.

15. ADP. Dated March 14, 1904.

16. ADP. Satolli to O'Connell, Nov. 22, 1903: ". . . in massima la S. Sede desidera non piu Ausiliari ma Coadjutori quando sia riconsciuto il bisogno. Temo che in Boston nascano partiti di personalita e cio saria impaccio di salutare elezione: speriamo che prevarra la parte piu saggia per quella Sede di somma importana."

17. Pius X was officially beatified June 3, 1951 and was canonized on May 29, 1954.
18. *Recollections*, pp. 4-6.
19. *Ibid.*
20. Bishop: *Theodore Roosevelt and His Time.* New York, 1920, p. 194
21. Griscom: *Diplomatically Speaking.* New York, 1940, p. 87.
22. *Recollections*, p. 263.
23. *Ibid.*, p. 230. The cathedral in Boston bears the name of the Holy Cross.

NOTES FOR CHAPTER FOURTEEN

1. Vide Sansom: *The Western World and Japan.* New York, 1950.
2. *Mittheilungen aus dem Deutschen Provinzen.* Vol. LX, 1927-29, p. 255 *et seq.* quoted by courtesy of Biblioteca Privata; Praep. Gen. Soc. Jesu, Rome.
3. Archives of Sophia University, Tokyo.
4. *Recollections*, p. 232.
5. HAB., iii, 478.
6. *Boston Sunday Journal,* Dec. 20, 1903. "Three candidates prominently mentioned. . . . Rt. Rev. John J. Brady, auxiliary bishop of Boston; Rt. Rev. Matthew Harkins, bishop of Rhode Island; and Rt. Rev. William H. O'Connell, bishop of Maine. . . . The *Journal* is led to believe that Bishop O'Connell will probably be . . . selected."
7. Hearn: *Glimpses of Unfamiliar Japan.* London, 1894, pp. 2-8.
8. *Recollections*, p. 254-5.
9. *Ibid.*, p. 234.
10. Griscom: *Diplomatically Speaking.* New York, 1940, p. 259.
11. *Recollections*, p. 238.
12. The Boston *Globe,* March 11, 1903.
13. Library of Congress. Papers of Theodore Roosevelt. This holograph from O'Connell, dated Jan. 24, 1906, would be one of the last letters he signed as "Bishop of Portland."
14. The Japanese envoys received in Rome by Pope Gregory XIII in 1585, had credentials not from the Emperor of Japan, but from the Shogun Hideyoshi.
15. *Recollections*, p. 241. Mutsuhito died in 1912. Since then, by Japanese custom, he has been spoken of by his post-obitum title of the Emperor Meiji.
16. *Ibid.*, p. 243.
17. *Ibid.*, p. 247.
18. *Ibid.*, pp. 252-53.
19. Katsura, Taro (1847-1913). Choshu clansman, famed general of the Japanese Army; Premier of Japan, 1901 with rank of Count; raised to the rank of Prince in 1911 for his services to the nation. He was Count Katsura when Bishop O'Connell met him in 1905.

20. *Recollections,* pp. 247-48.
21. *World Mission.* New York, Winter, 1952.
22. *Recollections,* p. 244.
23. *Japan Year Book,* 1939. Decorations for "distinguished or meritorious service to the State" were created in 1875. The system is complicated, each Order possessing nine classes, the grand cordon and classes numbered from one to eight. The highest decoration is the Supreme Order of the Chrysanthemum. The Rising Sun decoration, in varying classes, is that usually bestowed on foreigners. The Imperial Order of the Sacred Treasure, conferred on Bishop O'Connell, on its medallion represents the Mirror and Jewel of the historic Imperial Regalia. The cordon is a light blue ribbon with two orange stripes.
24. Governor Curtis Guild, a non-Catholic, referred to the mission to Japan in his Inaugural Address at Boston, Jan. 2, 1908: "The Vatican seeks a pioneer to transact the important and delicate mission of establishing necessary privileges at Tokyo. Among the prelates of the world, the ablest and fittest for the task is found to be a Massachusetts clergyman."
25. *Recollections,* p. 263.

NOTES FOR CHAPTER FIFTEEN

1. The Boston *Herald.* Jan. 26, 1906.
2. *Sermons,* X, 68-73.
3. *Recollections,* p. 265.
4. *Sermons,* III, 9-17.
5. *Recollections,* p. 268.
6. ADP. Letterbook, 1904.
7. *Ibid.* Letterbook, 1906.
8. *Recollections,* pp. 265-66.
9. *Ibid.*
10. *Sermons,* III, 61-71.
11. Lord, Sexton, Harrington: *The History of the Archdiocese of Boston.* 3 vol. Imprimatur dated Boston, Feb. 29, 1944.
12. *Sermons,* II, 361-66.

NOTES FOR CHAPTER SIXTEEN

1. Apostolic Constitution *Sapienti Consilio* of Pius X.
2. HAB., III, 522.
3. *Ibid.,* 521 *et seq.* Chapter Four. The Re-organization of the Archdiocese (1905-1911).
4. *Sermons,* III, 165 *et seq.*
5. *The Pilot,* observing in 1954 the 125th anniversary of its founding, was hailed as the oldest Catholic journal in the United States still in publication.

6. *Sermons,* XI, 168-69.

7. Father Fidelis, a convert, was the brilliant James Kent Stone of Brookline, Massachusetts.

8. Gabriel of the Seven Dolors, who died in 1862, had just been beatified in 1908; would be canonized in 1920.

9. Mother Filippi died at Boston, April 19, 1932. The Brighton Cenacle today has a handsome brick building containing convent, chapel and guesthouse thronged week after week with women retreatants.

10. *Sermons,* III, 408.

11. A story current in Boston when O'Connell first occupied the Granby Street residence concerned the frequent ringing of wrong doorbells by Catholics seeking the new home of their Archbishop. One irate Yankee neighbor was supposed to have called in person on the Archbishop to ask how this nuisance could be mitigated. "Why not put on *your* front door a sign reading 'To H—— with the Pope.' That might protect you," was reported to have been the Archbishop's smiling suggestion.

12. HAB., iii, 508.

13. *Sermons,* III, 122-39.

14. *Ibid.,* III, 105-07.

15. Psalm 120: 1. Douay version.

NOTES FOR CHAPTER SEVENTEEN

1. *Sermons,* III, 430-31.

2. AABO. One of the recipients was Mrs. Jack Gardner of Fenway Court who wrote: I am so grateful to Your Grace for the wonderful medal. . . . It rejoiced my heart."

3. *Sermons,* IV, 27.

4. *Ibid.,* IV, 29-31.

5. *Ibid.,* VIII, 212.

6. *Ibid.,* IV, 97-98.

7. Grant: *Fourscore: An Autobiography.* Boston, 1934, p. 258.

NOTES FOR CHAPTER EIGHTEEN

1. Berardis: *Italy and Ireland in the Middle Ages.* Dublin, 1944, p. 101.

2. Nolan, O.P.: *San Clemente in Rome.* Rome, 1914, p. 246.

3. It was not until after the death of Cardinal O'Connell that the Fathers of St. Columban's Missionary Society made a foundation at Milton, in the Archdiocese of Boston. The guestbook at Bobbio in 1953 showed that many Chinese priests, ordained at Rome, journeyed to the ancient Abbey to say their first Holy Mass, in gratitude to the mission-

ary efforts of the Columban Fathers in China, until expelled by Mao Tse Tung in 1950.

4. *Sermons,* IV, 18.

5. Mullooly, O.P.: *San Clemente and His Basilica in Rome.* Rome, 1873, p. 187.

6. Archives of the Irish Dominicans at San Clemente.

7. Lawrence: *Memories of a Happy Life.* Boston, 1926.

8. Boston *Globe,* Nov. 2, 1934.

NOTES FOR CHAPTER NINETEEN

1. Cardinal Hayes, Archbishop of New York, died suddenly, while saying his night prayers, Sept. 4, 1938.

2. Before his death, Cardinal O'Connell gave "The Hermitage" to the Bishop of the Bahamas. It was subsequently a girls' boarding school conducted by the Sisters.

3. *Sermons,* IV, pp. 198-200.

4. *Reminiscences,* pp. 15-16.

5. *Recollections,* p. 399. Cardinal O'Connell's aging memory, in 1934, betrayed him into giving in his *Recollections,* a description of the ceremony as he had seen it in St. Peter's at the crowning of Pius XI in 1922.

6. *Ibid.,* p. 342.

7. *Sermons,* IV, 203.

8. Morgan: *A Reporter at the Papal Court.* New York, 1937, p. 42.

9. *Recollections,* pp. 354-55.

NOTES FOR CHAPTER TWENTY

1. Benjamin F. Keith (1846-1914), native of Hillsboro, N. H. Learned the show business under P. T. Barnum; his Keith Theatre in Boston, 1885, first to offer continuous vaudeville. Eventually built a chain of more than 400 vaudeville houses. The familiar "R.K.O." initials of moving pictures stand for Radio-Keith-Orpheum.

2. *Recollections,* p. 205.

3. *Sermons,* X, 134-35.

4. *Ibid.,* III, 397-98.

5. *Ibid.,* IV, 128.

6. *Ibid.,* V, 116-17.

7. *Ibid.,* X, 161-66.

8. *Ibid.,* XI, 43. The list of Auxiliary Bishops in O'Connell's tenure of the See included Rt. Rev. Joseph G. Anderson (1909-27); Rt. Rev. John B. Peterson (1927-32); Rt. Rev. Francis J. Spellman (1932-39); and Rt. Rev. Richard J. Cushing (1939-1944). Bishop Spellman became Archbishop of New York, 1939; and Cardinal in 1946. Bishop Cushing succeeded O'Connell as Archbishop of Boston in 1944.

9. The Cardinal, in his bequests took pains to remember institutions serving each of the major racial groups in the Archdiocese, although without so designating them.

10. Luke xix; 12-26.

NOTES FOR CHAPTER TWENTY-ONE

1. *Letters,* 127.

2. The author is indebted to William Arthur Reilly of the firm of McLaughlin and Reilly, Boston, for data on the music compositions of the Cardinal.

3. The motet was sung at the Golden Jubilee of Cardinal O'Connell in Fenway Park, June 10, 1934 by a student from St. John's Seminary, later Father Joseph Monahan, chaplain in the South Pacific in World War II and subsequently director of the Boston bureau, Propagation of the Faith.

4. Johnson: *Symphony Hall, Boston.* Boston, 1950, p. 25.

5. HAB., iii, 681.

6. The artist's memory of the particular aria may be at fault. However, the Cardinal frequently studied operatic records, transposing the key to accompany himself in repeating them for his own pleasure.

7. The artist recalled that "the Cardinal always said my name 'Binnder,' though I pronounce it Buynda."

8. The Boston *Globe.* Oct. 20, 1933.

9. The Boston *Herald.* March 17, 1940.

10. Cardinal de Lai; O'Connell, tr.: *The Passion of Our Lord.* Boston, 1924. Preface.

11. Cardinal O'Connell: *The Letters of Cardinal O'Connell.* Vol. 1. Riverside Press, Cambridge, 1915.

12. Cardinal O'Connell: *Recollections of Seventy Years.* Houghton Mifflin Co. Riverside Press, Cambridge, 1934.

13. Cardinal O'Connell: *Reminiscences of Twenty-five Years.* Pilot Publishing Company, Boston, 1926.

14. *Recollections,* p. 7.

15. *Ibid.,* p. 369.

16. Draperies were added to Michaelangelo's figures in a later age.

17. *Recollections,* p. 186.

18. Howe: *Roma Beata,* p. 85.

19. Boston *Globe,* June 17, 1935. Report of a sermon by Cardinal O'Connell at the Cathedral of the Holy Cross at the Confirmation of 500 women-converts.

NOTES FOR CHAPTER TWENTY-TWO

1. HAB., iii, 488-773, gives a scholarly and detailed account of the progress of the Archdiocese of Boston under Cardinal O'Connell. It has been liberally and gratefully drawn upon for this short biography.

2. Boston *Post,* May 2, 1926.
3. *Sermons,* IV, 137.
4. *Ibid.,* IV, 142.
5. *Recollections,* pp. 61-63.
6. Archives, Maryknoll, New York. James Anthony Walsh to Father Price, dated Oct. 10, 1910.
7. *Sermons,* III, 144.
8. Kelley: *The Bishop Jots It Down.* New York, 1939, p. 142.
9. Goldstein: *Campaigning for Christ.* Boston, 1924, p. 24.
10. *Ibid.,* p. 54.
11. *Sermons,* III, 72-87.
12. *Ibid.*
13. *Quandoquidem* is dated April 25, 1922.
14. *Deus Scientiarum Dominus* is dated May 24, 1931.
15. *Sermons,* XI, 128. Dated Nov. 14, 1934.
16. *Ibid.,* XI, 127-35.
17. *Sermons,* VII, 186-199.
18. *Ibid.*
19. *Ibid.*
20. Pringle: *The Life and Times of William Howard Taft,* II, p. 102.
21. ACUA. Cardinal O'Connell to Archbishop Curley, Nov. 5, 1924.
22. *Recollections,* pp. 302-05.

NOTES FOR CHAPTER TWENTY-THREE

1. *Sermons,* IX, 276.
2. AABO. O'Connell to Harold J. Coolidge, Oct. 31, 1922.
3. Vide *Golden Jubilee.* Privately printed. Riverside Press, Cambridge, Mass., 1935.
4. *Sermons,* IX, 54-56.
5. Maurice J. Tobin, United States Secretary of Labor in the Truman administration, died July 19, 1953.
6. The Boston *Post,* Nov. 2, 1937.
7. *Sermons,* XI, 227. Addresses to the Catholic Alumni Federation. Oct. 28, 1937.
8. Dinneen: *The Purple Shamrock.* New York, 1940, p. 251.
9. Hennessey: *Four Decades of Massachusetts Politics.* Norwood, 1935, p. 257.
10. Wayman: *David I. Walsh: Citizen-Patriot.* Milwaukee, 1952, pp. 97-98.
11. The Boston *Herald,* Dec. 7, 1934.
12. The Boston *Herald,* Dec. 10, 1934.
13. *Sermons,* III, 96-97.
14. HAB., iii, 621.
15. *Sermons,* V, 153-67.
16. *Ibid.,* VI, 147.

17. *Ibid.,* VI, 195.
18. *Ibid.,* VI, 224-25.
19. *Ibid.,* X, 5-13.
20. The Boston *Globe,* Dec. 5, 1929.
21. *Associated Press* advance obituary, July, 1929.
22. *Sermons,* XI, 74.

NOTES FOR CHAPTER TWENTY-FOUR

1. *Sermons,* IX, 127.
2. *Ibid.,* III, 401.
3. *Ibid.,* VII, 170.
4. The Boston *Globe,* Dec. 13, 1923.
5. *Sermons,* VIII, 98.
6. The Mission Church, on Tremont Street in the Roxbury district of Boston, under the Redemptorist Fathers, has a replica of the shrine of Our Lady of Perpetual Help in the Church of St. Alphonsus in Rome where O'Connell said his First Holy Mass.
7. *Sermons,* IX, 207.
8. Sexton: *Cardinal O'Connell.* Boston, 1926, p. 355. "In times of mental anguish, he . . . knelt himself upright, not a lip moving, but with all that tremendous personality concentrated on the eternal reality."

NOTES FOR CHAPTER TWENTY-FIVE

1. Brooks: *New England: Indian Summer.* New York, 1940, p. 435.
2. The United States, with a population increased to 150,000,000, still had only some 7,000 free public libraries scattered over the country in 1950.
3. Behrman: *Duveen.* New York, 1952, p. 153.
4. AABO. Coolidge correspondence. Julian Coolidge was master of Lowell House at Harvard; Archibald a Harvard librarian. The Harold Coolidge home on Berkeley Street, Boston, frequently entertained the Cardinal.
5. AABO. O'Connell to Harold J. Coolidge, dated 1931.
6. *Sermons,* V, 186. Nov. 12, 1916.
7. *Ibid.*
8. *Ibid.,* IV, 206.
9. *Ibid.,* IX, 25-27.
10. AABO. The sequence of correspondence is in these archives.
11. *Ibid.,* dated Sept. 12, 1919.
12. *Ibid.,* dated Sept. 16, 1919.
13. *Ibid.,* dated Sept. 29, 1919.
14. Dr. James Bryant Conant retired as president of Harvard in 1952 to become U. S. High Commissioner in Germany.
15. *Sermons,* VIII, 181-82.

NOTES FOR CHAPTER TWENTY-SIX

1. The Apostolic Vicar of the Bahamas in 1939 was the Most Reverend John Bernard Kevenhoerster, O.S.B.
2. *Associated Press,* March 1, 1939.
3. Pope Pius XII decreed that in future conclaves, a majority of two-thirds plus one extra vote shall constitute election.
4. During the voyage, Cardinal O'Connell had confided to Monsignor Minihan his opinion that the new Pope should and would be Pacelli.
5. Matthew, xvi; 18.
6. The translation runs: Father of princes and kings, ruler of the earthly world, Vicar of Our Saviour.
7. When Mrs. Brady married, her 84-room mansion on Long Island, New York was given to the Jesuits.
8. Alfonso XIII was King of Spain from his birth to 1931 when he abdicated. His mother, Queen Christina was Regent until his majority in 1902.
9. The Boston *Globe,* March 31, 1939.
10. *Ibid.,* March 4, 1939.
11. O'Connell: *A Memorable Voyage.* Boston, 1939, pp. 49-50.
12. Translation: "Do not kneel." "But yes, Holy Father."

NOTES FOR CHAPTER TWENTY-SEVEN

1. The Latin reads: *Proh dolor quantus refert in quae tempora vel optimi . . . cuiusque virtus incidat.*
2. Nicholas Cardinal Wiseman (1802-1865) was educated at the English College in Rome from 1818; its Rector for twelve years. Consecrated bishop in 1840, he was created a cardinal in 1850.
3. Wiseman: *Recollections of the Last Four Popes.* New York, 1858. "The student at Rome so peoples his thoughts with persons, fills his memory with things seen and heard, that his studies are . . . rich as the tree in Spring in the assurance of future bloom and fruit. There literally sparkle beams of every hue, like flowers reflected in a running stream, from every monument and every record of the past there present, so as to make it truly an illuminated page. . . . Thus does Rome sink deep and deeper into the soul like the dew which finds its way to the root of everything beneath the soil, imparting there to every future plant its own warm tint, its own balmy fragrance, and its own ever rejuvenescent vigor." Pp. 273-75.